# A HISTORY OF LANDSCAPE ARCHITECTURE
## THE RELATIONSHIP OF PEOPLE TO ENVIRONMENT

# A HISTORY OF LANDSCAPE ARCHITECTURE
## THE RELATIONSHIP OF PEOPLE TO ENVIRONMENT

### G.B. TOBEY

Professor of Landscape Architecture
The Ohio State University

AMERICAN ELSEVIER PUBLISHING COMPANY, INC.

NEW YORK, LONDON, AMSTERDAM

AMERICAN ELSEVIER PUBLISHING COMPANY, INC.
52 Vanderbilt Avenue, New York, N.Y. 10017

ELSEVIER PUBLISHING COMPANY
335 Jan Van Galenstraat, P.O. Box 211
Amsterdam, The Netherlands

International Standard Book Number 0–444–00131–X

Library of Congress Catalog Card Number 72–87211

**Library of Congress Cataloging in Publication Data**

Tobey, George B
    History of landscape architecture—the relationship of people to environment.

    Bibliography:  p.
    1. Landscape architecture—History.    2.    Civilization—History.    I.    Title.
SB470.5.T6                712'.09              72–87211
ISBN 0–444–00131–X

*Manufactured in the United States of America*

# CONTENTS

# Preface

As only about one-ninth of an iceberg shows above the surface of the waters in which it floats, so appears in this little book a small portion of the history of man's attempts to control his environment. Much of the text attempts to describe the who, what, when, where, and why of man in a context of scale relationships.

You will find described here brief studies of the multifarious scales of man's life, from the smallest, man himself, through the kinds of spaces he occupies; from the family, the smallest biological and social unit, on up the scale through town, city, state, region, and continent to the world as a total ecosystem.

The major thrust of the text moves in the direction of scale comparison, especially in the illustrations it contains. In many cases, the attempt has been more to describe the cultural "flavor" of a specific event, rather than to achieve archeological or geometric accuracy. That this is so may be explained by the facts of the matter. History itself consists of a complicated system of related incidents. The interpretation of historical fact by those who prepare histories makes the study of history just that much more fascinating.

You will find contained in this volume one man's interpretation of the history of mankind translated into examples drawn to comparative scale indicating, in some small way, the impact mankind has had on the surface features of the world during the geologically brief period of his existence on this planet.

It can by no means be considered the work of a single author, however. Many have had major influence on this work. Bremer W. Pond, scholar and teacher at Harvard Graduate School of Design, first opened my eyes to the fascination of history, along with Dean Joseph Hudnut. Katherine McNamara, School of Design librarian, showed me the path, while Mary Pence, librarian of the School of Architecture at The Ohio State University, proved invaluable in finding esoteric references.

Charles R. Sutton, teacher of landscape architecture for many years at Ohio State, generously permitted me to choose, as a neophyte teacher, those subjects I wished to explore.

Although they are too numerous to call by name, the important contributors to this volume are the hundreds of students of architecture, planning, and landscape architecture who, during the background years of preparation for this work kept it alive by their abiding interest in the subject. Any teacher will tell you that he learns far more from interpersonal relations with his students than they can possibly gain from him.

Therefore, this work must in all honesty be dedicated to them and to students everywhere, who by their intellectual curiosity keep alive the thirst for just a little more understanding of what makes man tick.

I would be remiss if I did not acknowledge those others, who, though in the background, made this all possible. Laurence Gerckens, Professor of City and Regional Planning, and now Director of the School of Architecture at O.S.U., set the stage by the thoroughness with which he prepares course manuals and sets course objectives. Harold Bolz, Dean of O.S.U.'s College of Engineering, gave more than encouragement in making this effort fruitful.

Then there are the women in the typing pool, who uncomplainingly took on the preparation of the typescript as an overburden. Most especially Connie Darrah, who did most of the typing, deserves credit for putting up with constant pressures, such as "Where's Chapter—?"

Last, but by no means least, my wife deserves a gold star for learning to live with a virtual recluse over the past couple of years.

Here, then, for what you may gain from it, is a much too brief outline of people, places, and events that have shaped the course of history.

George B. Tobey, Jr.
Columbus, Ohio

# Introduction

This book describes shifts in man's attitudes toward himself and his relation with nature (his environment) from his beginnings as a sentient being to the present, the commencement of a future controlled by an ethical attitude toward conserving spaceship earth.

The appearance of early man corresponds roughly with the Pleistocene epoch, beginning about 1 million years ago (see Appendix A). Through the continuing investigations of paleontologists, anthropologists, and geneticists, more accurate information about the origins of man will become known. As far as we know now, *Homo sapiens*, modern man, probably appeared about 75,000 years ago.

Early man first found need for shelter from the elements. As a hunter, his need was for protection from wild beasts. One of man's first "castles" was a rough enclosure of thorny plant material, in which his basic need for sleep after effort could be fulfilled in safety. As man became a nomadic herdsman, the thorny shelter became protection from trampling by the herd animals.[1] This became more elaborate—for protection not only from other animals, but from his own species—in the form of castles or forts (the semantic derivation of the phrase, "A man's home is his castle").

Once man's basic needs for food, fiber, and shelter had been resolved, he had time to develop more philosophical attitudes in relation to environment. The "garden" then became man's Garden of Eden. ("Paradise" comes from Persia by way of Greece, and means "garden.") Association with environment was no longer a purely "economic" relationship, but one of need for shade from sun, a place (water involved, too) of refreshment after hunger and thirst, coolness after heat, love after fear, sleep after exhaustion.

Another source of early attitudes was the sense of awe felt in certain natural scenery. This awe translated itself into nature worship; for example, the dryads (wood nymphs) of the Greeks. This sense of awe still exists—witness the feeling of being "in a cathedral" that steals over visitors to the great Redwood National Parks.

Mankind's sense of the awesome character of his environment must have lasted throughout his "childhood" (from 75,000 years ago until about 10,000 years ago). During this long period of incubation man progressed from savagery to barbarianism. V. Gordon Childe[2] classifies savagery as a part of the Paleolithic era, during which society consisted of small roving bands collecting natural resources where they found them. Then, about 20,000 years ago savage bands began to supplement natural foodstuffs by cultivating edible plants and domesticating animals. Barbaric societies then came into existence,

---

[1]Clifford, Derek, *A History of Garden Design*, New York, Praeger, 1963.

[2]Childe, V. Gordon, "The Urban Revolution," *Town Planning Review*, Vol. XXI, No. 1, (April 1950), pp. 3–17.

forming villages of from 200 to 400 persons, all cooperating in the common goal of producing the means to survive the rigors of inimical nature.

Civilization, according to Childe, probably began about 5,000 years ago in what we now call the Fertile Crescent. Through gradual accretion of knowledge and technical skills men learned to live together in cities of upwards of 10,000 to 50,000 people, with a complex societal structure involving specialization of work, taxes, writing. At this point history begins. Civilization, or concentration of population in urbanized centers, has been since about 4000 B.C., the common denominator of culture, rising in Mesopotamia and spreading from there throughout the Mediterranean world by way of Egypt and Phoenicia to Crete, and thence to Greece.

If we conceive of the Greeks in the time of their greatest glory (about 500 B.C.[3]) as the first cosmopolitan people, we understand their environmental attitudes. Living in a lean land, of necessity they became mariners, traders, and world travelers. Their cities were truly urban in character. But, among the Greeks, gossip, public talk, and observing athletic contests were important aspects of life. Thus, groves of trees became places to gather, to watch, and to exchange gossip. Here were the origins of today's public parks.

To the Romans, fine growths of trees, contrast in foliage, the sensation of coolness and peace became ends in themselves, which they enjoyed as countrymen. Forests, as such, on the other hand, were sources of sport and hunting to the civilized Romans. (We can trace this attitude back to the Persians, Assyrians, and probably the Babylonians, who had great royal game preserves. The attitude persists today, modified to fit our western democratic concepts, in federal, state, local, and private hunting preserves.)

After the "fall of Rome" (which was not a sudden, calamitous event but came gradually as a period of transition from one life style to another), man's attitudes toward environment were colored by mysticism and magic (as in earlier cultures). Cities were for protection. The forest was the enemy, full of robbers, murderers, and savage beasts, both real and imaginary. Man withdrew into a spiritual world, in which personal and domestic defense was primary.

With the arrival of the succeeding era, which we have come to call "Renaissance," man again regained his sense of individual worth, his dominance through intellectual processes over the forces of nature. Old forms were renewed and modified to fill new life styles. An earlier concept of a disciplined nature ordered for man's use was revived, yet modified by opening out of geometric gardens to vistas over the surrounding countryside.

These expressions of dominance spread over all Europe, and persisted well into the eighteenth century. The most striking example of this lengthy period, and one which had a significant influence on attitudes toward environment, was Versailles. Built by and for Louis XIV (1643–1715), the palace and gardens epitomized the then prevalent attitude that man was monarch of all he surveyed.

Such writers as Addison (1672–1719) and Pope (1688–1744) in early nineteenth-century England created a revolution in taste and attitude toward nature. The industrial-scientific revolution was beginning to affect life styles, and the face of England had

---

[3]There have been devised several systems for segregating historic eras. We will use throughout the presently widely understood system based on the Gregorian Calendar. B.C. refers to periods prior to the year 0 in the Gregorian Calendar; A.D. to years after year 1.

already the appearance of a man-modified nature. The Englishman could afford to turn about, look upon and think about nature and nature's forms as something controllable, friendly, and capable of inspiring lofty flights of imagery; thus, the three-dimensional landscape painting, the contrived visual picture of an idealized nature became the dominant attitude.

Beginning with the executed works of Sir William Kent (1684–1748), Bridgeman and Wise (1680–1738), and Lancelot "Capability" Brown (1715–1783), and carried on by Sir Humphrey Repton (1752–1818), the romantic attitude toward nature extended well into the present century and still exists in many minds.[4]

Attitudes toward nature regressed during the Colonial period in the United States. This was naturally so because, first, the forests of the eastern seaboard were a deterrent to agriculture. Second, the forests harbored savages who (although initially courteous and helpful) soon realized that the white man intended to destroy the Indians' way of life and occupy their traditional hunting grounds. As an urban life style grew on the eastern seaboard, the Colonial gentleman, to seem "cultured," accepted geometric garden forms (man-dominated nature) as the only way to feel civilized. As the new nation expanded, so did an "English" cultured landscape. Gone were the bears, wolves, and (by this time) the "noble savage" (James Fenimore Cooper).

Andrew Jackson Downing (1815–1852), cultured Hudson River Valley esthete, espoused the causes of Brown and Repton, and introduced the attitudes long prevalent in England toward nature—that it should be beautiful and picturesque. Admittedly, these ideals could only be achieved through man's intervention (the wilderness was still too rough and uncouth to be considered a valid place to spend time).

The romantic tradition persisted throughout the nineteenth century, and there is substantial evidence that the attitude still persists in the layman's mind. Study, for example, the naming of real-estate developments, and read the advertisements published by residential sales agencies.

Such major figures as Olmsted, Eliot, and Hubbard fostered the romantic attitude as a means of "refining, elevating, and affording enjoyment to the people at large."[5]

Eliot, for example, referred to "the comfort, convenience, and health of urban populations, which have scanty access to rural scenery, and urgently need to have their hurrying, workday lives refreshed and calmed by the beautiful and reposeful sights and sounds which nature, *aided by the landscape art*, can abundantly provide."[6]

Concepts such as these were the real basis of the nineteenth-century park movement. Added to these was another attitude which showed up as the playground movement. It began in Boston in the 1880s with sand gardens. Jane Addams in Chicago in 1893 established at Hull House the first playground. The play motif was urbanized, "the kind of play that makes for wholesome moral and ethical life."[7] This was social awareness

[4]Hussey, Christopher, *English Gardens and Landscapes, 1700–1750*, New York, Funk & Wagnalls, 1967.

[5]Schmitt, Peter J., *Back to Nature: The Arcadian Myth*, New York, Oxford University Press, 1969, p. 66.

[6]Schmitt, *op. cit.*, p. 66, as quoted in Henry Vincent Hubbard and Theodora Kimball, *An Introduction to the Study of Landscape Design*, New York, Macmillan, 1938, p. 1. First published in 1917.

[7]Gulick, Luther, *Play and Democracy*, Playground Association of America, Proceedings 1, August, 1907, p. 12, as quoted in Schmitt, *op. cit.*, p. 75.

brought into children's play. Solitary activities were *out*, active (even frenzied) social recreation was *in*.

Another aspect of the romantic attitude affecting housing. Andrew Jackson Downing, in 1848, wrote: "In the United States, nature and domestic life are better than society and the manners of towns. Hence, all sensible men escape, earlier or later, and partially or wholly, from the turmoil of cities. Hence, the dignity and value of country life is every day augmenting. And hence, the enjoyment of landscape or ornamental gardening—which, when in pure taste, may properly be called *a more refined kind of nature*—is, every day becoming more and more widely diffused."[8]

Nature writers of the last quarter of the nineteenth century and the first quarter of the twentieth, established the idea of Arcadia (which Webster defines: "A mountainous district of Greece, celebrated as the abode of a simple contented pastoral people; hence, any scene of simple pleasure and quiet"). Landscape architects, with their prestige resting on the existence of the Arcadian myth, tried to reconcile the literary Arcadia and the suburban estate. The landscape garden, in the suburban subdivision, became, during the first half of the twentieth century, an island of nature in a mechanized world.

F. L. Olmsted's Riverside, a railroad subdivision outside Chicago (still existing in its original form, but now based on automobile commuting), perhaps best expressed the romantic attitude and tradition.

Landscape Architecture, having come of age under the romantic tradition, had, in the 1930s, 1940s, and 1950s, a minor revolution of its own. Influenced by architecture (the Bauhaus, Le Corbusier, Frank Lloyd Wright), functional relationships, overlaid by a pseudo-understanding of Oriental attitudes toward nature (especially as an art form, applied as occult balance), produced attitudes of reversion back to man-structured definition.

Garrett Eckbo, California landscape architect and teacher, could, by 1950, influence landscape design significantly as he described the use areas of any site in terms of their functions, and the ways in which the surfaces, walls, and enclosures should be brought under control.[9]

This is contemporary urban design expressed in simple terms, made necessary by urban concentrations (76 percent of the U.S. population lives in metropolitan areas). Such intense urbanization, so rapidly changing the face of the earth in the "developed countries," has caused disturbing retrospect.

Soon after World War II, with its resulting population explosion and building boom, it became apparent that man was "fouling his own nest."

Eckbo would now write:

> Pedestrian though the act of arranging growing plants on and
> in the ground may seem in relation to the abstruse esthetics of
> painting, poetry or composing, it is nevertheless design in form,

[8]From "Hints to Rural Improvers," *Horticulture*, July, 1848, as quoted in Schmitt, *op. cit.*, p. 56.

[9]Eckbo, Garrett, *Landscape For Living*, New York, F.W. Dodge Corp., 1950.

texture, color, and time; it is our poetic lifeline back to Mother Nature, in an increasingly denatured world. And being design in both time and space, it has symphonic and architectonic potentials which are very great because they are so difficult to achieve. Every act of planting design, from potted geranium to major park, is an *act of science,* because the plant we select and maintain is a product of genetics, propagation, soil technology, plant nutrition, pruning, and plant pathology. It is an *act of art,* because it involves a choice among form, colors, and textures which cannot be made upon technical or functional bases alone. And it is an act of nature because when art and science have done all they can, the growth process which produces the effect envisioned by the designer is the same process which produced the original and continuing wilderness.[10]

What is implied here is a blending of art (choice) with science (specific factors) in the modification of environment for man's needs.

Others see environmental problems differently. Aldo Leopold has written: "The outstanding scientific discovery of the twentieth century is not television or radio, but rather the complexity of the land organism. The last word in ignorance is the man who says of a plant or animal 'what good is it?' If the land mechanism as a whole is good, then every part of it is good, whether we understand it or not."[11]

Leopold was beginning to define a "land ethic." Perhaps the idea was best expressed in the following, which appeared in the *Tennessee Conservationist,* January 1962:

A deserted farmhouse in a gullied field was pictured in a farm journal which offered a prize for the best 100-word description. An Indian took the prize with this:

"Picture show white man crazy. Cut down trees. Make big tepee. Plow hill. Water wash. Wind blow soil. Grass gone. Door gone. Windows gone. Whole place gone. Buck gone. Squaw gone. Papoose too. No chuckaway [food]. No pigs, no corn. No plow. No hay. No pony.

"Indian no plow land. Great Spirit make grass. Buffalo eat grass. Indian eat buffalo. Hide make tepee; make moccasin. Indian no make terrace. All time eat. No hunt job. No hitchhike. No ask relief. No shoot pig. No build dam. No give damn. Indian waste nothing. Indian not work. White man crazy."

[10]Eckbo, Garrett, *The Landscape We See,* New York, McGraw-Hill, 1969, p. 141.

[11]Frome, Michael, *Whose Woods Are These?* New York, Doubleday, 1962, p. 170.

As early as the 1850s, Henry David Thoreau recommended that the United States have "our national preserves, where no village need be destroyed; in which the bear and panther may still exist, and not be civilized off the face of the earth—our own forests . . . for inspiration and our own true recreation."[12]

We are, today, on the threshold of an era in which the new and intelligent role of the citizen is that of a practicing ecologist. A basic human need is for an orderly, beautiful, natural environment.

Our surroundings can be healthier, more livable, and more beautiful if we learn to weigh environmental alternatives. Whereas malfunction is ugliness, a beautiful environment is one that is functioning properly.

We are learning that, to conserve ecological systems, we must distinguish between hardy and fragile environments. A hardy environment is one in which natural succession takes place easily; a fragile environment is one in which succession takes place slowly and with difficulty.

While too many decisions are still being made on economic determinism alone, we have reached a point in time where it lies within the power of coming generations to develop fully a land ethic in which man sees himself not as the dominant living species, but as steward of all life.

[12]Frome, *ibid.*

# 1 In The Beginning

## (5,000,000,000–11,000 Years Ago)

[1]In the beginning God created the heaven and the earth.

[2]And the earth was without form, and void; and darkness was upon the face of the deep. And the Spirit of God moved upon the face of the deep. And the Spirit of God moved upon the face of the waters.

[3]And God said, Let there be light; and there was light.

[4]And God saw the light, that it was good and God divided the light from the darkness.

[5]And God called the light Day, and the darkness he called Night. And the evening and the morning were the first day.

[6]And God said, Let there be a firmament in the midst of the waters, and let it divide the waters from the waters.

[7]And God made the firmament, and divided the waters which were under the firmament from the waters which were above the firmament: and it was so.

[8]And God called the firmament Heaven. And the evening and the morning were the second day.

[9]And God said, Let the waters under the heaven be gathered together unto one place, and let the dry land appear: and it was so.

[10]And God called the dry land Earth; and the gathering together of the waters called he Seas: and God saw that it was good.

<sup>11</sup>And God said, Let the earth bring forth grass, the herb yielding seed, and the fruit tree yielding fruit after his kind, whose seed is in itself, upon the earth: and it was so.

<sup>12</sup>And the earth brought forth grass, and herb yielding seed after his kind, and the fruit tree yielding fruit after his kind, whose seed is in itself, after his kind: and God saw that it was good.

<sup>13</sup>And the evening and the morning were the third day.

<sup>14</sup>And God said, Let there be lights in the firmament of the heaven to divide the day from the night; and let them be for signs, and for seasons, and for days, and years:

<sup>15</sup>And let them be for lights in the firmament of the heaven to give light upon the earth: and it was so.

<sup>16</sup>And God made two great lights; the greater light to rule the day, and the lesser light to rule the night: he made the stars also.

<sup>17</sup>And God set them in the firmament of the heaven to give light upon the earth.

<sup>18</sup>And to rule over the day and over the night, and to divide the light from the darkness: and God saw that it was good.

<sup>19</sup>And the evening and the morning were the fourth day.

<sup>20</sup>And God said, Let the waters bring forth abundantly the moving creature that hath life, and fowl that may fly above the earth in the open firmament of heaven.

<sup>21</sup>And God created great whales, and every living creature that moveth, which the waters brought forth abundantly, after their kind, and every winged fowl after his kind: and God saw that it was good.

<sup>22</sup>And God blessed them, saying, Be fruitful, and multiply, and fill the waters in the seas, and let the fowl multiply in the earth.

<sup>23</sup>And the evening and the morning were the fifth day.

<sup>24</sup>And God said, Let the earth bring forth the living creature after his kind, cattle, and creeping thing, and beast of the earth after his kind: and it was so.

**25**And God made the beast of the earth after his kind, and cattle after their kind, and every thing that creepeth upon the earth after his kind: and God saw that it was good.

**26**And God said, Let us make man in our image, after our likeness: and let them have dominion over the fish of the sea, and over the fowl of the air, and over the cattle, and over all the earth, and over every creeping thing that creepeth upon the earth.

**27**So God created man in his own image, in the image of God created he him; male and female created he them.

**28**And God blessed them, and God said unto them, Be fruitful, and multiply, and replenish the earth, and subdue it: and have dominion over the fish of the sea, and over the fowl of the air, and over every living thing that moveth upon the earth.

**29**And God said, Behold, I have given you every herb bearing seed, which is upon the face of all the earth, and every tree, in which is the fruit of a tree yielding seed; to you it shall be for meat.

**30**And to every beast of the earth, and to every fowl of the air, and to every thing that creepeth upon the earth, wherein there is life, I have given every green herb for meat: and it was so.

**31**And God saw every thing that he had made, and, behold, it was very good, And the evening and the morning were the sixth day.[1]

Thus The Bible chronicled the creation story. And a remarkably accurate story it was, considering that the "myths" of creation, as recorded by Old Testament writers were based on creation tales from earlier, Mesopotamian oral sources.

Much later, Christian theologians came up with a variety of dates for the creation. "The most familiar of these is one worked out by James Ussher, an Anglican Archbishop of Armagh, Ireland. In 1654 A.D., he decided that the creation had taken place in 4004 B.C. (at 9 A.M. of October 23 of that year, according to some)."[2]

---

[1] *The Holy Bible, King James Version* (text conforming to the edition of 1611), Cleveland, World, n.d., pp. 5,6.

[2] Asimov, Isaac, *Asimov's Guide to the Bible, Vol I, The Old Testament*, New York, Doubleday, 1968, p. 36.

We now, of course, believe that the earth is some 5 billion years of age. (See Appendix A). In fact, historians and philosophers have long been aware that the Christian fundamentalist chronology could not be accurate.

Herodotus, in the fifth century B.C. concluded from the large numbers of fossil shells and beds of salt in Egypt that much of the present land had once been under water. Aristotle, a century later, voiced the same conclusion, attributing geologic process to natural rather than supernatural causes.

Eratosthenes in the third century B.C., announced from Alexandria the first approximation of Earth's circumference. Strabo and other Roman scholars cited seashells in rock formations as proof of earlier extensions of the seas.

Leonardo da Vinci (1452–1519 A.D.) observed that surface waters carried salts from land to sea, and that muddy water flowing into marshy ground emerged clear. His conclusion: sediment would in time change the marsh into dry ground. He further observed that fossil shells even at high land altitudes included representatives of living marine animals. However, tenacious biblical doctrine of Da Vinci's time and later attributed these shell deposits to the flood made famous in the story of Noah and the ark.

By the seventeenth and eighteenth centuries A.D., philosophers demonstrated through careful investigation the truths of geologic process as we know it today.

During the eighteenth Century, before Darwin, there were two schools of thought, in reference to geologic process. The Neptunian School believed all rocks to be precipitates from the waters of a primeval, universal ocean. Their first precipitate was granite as oldest, then later came gneiss, slate, basalt, porphyry and syenite. Limestones and sandstones were, to the Neptunists, transition rocks.

The opposing school, the Plutonists, believed granite and basalt to be of igneous nature, and that natural agents now at work on and in the earth had been operating through immense periods of time.

Then, in March, 1835, Charles Darwin, climbing the Andes, found fossil shells protruding from a broad band of limestone at an elevation of 13,000 feet! On the eastern slopes, Darwin also found petrified tree stumps that had once been under water. He wrote to a scientist friend, "I know some of the facts of the truth of which I in my own mind feel fully convinced, will appear to you quite absurd and incredible."[3]

These finds and others Darwin made during his voyages in the *Beagle* led to twenty years of work, resulting finally in his *Origin of the Species,* forming the basis of our present theories of the evolution of the world of man.

While astronomers almost daily discover more of the billions of suns scattered throughout the vast universe, and any one of these suns can conceivably have associated with it life-supporting planets, we know for sure of only one such planet, the third planet from our sun which we call Earth.

[3]Moore, Ruth, The Record in the Rocks, *Audubon Magazine,* vol. 73, no. 1, (January 1971), p. 14.

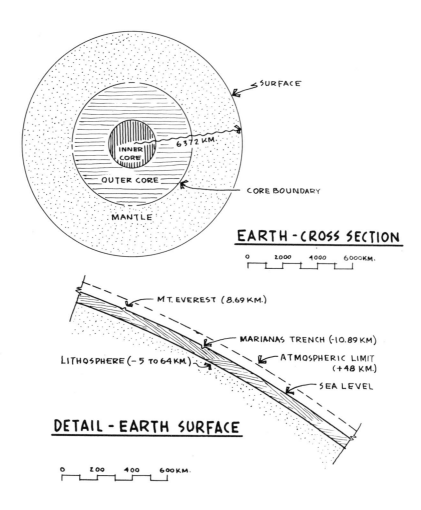

EARTH - CROSS SECTION

DETAIL - EARTH SURFACE

FIGURE 1

Earth is, for us (as Buckminster Fuller concludes), our own spaceship, spinning at 1,000 miles per hour, revolving around the sun every 365 days and the entire planetary system moving at speed, along with "our" galaxy, to an ultimate destination we do not yet know.

To understand man's brief history on this planet (*Homo sapiens* as a species has existed 75,000 years, as opposed to present understanding of the planet's life of 5 billion years), we need to know the characteristics of the narrow envelope on Earth's surface capable of supporting life.

This narrow band of seas, lands, and atmosphere is, to our eyes, a vast territory. The land surface (and, according to recent marine soundings, the surface under the seas) is quite wrinkled. Mt. Everest, in the Himalayas rises 8.69 kilometers (5.4 miles)[4] above mean sea level, while the Marianas Trench, shown close to Everest in Fig. 1, but actually 7,562 kilometers (4,700 air miles) distant, penetrates beneath the sea 10.95 kilometers (6.8 miles).

---

[4]In view of the impending shift to the metric system, measurements will be given in the metric system, with the "English" system appended for comparison.

Because without special equipment, mankind has difficulty breathing above the 3,962.4-meter (13,000-foot) elevation, and the pressures beneath the surface of the waters require even more specialized life-supporting devices, we are confined to the earth's surface.

This surface of 512,000,000 square kilometers (197,000,000 square miles), 70 percent water, 30 percent land, comprises a self-contained ecosystem of rocks, soil, water, plants, animals, and a thin 48-kilometer (30-mile) envelope of atmosphere, ultimately dependent on the sun for the energy to function as a viable life-system for mankind.

Earth's ecosystem is made up of many delicately balanced, complex energy relationships. The geologic foundation of the earth's surface, the rocks, release their

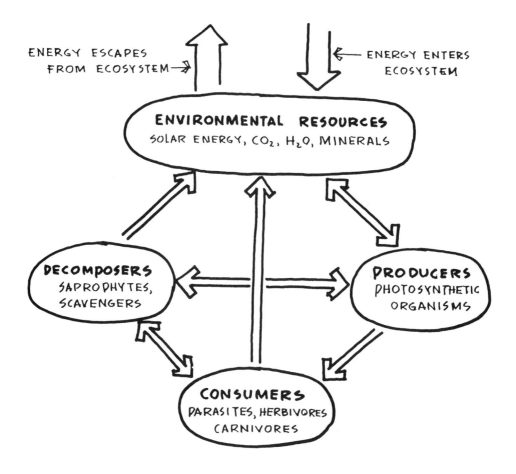

# TROPHIC-DYNAMIC INTERRELATIONS IN THE ECOSYSTEM

FIGURE 2

After Daubenmire, Rexford, *Plant Communities*, New York, Harper and Row, 1968, p. 15.

energy in a complex cycle of destruction, the three basic energy constituents of which are frost action in cold regions, temperature differentials in hot areas, and chemical interactions (solution) among air, water, and the rocks themselves.

One of the most important physical energy transfers producing soil from the rocks is erosion by water, and, to a lesser extent, winds. Once soil is formed, whose composition depends on the mineral content of the stones themselves, and once life forms (biological soil organisms, including earthworms and soil bacteria) have begun their own complicated energy transfers, the composition, both chemical and physical, of that soil continues to modify.

Physically, soils are deposited on rock surfaces by alluviation (erosion by water), glaciation (deposition by vast weights of ice of large ungraded volumes of clays, silts and gravels), and aeoliation (deposition of very fine, wind-borne particles).

Soils may be residual (weathered in place), cumulative (organic accumulation), or transported (by glaciers, floods, wind, gravity, volcanic action, and, a recently significant factor, man-made cuts and fills).[5]

Climate, the intricate energy system of air-mass movement over the surface of the globe as modified over large areas and over time by variations in sun evergy levels, the rotation of the earth, intricate topographic differences and the presence or absence of moisture, further modifies soils as the basal medium for growth of the vegetative cloak upon which all life depends.

Climate and weather are closely entwined to produce the hydrologic cycle, involving solar energy, wind, precipitation, surface runoff, ground water percolation, and evaporation. The hydrologic cycle, upon which all plant and, therefore, all animal life depends in all its variations from superhumid to arid, has created the wide variety of plants and animals (including man) that people the surface of the earth.

Figure 2[6] represents, briefly and generally, the energy systems that have, over geologic time, produced the present surface structure of the earth, that mankind has known as he evolved from an arboreal mammal to a two-legged, upright walking predator upon other life systems—a predator who, through his ability to think and to utilize tools, has had profound effects in changing the face of the globe.[7]

---

[5]For a more complete description of soils, see Monkhouse, F.J., *Principles of Physical Geography*, Totowa, New Jersey, Littlefield, Adams, 1962, Chapter 9.

[6]Trophism pertains to the nutritional cycle of plants and animals. See Rexford Daubenmire, *Plant Communities, a Textbook of Plant Synecology*, New York, Harper & Row, 1968, for a more complete explanation. See also Warner L. Marsh, *Landscape Vocabulary*, Los Angeles, Miramar, 1964 for oxygen, nitrogen and hydrologic cycles.

[7]See Appendix A for Geologic Timetable. G. Dury, *The Face of The Earth*, rev. ed., Baltimore, Pelican, 1966, provides a detailed description of geologic process. Rexford Daubenmire, *Plant Communities: A Textbook of Plant Synecology*, describes another aspect of the stage setting for man, in terms of the ecological relationships of plant and animal communities.

# 2          From Hunter to Farmer

Computer analysis has recently confirmed a concept long held by anthropologists and geneticists. Laboratory scientists, working with the amino acid chains that make up the subunits in the nucleic acids of genetic material, have produced a phylogenetic tree showing that all biological organisms contain only minor differences in their protein nuclei. Relatively simple mutations occurring in the chains of nucleic acid molecules have, over billions of years, produced all life on earth.[1]

Paleobiologists, who study fossilized remains of ancient organisms, have discovered, in rocks calculated to be 3 billion years old, bacteria that can be classified neither as plant nor animal. In rocks 2 billion years old in Ontario, investigators found an organism which used photosynthesis to fix nitrogen, one of the building blocks of protein. As early as 500 million years ago, plants and animals had begun to follow divergent evolutionary paths, but only half a million years ago did man emerge as a tool-user (see Fig. 3).

Among geologists this period in prehistory goes by the name Pleistocene, and among anthropologists Paleolithic, or early Stone Age. In other words, present definitions classify our earliest ancestors as men, by virtue of the fact they manufactured tools to assist them in surviving in a period of major climatic fluctuations. As far as we know from available geologic, geographic, and climatic information, the Pleistocene epoch has been characterized by a series of cyclic climate changes, at times producing great ice sheets in temperate zones, with corresponding very moist climates in those areas near the equator. The glacial cycles were inevitably followed by warming trends, producing interglacial (warmer) climates north and south, and corresponding drier, warmer periods in what we now call tropical zones. The climatic cycles were accompanied with earth movements, creating uplifts, including mountain formation, and, especially in glacial periods, land bridges between continents.[2] We theorize that these geologic and climatic cycles were major factors in causing man, following shifts in available supplies of food, to migrate widely.

It is conjectured that in Africa, where a large enough land mass and suitable climate produced foodstuffs in the form of vegetation and associated animal life man first became a toolmaker, then, through time, an even more efficient maker and user of tools. Why Africa, rather than the Indian peninsula or South America? ask the investigators.

---

[1]Dayhoff, Margaret O., "Computor Analysis of Protein Evolution," *Scientific American*, July 1969.

[2]Leakey, L. S. B., *Adam's Ancestors, The Evolution of Man and His Culture*, New York, Harper & Row, 1960.

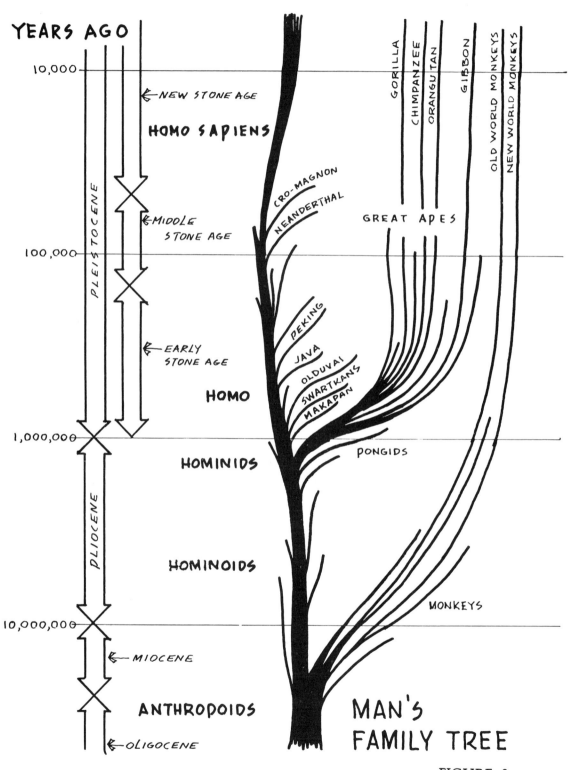

MAN'S
FAMILY TREE

FIGURE 3

The only explanation so far available indicates that the proper combination of circumstances just did not happen in those other regions.

So far as we know, the population of men expanded as they became more adept at making tools to provide better and more assured food supplies, more efficient shelters, and means of storing and transporting food supplies during long migrations. By 300,000 years ago, world population had expanded (estimated) to 1 million individuals, scattered over Africa, Europe, and Asia.

Apparently, too, man arrived in the Western Hemisphere some time between 25,000 and 10,000 years ago, thus making man the most widely distributed single species of animal in the world.[3]

Man, as an animal, had certain definite disadvantages in enabling him to adapt to environment. He had no fur coat to protect him from cold. His strength, speed, and agility were much at a disadvantage as opposed to many other life forms. These disadvantages made it necessary for man to devise ways of clothing himself, except in uniformly warm climates. Only regions near the equator maintain an evenly warm temperature range, but these areas consist primarily of tropical rain forest. Though tropic vegetation is lush, rainforests harbor a surprisingly small supply of edible foodstuffs. The most suitable environment for man's evolution occurred near the edge of forested areas, where dense vegetation provided protection, yet open, grassy plains provided large numbers of herbivores, making available supplies of protein.

Thus did primitive man become hunter. As animal herds moved seasonally, as do the wild herds of the Serengeti in Kenya, East Africa, so man migrated in small bands, following the herds and discovering along the way edible roots, nuts, berries and seeds. As these small bands of savages trailed their mobile food supplies, they had to create tools.

The first tools may have been sticks, used as clubs. It followed, however, that means of tearing apart killed animals had to be devised. Certain hard stones such as flint and volcanic glass (obsidian) tend to shatter in ways that leave sharp edges. With these primitive tools, man learned to cut through animal skins to make available the meat within. Over many millennia these stone tools evolved into a remarkable variety of implements, including axes, knives, awls, spearheads and arrowheads.

It follows logically that migration tended toward areas providing "mines" where sources of toolmaking materials lay. Exposed flint beds sometimes occurred along, or near, stream banks. Since man can survive only where water is available, migrating bands of hunters tended to settle briefly near lakes or streams. Shelter from the elements was a concomitant need. Thus we often find remains of our paleolithic ancestors buried beneath the debris of cave floors.

One of the more fascinating aspects of man's evolution had to do with the development of storage and carrying devices. The migrants could not have traveled far without carrying food, water, and weapons across the relatively barren stretches between water courses. Food storage and transport devices evolved from use of animal

---

[3]Deevey, Edward S., Jr., "The Human Population," *Scientific American*, September 1960, p. 4. See Fig. 4.

skins through basket weaving to pottery. Pottery-making required knowledge of the uses of fire. We do not know the long series of events which led to technical competence in producing and using fire, but we know it followed as a necessary part of the evolutionary process.

Sometime between 10,000 and 7,000 years ago, men thought of a way to provide surer food supplies. Certain kinds of animals, including dogs, pigs, sheep, goats, cattle and chickens seemed willing to live near men. Thus began the domestication of animals.

The slow process of evolution received, at this point, a remarkable impetus. Not only did man become a herdsman, or guardian over flocks and herds, but another discovery for the first time tied man to a particular plot of ground. Conjecture has it that some unknown herdsman noticed that grain seeds which had been trampled into a particularly fertile spot of ground by his goats (or sheep) sprouted, grew, and produced seed in their turn. Another means for assured food supplies had occurred to man.

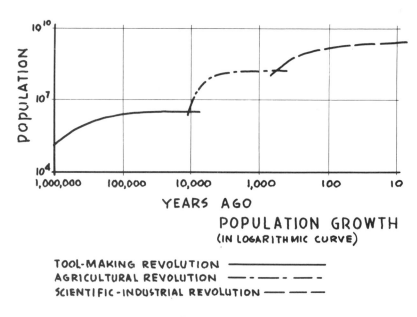

FIGURE 4

These events took place during a geologic cycle which had produced an environment favorable to agriculture. The last known glacial epoch had come to an end, accompanied by a warming, drying trend in climate. We have ample evidence of this climatic trend. Elephants, lions, and other moisture-dependent animals once roamed what is now the Sahara desert.

Man and his associated plants and animals were forced into relatively restricted locations, most notably into fertile river valleys. At the time of the agricultural revolution (about 7,000 or 8,000 years ago), man's technical and social skills were quite advanced. Whereas, as a primitive savage, mankind was purely a predator, destroying his own or other species for survival, the agricultural revolution changed man's role into one of mutualism. While man was dependent on animals and plants, in turn these same

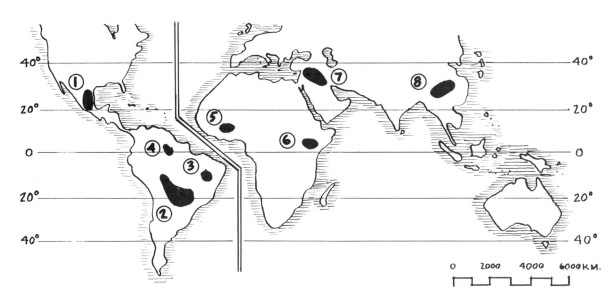

# ORIGINS OF AGRICULTURE

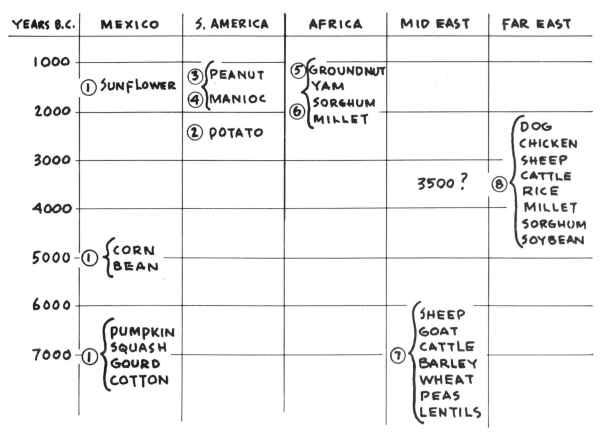

| YEARS B.C. | MEXICO | S. AMERICA | AFRICA | MID EAST | FAR EAST |
|---|---|---|---|---|---|
| 1000 | ① SUNFLOWER | ③ PEANUT<br>④ MANIOC | ⑤ GROUNDNUT<br>YAM | | |
| 2000 | | ② POTATO | ⑥ SORGHUM<br>MILLET | | |
| 3000 | | | | | ⑧ DOG<br>CHICKEN<br>SHEEP<br>CATTLE<br>RICE |
| 4000 | | | | 3500 ? | MILLET<br>SORGHUM<br>SOYBEAN |
| 5000 | ① CORN<br>BEAN | | | | |
| 6000 | | | | | |
| 7000 | ① PUMPKIN<br>SQUASH<br>GOURD<br>COTTON | | | ⑦ SHEEP<br>GOAT<br>CATTLE<br>BARLEY<br>WHEAT<br>PEAS<br>LENTILS | |

FIGURE 5

animals and plants became dependent on man. For example, corn (used as food as early as 5000 B.C. in Mexico) has been genetically modified into purely man-made strains. Paleobotanists have not yet discovered fossil remains of the original, wild corn.

As mentioned earlier, men found it necessary, as hunters and food gatherers, to band together in rudimentary societies, thus making food supplies for all more ample. Social anthropologists classify this simple social structure as Savagery. The social structure was comprised of small, roving bands having fairly close genetic relationships. The Pygmies of Africa and the Aborigines of Australia are contemporary residual survivors of this form of culture, which apparently developed some 20,000 years ago.

Then, about 10,000 years ago Neolithic (New Stone Age) societies were formed. Known as barbaric societies, these relatively larger clusters of families supplemented natural food resources by cultivating edible plants and domesticating animals. As these processes (agriculture; see Fig. 5) gradually evolved, population could increase radically. Irrigation of cropland became common, and the land area needed to support one person was reduced to about 1.3 square kilometers (½ square mile).

Barbaric societies were characterized by permanent villages of from 200 to 400 people. Population growth occurred, not by increasing village size, but by increasing the number of villages. Barbaric societies were much more complex than under earlier cultures; because to irrigate and farm cropland and to herd domestic animals required it, nearly everyone in the village population cooperated in the community interest, producing not only enough foodstuffs for survival, but actually, in good times, surpluses of food. Maintenance of food surpluses led to the next revolutionary step, the development of civilization.

# 3        The Fertile Crescent
## (4000–2000 B.C.)

"During evolutionary time the avenues of possible progress have become progressively restricted, until today only one remains open . . . Man . . . has been suddenly appointed managing director of the biggest business of all, the business of evolution."[1]

From this point on, we concentrate our attention on man and his progress toward environmental control. Control over environment, had, by 10,000 years ago, produced rudimentary agriculture, the domestication of plants and animals, the procurement of a reasonably assured food supply.

The world map (Fig. 5) shows the several locations in which agricultural practices had their origins. In these areas, complex societies gradually evolved into what we call "civilization." Present knowledge indicates that civilization first appeared in that geographic area known as the Fertile Crescent. Between 10,000 and 5,000 years ago agriculture and irrigation culture appeared, due to a combination of mild climate, adequate moisture, and the presence of wild plants and animals adaptable to man's use. Excavations at Jarmo, Jericho, and Helwan all indicate incipient farming cultures.

Yet, it was in the several great river valleys themselves where circumstances combined to produce that gradual evolution toward a new economic structure and social organization causing a startling upward bend in the population curve. A fortuitous set of circumstances led to what V. Gordon Childe has termed the "Urban Revolution."[2] As the last of the Pleistocene glaciers receded, the lands between the 20th and 40th parallels of North latitude gradually became warmer and drier. While the previously discussed "agricultural revolution" (Chapter 2, Figs. 4 and 5) took place generally in higher, grassy plains, where lived edible grains and animals conducive to domestication, the warming, drying climatic trend gradually forced the farmers closer to the three river systems noted in Figure 6. Down from the highlands migrated the villages to establish permanent farms in the fertile river valleys. Figure 7 indicates a land form system consisting of low-lying fertile valleys with higher land between.

In these valleys, with their relatively consistent water supply, agriculture evolved into a regularized system, producing assured supplies of life-supporting food. Paleoclimatolo-

[1]Huxley, Julian, *New Bottles for New Wine*, New York, 1957, p. 13, as quoted in Wagar, W. Warren, *The City of Man*, Baltimore, Md., Penguin, 1967, p. 75.

[2]Childe, V. Gordon, "The Urban Revolution," *Town Planning Review*, Vol. 21 (April 1950), pp. 3–17.

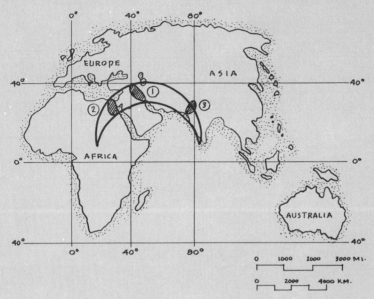

## THE FERTILE CRESCENT

① TIGRIS-EUPHRATES RIVER VALLEY.
② NILE RIVER VALLEY.
③ INDUS RIVER VALLEY.

FIGURE 6

## PHYSIOGRAPHY - FERTILE CRESCENT

3000 + M
1500 - 3000 M
300 - 1500 M
0 - 300 M

FIGURE 7

gists claim that in this period of cultural development, the fertile crescent, which today has a hot, dry climate, at the dawn of civilization had cyclonic weather patterns similar to those of Central Europe today. Rainfall in the crescent latitudes was reasonably abundant and evenly distributed.

Nature's provision of easily available bounty induced formerly nomadic man to settle in permanent locations, for the first time tied to the land. Whereas before, Paleolithic cultures had followed migratory food supplies, and Neolithic peoples had learned to supplement hunted food by herding animals and domesticating crops, now arose, along the Nile, the Tigris-Euphrates, and the Indus, a new kind of culture, far more complex in nature.

The environmental factors existent in the period from 4000 to 1700 B.C. produced an astonishing series of results. An economy that could finally produce food surpluses for the first time permitted men to specialize in varied tasks, as opposed to the former need for everyone to work at the task of producing food, clothing, and shelter. Though the bulk of the population consisted of peasant farmers, there were now also craftsmen, tradesmen, and administrators to account for the amounts of agricultural surpluses that went to support those who performed the tasks of thinking and planning.

While savage and barbaric tribes had a chieftain of sorts, who made the clan decisions, society now involved a ruling class, who decided; transport workers, responsible for moving goods; tradesmen who bought and sold "foreign goods." Archeologists have proven that trade between tribes had for many millennia previously been a fact, because no geographic location could provide all of the felt needs of any group. Trade now became a formalized necessity of society. While early trade had been in luxury goods, civilization demanded trade in hard goods, such as various woods, metals, and fabrics.

Formalized trade required clerks and administrators to keep accounts of available supplies, their locations, and their distribution. Above them were the administrators, and even higher on the social scale, those who made the decisions. Conjecturally, tribal chieftains had often made decisions for future clan action, whether based on instinct or intuition, that mystified the people. Men who could make such intelligent predictions must have direct contact with higher powers. Imagine, if you will, an intelligent observer of nature, living along the Nile River 3,000 or 4,000 years B.C. He began, over the years, to note that on a certain day, when the sun rose at a particular spot on the eastern horizon, the river would bring flood waters, which spread fertile silt over the adjacent fields. Then one year, just before the annual flood, he announced to an unbelieving populace that Mother Nile would next week make the fields ready for planting; on the day our wise man had predicted, down came the floods. It was this man, or his counterpart in other valleys of the fertile crescent, who, because of his supernatural powers, probably became the first priest-king. Thereafter, every important decision for the destiny of his people came to him for judgment.

As cities grew in size, governance became necessarily more complex. One man could not possibly have time to make every decision. Thus, as urban living progressed, a whole hierarchy of social strata arose, producing the rudiments of culture as we know it today.

First, systems of recording and "exact" sciences had to be devised. How many bushels of wheat were stored in the granaries? How much land could a farmer plow in a day?

# PICTOGRAPHS REPRESENTING CULTURAL DEVELOPMENT – FERTILE CRESCENT

DEVELOPMENT OF THE ARCH

MILITARY FORCE

KINGS SEPARATE FROM PRIESTS

WHEELED TRANSPORT

SOPHISTICATED BUILDING TECHNIQUES

PRIEST-KINGS

WRITING; HISTORICAL RECORDS

CIPHERING; EARLY SCIENCES

BOATS; WATER TRANSPORT

METAL-WORKING

TRADE

IRRIGATION AGRICULTURE

ADVANCED POTTERY

FOOD SURPLUS STORAGE

AGRICULTURE

DOMESTICATION OF ANIMALS

PRIMITIVE MAN-MADE SHELTERS

FOOD STORAGE; PRIMITIVE POTTERY

FOOD GATHERING

FIGURE 8

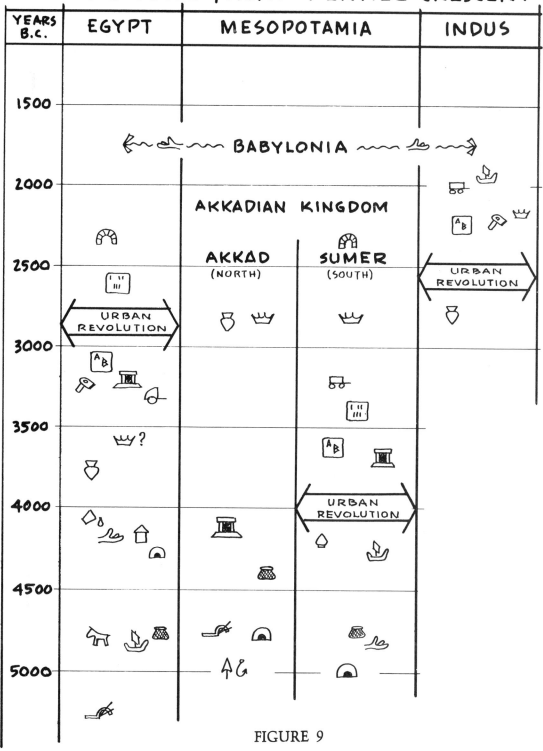

FIGURE 9

How many bricks would it take to build a temple to the local god? How many men would it take to dig an irrigation canal to prepare more land for cultivation? How could a caravan sent into the northern hills of Mesopotamia to cut cedar trees know where it was or how to get back with the wood?

All these problems were early solved by numbering systems and some of the rudiments of exact sciences we know today. The early Sumerians, for instance, invented trigonometry to measure angles between the stars in the heavens.

Then, too, even priest-kings, though professedly immortal, did not live forever (even though early Sumerian King lists recorded on clay tablets ascribed reigns of the most exaggerated length, three of whom supposedly ruled for 64,800 years). Therefore, systems of recording events evolved from earlier pictographic recording of ideas.

Whether the early priests or the populace itself decided, a grandiose house for the local god evolved as cities became established. Though we have yet to discover, for example, where lived the thousands of workmen who built the temple complexes of Chichenitza or Uxmal in Central America, those temples remain as examples of a high culture. The pyramids at Gizeh on the Nile stand as the sole reminder of the Seven Wonders of the World known to Alexander the Great. Excavations in Mesopotamia at Uruk (Fig. 10) show that the White Temple had been reconstructed numerous times on the same site, each time larger and more magnificent.

We know, then, that the factors of civilization included monumental public buildings, which with time and accumulation of wealth became larger and more sophisticated in artistic expression. In other words, once the problems of survival were solved, individuals found time and energy to add beauty to their lives. Princely tombs have produced, at astonishingly early periods, purely ornamental objects of gold, silver and precious stones.

Not all found objects were of local origin, however. Recent investigations have proved that trade in all sorts of goods must have appeared early. By the time of Hammurabi, King of Babylon in c1790 B.C., extensive trade existed across the some 4,000 kilometers between Memphis on the Nile and Harappa on the Indus.

A necessary resultant of the urban revolution, then, included interdependence. Tied to specific geographic locations as cities were, even though they might be in a fertile agricultural area near a constant source of water, their achievements in city building for large populations meant they could never completely supply themselves from local sources. This was especially true among the earliest known cities, those of Sumer, in the southern plains of the Tigris-Euphrates valley, at the head of the Persian Gulf. The Sumerians were the first literate inhabitants of Mesopotamia, and their cuneiform language, indented on clay tablets, is the oldest known.

The Epic of Gilgamesh, Priest-King of Uruk, is the earliest piece of recorded literature. Whether it is fictional or fact matters little. Anthropologists have long studied oral sagas, describing the part real, part mythical, origins of peoples. This epic, like others (read the creation story in Genesis, Chapter 1, or read the biblical story of Daniel, Shadrach, Meshach, and Abednego), originally was part of Sumerian oral tradition, recorded much later, probably in about 2000 B.C.

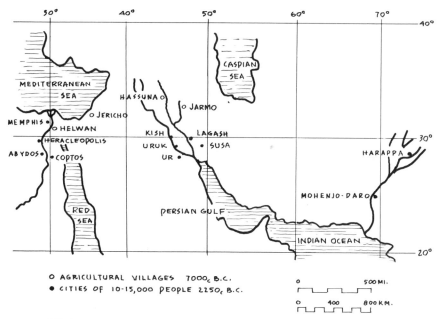

**THE FIRST CITIES**

O AGRICULTURAL VILLAGES 7000₂ B.C.
● CITIES OF 10-15,000 PEOPLE 2250₂ B.C.

FIGURE 10

Fortunately for us, a much later Assyrian King, Assurbanipal, (669–633 B.C.), built a great library in his capital, Nineveh, and there the clay tablets were excavated which record the story of one of the earliest kings of recorded history. The prologue to this recorded tale reveals a great deal about the first cities.

> O Gilgamesh, lord of Kullab, great is thy praise. This was the man to whom all things were known; this was the king who knew the countries of the world. He was wise, he saw mysteries and knew secret things, he brought us a tale of the days before the flood. He went on a long journey, was weary, worn-out with labour, and returning engraved on a stone the whole story.
>
> When the gods created Gilgamesh they gave him a perfect body. Shamash the glorious sun endowed him with beauty, Adad the god of the storm endowed him with courage, the great gods made his beauty perfect, surpassing all others. Two thirds they made him god and one third man.
>
> In Uruk he built walls, a great rampart, and the temple of blessed Eanna for the god of the firmament Anu, and for Ishtar the goddess of love. Look at it still today: the outer wall where the cornice runs, it shines with the brilliance of copper: and the inner wall, it has no equal. Touch the threshold, it is ancient.

> Approach Eanna the dwelling of Ishtar, our lady of love and war,
> the like of which no latter-day king, no man alive can equal.
> Climb upon the wall of Uruk; walk along it, I say; regard the
> foundation terrace and examine the masonry: is it not burnt
> brick and good? The seven sages laid the foundations.[3]

Uruk, the "capital" of a prosperous Sumerian city-state, had a well-organized irrigation system, even in the time of Gilgamesh, fifth ruler of the dynasty. Close to the Euphrates, whose flood plain was a land of marsh and plain, the state had no timber, other than the date palm, or metals. Economic necessity led, therefore, to the establishment of merchant colonies (the first "suburbs," since until recent times foreigners were usually prohibited from living within the walls of cities). The presence of merchants implied bringing necessities from remote areas. Timber, copper, stone from distant quarries, and natural bitumen to waterproof foundations all had to be imported.

The epic also implies a highly developed class structure. At the top, the royal family, living in a palace, part dwelling, part temple. Next came the counsellors, an elected or appointed group of important men giving advice in matters domestic and foreign. There was a warrior class, defenders of the city-state and its trade routes. Military conscription existed, of course, unpopular then as now. Then there were craftsmen, armorers, copper- and goldsmiths, as well as stoneworkers. Below these were the tillers and harvesters, shepherds, gardeners, bakers, bearers of burdens, and the servants of the mighty.

Except in periods of drought (the epic mentions a 7-year dry period) the people ate well. Bread was the staff of life. Wine, both red and white, was the customary beverage. Besides domesticated cattle, sheep, and goats for meat, these riverine people often ate fish and river fowl.

Dwelling along the Euphrates as they did, Gilgamesh's people not only made journeys to the mountains for timber and stone, they also used the river for travel (even though their belief at the time was that the great ocean was uncrossable). Shipwrights, steersmen, and navigators were an important class, and the epic describes in detail boatbuilding, including keel, ribs, caulked planking, decks, masts, and sails.

Early literature, of the kind described above comprised the smaller part of the written and graphic documents of the period. The earliest city map of which we have knowledge is a clay tablet dating from about 1500 B.C., which shows with remarkable accuracy a plan of the city of Nippur, which lay on the left bank of the Euphrates, about halfway between Uruk and Kish (see Map, Fig. 10).

It shows a strongly fortified enclosure with access to the river, and, further, canals leading around and through the city. Although there is no scale attached, from excavations of other cities of the area, we know that such cities were densely built up and had quite large populations. For example, by the period from 3000 to 2500 B.C., Uruk extended over 445 hectares (1,100 acres) and contained possibly 50,000 people.[4]

---

[3]Sandars, N. K. tr, *The Epic of Gilgamesh*, © N. K. Sandars, Baltimore, Md., Penguin, Prologue, p. 59.

[4]Adams, Robert M., "The Origin of Cities," *Scientific American*, September 1960, p. 10.

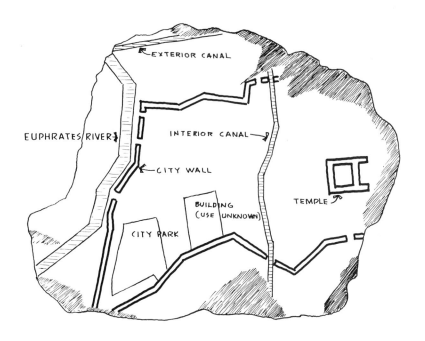

**THE FIRST CITY MAP**
MAP OF NIPPUR ON A CLAY TABLET
DATES FROM 1500, B.C.

FIGURE 11

Nippur's massive fortifications protected the city against nomadic raids, but also against the more formidable campaigns of neighboring rulers. Outside the walls clustered animal shelters, irrigated fields, and subsidiary villages.

Civilization, as it originated and flourished in Mesopotamia, contrasted sharply with that of the Nile and Indus River Valleys, perhaps because of the less-predictable character of the Tigris-Euphrates Valley. Egypt early developed a rigid, monolithic culture under absolute pharaonic rule perhaps due to the absolute predictability of the Nile floods. Though we know far less of the culture of Mohenjo-daro and Harappa, no city walls have been found, and, despite the fact the two centers were 600 kilometers apart, culturally the cities were identical. This is remarkable, when Akkadia (North Mesopotamia) and Sumer (South Mesopotamia) were less than half that distance apart, and yet, until consolidated under Babylonian rule, consisted of a relatively large number of independent city states.

The early Mesopotamian civilization, through its cultural relations with the Mediterranean world, left us enduring sets of values. The Sumerians respected private property, and individuals were permitted to cross the by no means rigid class lines. In Sumer, syllabic (as opposed to pictographic) writing began. A thousand years later, building on the syllabic base, Phoenicia created an alphabet. Chaldean astronomers developed the sexagesimal system of mathematics we use today in trigonometry.

As early as 1790 B.C., Hammurabi had codified laws controlling the adjudication of urban affairs. Religion here in the fertile crescent acquired complexity, explaining creation and providing for a destiny beyond the grave. The concept of citizenship, attributed earlier to the Greeks, in actuality first appeared here.

Because cities first appeared in the Tigris-Euphrates valley, here first grew bureaucracy, primarily for control over public works. Irrigation systems, so vital to the economy, became state-managed projects in view of their magnitude. Here too, a rudimentary form of monetary exchange, in the form of weighed quantities of gold and silver, controlled the economy. In fact, biblical texts often refer to Babylon when referring to capitalistic money concepts.

In short, almost every one of the complexities of modern society, including separation of church and state, was fairly completely developed among these earliest cities.

# 4

# Citadels and Gardens
## (2500–600 B.C.)

> King Nebuchadnezzar made an image of gold, whose height was sixty cubits and its breadth six cubits. He set it upon the plain of Dura, in the province of Babylon. Then King Nebuchadnezzar sent to assemble the satraps, the prefects, and the governors, the counselors, the treasurers, the justices, the magistrates, and all the officials of the provinces to come to the dedication of the image which King Nebuchadnezzar had set up. Then satraps, the prefects, and the governors, the counselors, the treasurers, the justices, the magistrates, and all the officials of the provinces, were assembled for the dedication of the image that King Nebuchadnezzar had set up; and they stood before the image that Nebuchadnezzar had set up. And the herald proclaimed aloud, You are commanded, O people, nations, and languages, that when you hear the sound of the horn, pipe, lyre, trigon, harp, bagpipe, and every kind of music, you are to fall down and worship the golden image that King Nebuchadnezzar has set up . . .[1]

The paragraph quoted above is a part of the biblical story of Daniel, Shadrach, Meshach, and Abednego. The sequel, of course, to the setting up of the golden image, and the insistence on the part of Nebuchadnezzar, king of Assyria, that all people fall down and worship it, was that Daniel and his three companions, refused to do this. The penalty for such refusal was that the four Jews were cast into a "burning fiery furnace." Nebuchadnezzar, full of fury, ordered the furnace heated seven times hotter than normal. But, when the four emerged unscathed, the king, recognizing the superior powers of the God of Israel, promoted Daniel, Shadrach, Meshach, and Abednego, in the province of Babylon.

The story shows the relative sophistication of the high cultures of the Middle East of the period. It also reveals the great wealth of the Assyrians. The golden image, for

---

[1] *Holy Bible: Revised Standard Version*, New York, Nelson, 1952, Daniel, Chapter 3.

example, is described as standing sixty cubits in height, and six in breadth. Even if the image were made of bronze and gold plated, or covered with gold leaf, this image represented substantial wealth. Sixty cubits was, according to Webster, equivalent to 27.4 meters (90 feet). That amounts to a substantial quantity of the precious metal, which leads to further deductions about the complex civilization described.

The closest source of gold was in Africa, some 1,600 to 1,800 kilometers (1,000 to 1,100 miles) to the south and west of Assyria. Copper for the bronze could have come from Palestine, or perhaps the Island of Rhodes in the eastern end of the Mediterranean, while tin, the other ingredient of bronze, must have come from the lands between the Black and Caspian Seas.

The story of Daniel also portrays a highly complex bureaucracy, including provincial governors (satraps), treasurers, and magistrates. The presence of judges and, by inference, lawyers, in Nebuchadnezzar's court was nothing new to Mesopotamia, since Hammurabi had earlier recorded laws, many of them quite equitable, to make city life endurable.

By 600 B.C., then, the Fertile Crescent had a long history of urban life. Figure 12 shows the location of major centers of the periods, while Figure 13 describes in more detail the way in which the closely packed residential areas throughout the region were organized. All exhibit, from early to late in the period, several characteristics in common. Each had its street patterns oriented generally north-south, east-west; whether for mystical reasons or not, we cannot tell. We know, for example, that soothsayers decided on the exact location of Peking,[2] and its precise north-south street orientation. On the other hand, a reasonably logical explanation for such street-pattern orientation is that the builders took full advantage of summer and winter sun angles and probable prevailing winds during the hottest and coolest months (see also Fig. 17).

Generally, too, the scale of residential area blocks was small, reflecting an agriculturally based economy in which cities and villages alike were densely built to retain the fertile fields as close to the city walls as possible.

These examples also reveal differences which are not apparent in the sketches. Palaikastro, on the island of Crete, for instance, was, unlike Babylon (Fig. 18), entirely without walls. The explanation lies in the fact that Crete is an island, and the island itself, in the minds of these insular dwellers (whose culture disappeared in some as yet unknown cataclysm in about 1400 B.C.) had all the character of a fortress, while the Minoans relied on their fleet for protection.

That thesis does not explain, however, the fact that Mohenjodaro and its companion city Harappa in the Indus River valley were likewise unwalled cities, denoting an extremely peaceful way of life.[3]

---

[2]Originally Kublai Khan's capital, named Cambulae, sometime between 1260 and 1290 A.D.

[3]The Indus River valley cities of antiquity vanished about 1100 B.C. One explanation has it that a warlike tribe from the north destroyed that civilization. However archeological evidence shows many of the cultural facets of life in Mohenjo-daro persist in India and Pakistan today.

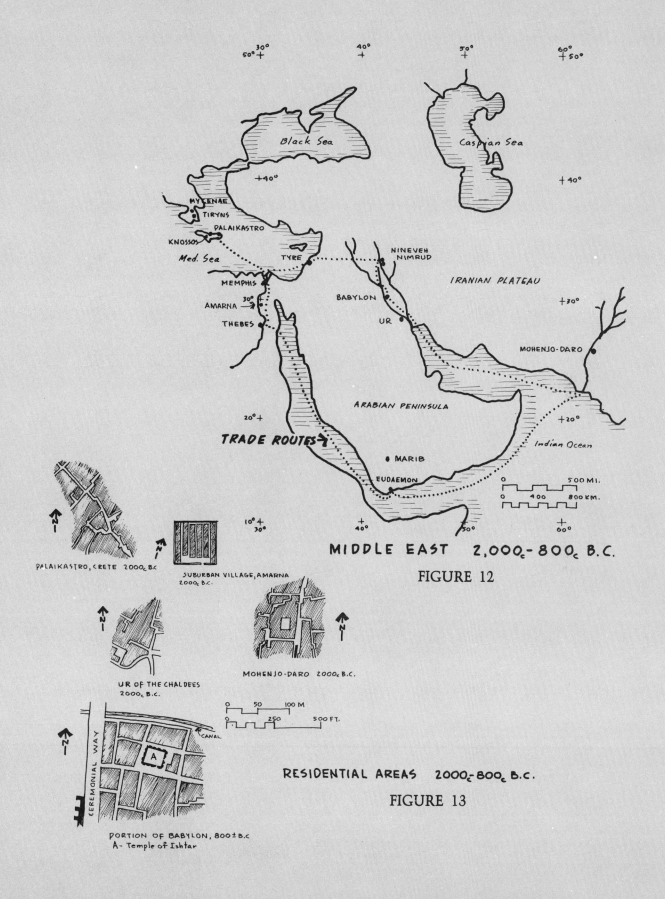

Black Sea

Caspian Sea

+40°

MYCENAE
TIRYNS
PALAIKASTRO
KNOSSOS
Med. Sea

IRANIAN PLATEAU

NINEVEH
NIMRUD

TYRE

MEMPHIS

BABYLON

+30°

AMARNA
30°

UR

THEBES

MOHENJO-DARO

ARABIAN PENINSULA

20° +

TRADE ROUTES

Indian Ocean

+20°

MARIB

EUDAEMON

500 MI.

400    800 KM.

10° +
30°

+
40°

+
50°

+
60°

MIDDLE EAST 2,000c-800c B.C.

FIGURE 12

PALAIKASTRO, CRETE 2000c B.C.

SUBURBAN VILLAGE, AMARNA
2000c B.C.

UR OF THE CHALDEES
2000c B.C.

MOHENJO-DARO 2000c B.C.

RESIDENTIAL AREAS 2000c-800c B.C.

FIGURE 13

50    100 M
250    500 FT.

CEREMONIAL WAY
CANAL
A

PORTION OF BABYLON, 800±B.C
A- Temple of Ishtar

On the other hand, the village at Amarna, Lavedan[4] describes as a *ville ouvrier*. Translated from the French, this title makes the walled, rigidly rectangular village a workers' city. In view of the fact that Egypt had, by 2000 B.C., a long history of Pharaonic control in which the Pharaoh had absolute power of life or death over the people and a strong army to defend the kingdom's borders, the explanation of the wall probably has a climatic connotation.

Just as was the case of the estate of an Egyptian nobleman, (see Fig. 14) the wall of the Amarna village probably protected the inhabitants from the harsh desert winds, the dominant climatic factor in Egypt at any distance away from the Nile since the recession of the last ice age.

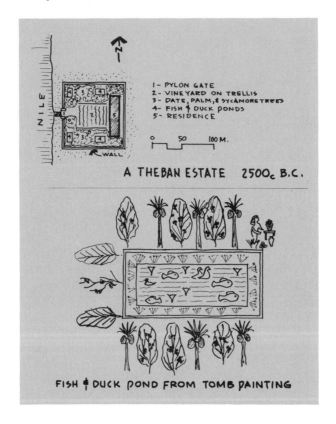

FIGURE 14

Most of what we know about life in Egypt in 2500 B.C., we have learned from translation of hieroglyphs, and from tomb paintings. Further explanation of the cultural and environmental factors inherent in the illustration (Fig. 14) seems necessary.

95 percent of Egypt's population occupied perhaps 3 percent of the land area because of the absolute dependence for survival on the irrigable lands along the Nile. The predictability of annual flooding, and the necessity to irrigate, tended to dictate the

[4]Lavedan, Pierre, *Histoire de L'Urbanisme, Vol I*, Paris, Henri Laurens, 1966.

monolithic culture of prehistoric and historic Egypt. The Pharaohs were absolute monarchs, ruling over a pantheistic hierarchy of the priesthood, with the exception of the time of Ahkneton, who introduced monotheism.

Egypt produced a high level of culture, noted for its artistic and intellectual achievements. The hot climate permitted two to three crops per year, thus establishing a ruling class with great public wealth, and encouraging the production of incredible public monuments (for example, the great pyramids at Gizeh).

Vegetation, in view of the semidesert climate, was extremely sparse. The necessity for irrigation tended to produce strict geometric order in the establishment of communities and public facilities. In fact, one's basic impression of Egypt from 3500 to 500 B.C. is of almost total bilateral symmetry.

The Egyptian concept of the universe reflects this symmetry. To them, the earth was a disk, with the flat plains of Egypt the center. Mountainous "foreign" lands formed a rim surrounding and supporting the disk. Below were the deep waters of the underworld and above, the plane of the sky. In pharaonic reference, the universe had been created by bringing order and justice to replace primeval chaos.

For our purposes, perhaps a significant aspect of this early civilization is the fact that those high in the power structure were permitted to amass great wealth and to live on a sybaritic level. Most significant, however, is the highly functional organization of the estate of an Egyptian noble illustrated in Figure 14.[5]

The little we know about such an establishment indicates that it was extremely functional. The estate was walled, both for privacy and for protection from the hot, drying desert winds. It faced the Nile, the principal communication route. The elements contained within the walls were thoroughly organized in an architectonic manner, expressing man's dominance over nature in its time. The vineyard not only provided grapes for eating and making wine; the date and palm trees added shade as well as food. The pools lent a feeling of coolness to the air, as well as serving as live storage for protein. The house was built with a flat roof, upon which were tent-like awnings, where the family could enjoy the cool evening breezes.

Still another indication of the wealth of Egypt at this period is illustrated by Figure 15. The "Incense Tree" to which the sketch refers may be either one of two trees known throughout the near East from at least as early as 1300 B.C. These are *Boswellia carteri*, the frankincense tree, and *Balsamodendron myrrha*, a tree resembling a low, spreading cedar and producing the aromatic resin, myrrh. Both these gum resins had, in antiquity, many uses. "Frankincense was used primarily as incense in offerings to the gods. . . . Myrrh was used primarily in cosmetics and perfumes."[6]

Population pressures and movements in the fertile crescent had, by this time, induced immigrants from the southern Tigris-Euphrates valley to move to the southwest tip of

[5]For further details, see Clifford, Derek, *A History of Garden Design.* New York, Praeger, 1963, Chapter 1.

[6]Beck, Gus, "The Rise and Fall of Arabia Felix," *Scientific American,* December 1969.

## WORKERS CARRYING INCENSE TREE
### FROM THE LAND OF PUNT

FIGURE 15

the Arabic peninsula, where, along with a corresponding climatic environment across the Red Sea in Africa, was the single region to which the frankincense and myrrh trees were indigenous.

These migrants must have known the value of these native trees, and therefore settled there to establish large-scale irrigation systems as at Marib (Fig. 16). The environmental situation here, at the southern tip of Arabia, was quite different from that of the river valleys. *Arabia Felix* (called thus by the Romans, who assumed the southern interior of the peninsula to be as fertile as the coastal areas), and especially the region producing the expensive resins, lay in the rain shadow of a 1,500-meter (4,900-foot) coastal range of mountains to the west. No rivers came out of these mountains, but there were many short wadis (eroded valleys), dry for most of the time, but subject to short, sharp flooding. The cultivators learned how to trap these infrequent floods behind impressive dams and sluices, feeding the irrigation canals which assured bounteous crops of the aromatic resins so sought after by the peoples of the fertile crescent, and later by the Romans. In fact, the 4,000 acres of irrigated land at Marib made possible by the long stone dam at Wadi Dhana may have provided life-giving sustenance to the people until the triumph of Christianity in 323 A.D. caused the frankincense market to collapse.

In sharp contrast to the irrigation cultures of the fertile crescent was, at this time, the semi-barbaric culture of early Greece. Tiryns and Mycenae, two similar citadels built on the crowns of low hills and heavily walled for protection, exhibit much less sophistication than Ur of the Chaldees, Abraham's early home, or later Babylon (See Fig. 18). Best known to us through the tales of Troy told by Homer, acropoli (for that is what both Mycenae and Tiryns were: "high cities") already showed environmental control. Note (Fig. 17) how the megaron (living room) faced to the east of south, to take full advantage of the sun in the cold winters of the Greek peninsula, and opened by way of a porch into a courtyard, the later Greek and Roman peristyle.

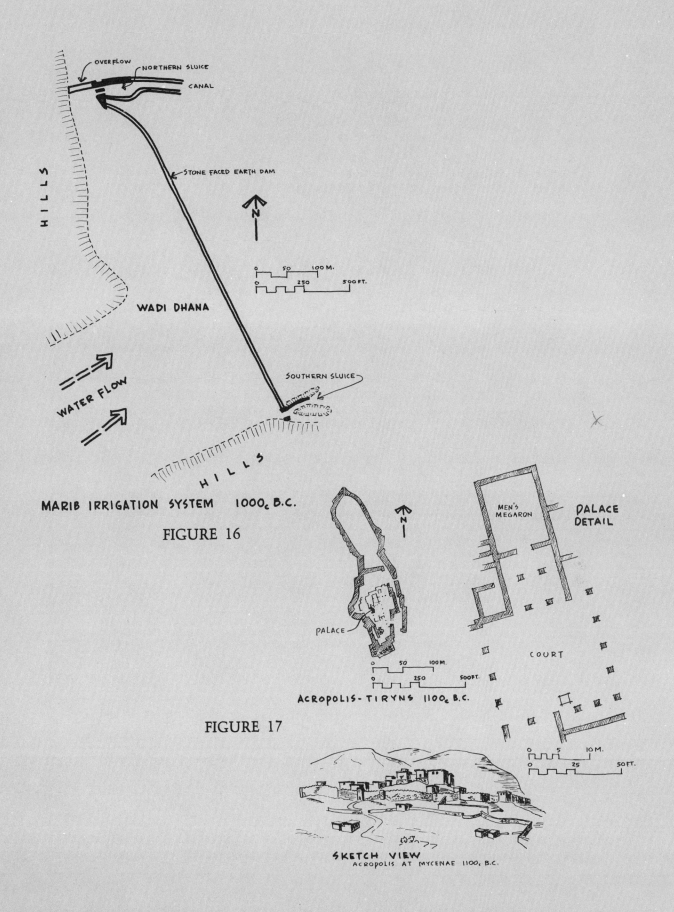

OVERFLOW   NORTHERN SLUICE

CANAL

HILLS

STONE FACED EARTH DAM

N

50   100 M.

250   500 FT.

WADI DHANA

WATER FLOW

SOUTHERN SLUICE

HILLS

MARIB IRRIGATION SYSTEM   1000ₑ B.C.

FIGURE 16

N

PALACE

50   100 M.

250   500 FT.

ACROPOLIS - TIRYNS 1100ₑ B.C.

FIGURE 17

MEN'S MEGARON

PALACE DETAIL

COURT

5   10 M.

25   50 FT.

SKETCH VIEW
ACROPOLIS AT MYCENAE 1100ₑ B.C.

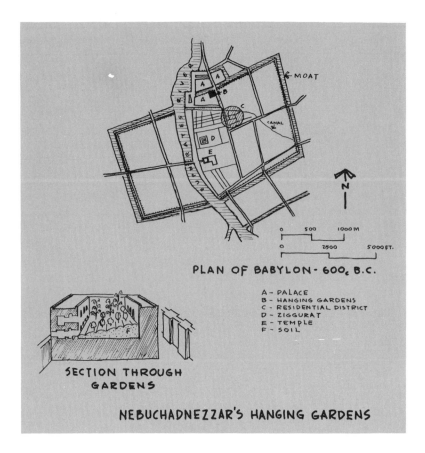

PLAN OF BABYLON - 600₂ B.C.

A - PALACE
B - HANGING GARDENS
C - RESIDENTIAL DISTRICT
D - ZIGGURAT
E - TEMPLE
F - SOIL

SECTION THROUGH
GARDENS

NEBUCHADNEZZAR'S HANGING GARDENS

FIGURE 18

The Greeks, early influenced by the older civilization on the island of Crete, and later by the influx of Dorians and Ionians, were in the process of developing the demotic city-states for which Greece is best known. At the same time, the older cultures of the Tigris-Euphrates river valley continued the process of historic change.

Babylon, according to the Greek historian Herodotus (fourth century B.C.), was a fabulous city, miles in extent. More recent scientific investigation reveals the walled city to have been less than 3 kilometers (1.8 miles) in its broadest extent. Yet, to an Athenian, Babylon,[7] with its broad ceremonial way, its extensive palace confines, and its world wonder, the hanging gardens, must have seemed immense. The curious traveler having heard at home tales of the famous hanging gardens must have made every effort to be invited by the great king's guardians to inspect these world-renowned terraces. Archeological investigation reveals that they resembled a contemporary roof garden of several acres. An ingenious structural system was invented by the Babylonians; the roofs were supported by large, hollow columns filled with earth, to permit sufficient soil

[7]Compare Babylon, Figure 18, with Athens, Figure 27, in terms of their relative size during the periods of their greatest area in antiquity.

volume for tree-root development. Several explanations have been offered as to how the gardens were watered; one is that lines of bucket-carrying slaves climbed up and down hidden stairways from the adjacent moat.

During its heyday, Nebuchadnezzar, the reported builder of the hanging gardens, commanded a kingdom large for its time. The Assyrians had overrun Egypt, Palestine, and the eastern Mediterranean coastline, with the exception of the small Phoenician kingdom of Tyre. This oriental despot had built a second capital at Nineveh with its twin city Nimrud adjacent. The Assyrians, a warlike people in contrast to the more peace-loving Babylonians (the cultural descendants of the Sumerians), despite their predilection for military conquest, performed a distinct service to posterity. The great library at Nineveh revealed, upon recent excavation, a treasure of cuneiform tablets, including most of the chapters of the dawn-world Epic of Gilgamesh.

The sophistication of the Near-East kingdom of Assyria is further revealed by evidence of man-made parks, devoted to the kingly sports of hunting and riding and to the development of war skills with the bow and javelin.

A fragment of an illustration of one of these parks has come down to us. The regular spacing of the trees may be artistic license, but, in view of the environment, anywhere away from the riverbanks themselves, a more logical explanation is that the trees were in plantation rows. The hills shown could have been natural or artificial, but the lake, on which boats rode, probably was man-made.

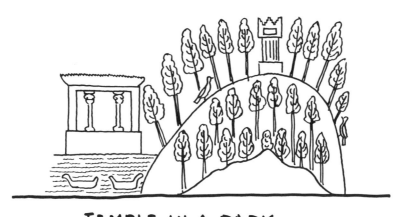

TEMPLE IN A PARK
ASSYRIA    700c B.C

FIGURE 19

Here may be revealed the origin of the great royal parks of the succeeding Oriental culture that was to have such environmental impact on the future—the Empire of Darius I, of Persia.

# 5        City States and Empire
## (1000–335 B.C.)

In 490 B.C., on the plain of Marathon, about 40 kilometers (26 miles) northeast of Athens, Miltiades, a Greek general, with 10,000 Greek hoplites, defeated a much larger Persian army. A fast runner named Phidippides, according to tradition, carried the news of the Persian defeat to Athens.

Then years later, Darius' Persian successor, Xerxes, marched with his huge army across Thrace and into Macedonia to the north of the Attic peninsula and thus again threatened Athens. In 481 B.C. at Corinth, Sparta and Athens formed a union of Greek city states to meet the Persian threat.

At the pass of Thermopylae, about 160 kilometers (100 miles) northwest of Athens, 7,000 Spartans fought and were finally defeated by Xerxes' huge army (thought to be 300,000 strong.) Shortly thereafter, Xerxes occupied and burned the city of Athens itself. But there were no Athenians in the city; they had taken ship and escaped. Themistocles of Athens had somehow been forewarned and developed a strong fleet of triremes (galleys with three banks of oars). The Persian fleet met the Greeks in a narrow water passage at Salamis, and the Greeks destroyed the Persian fleet. Thus, three days after Xerxes had stood in triumph on the Acropolis in Athens, he withdrew from the Greek shores, never to return.[1]

Two land battles, one at Marathon and one at Thermopylae, and one naval engagement, at Salamis, constitute a trio of perhaps the most important military engagements in history. The defeat of Xerxes at Salamis decisively changed the course of the river of history and caused the Western World to remain Western rather than Oriental.

In 612 B.C. the Medes[2] from the north and the Chaldeans from the south conquered Assyria and destroyed Nineveh. A little more than 100 years later Cyrus (later termed "the Great") of Persia, an obscure nation to the south and east of Babylon, conquered the Medes, thus establishing the Persian Empire, the first known in our world.

From 550 B.C. to the time of Xerxes' defeat at Salamis, Persia dominated Asia Minor and the lands to the east as far as India and Afghanistan. Cyrus and his successors, Cambyses, Darius, and Xerxes, were unlike previous conquerors. The success of the

---

[1] Asimov, Isaac, *The Greeks, A Great Adventure*, Boston, Houghton Mifflin, 1965.

[2] Medes, a people living to the north of Assyria south of the Caspian Sea.

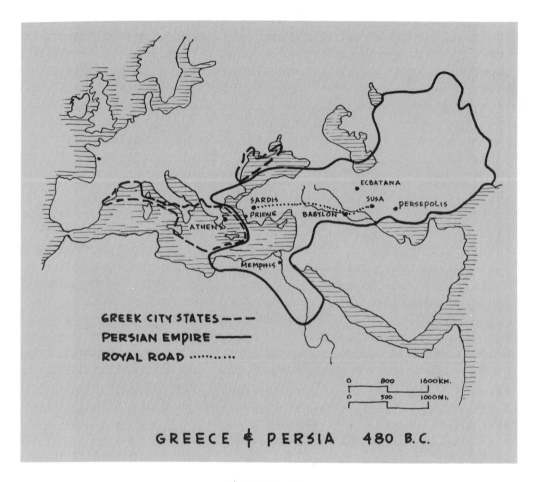

FIGURE 20

Persian Empire lay in allowing conquered people self-respect and considerable home rule. The result was that Persia was an administrative as well as a territorial success.

Darius, after he became king in 521 B.C. reorganized his huge empire, dividing it into satrapies (provinces), created an excellent road system (see Royal Road, Fig. 20), adopted the Lydian system of using coinage as a medium of exchange, and, in all, created a strong and efficient government.[3]

Under Cyrus, one of the Persian provincial capitals had been Ecbatana in the north, the earlier capital of the Medes. Susa, the seat of Fars (Greek *Persis,* thus Persia) became the winter capital, and Ecbatana was utilized during the summer.

Darius, however, perhaps to express the greatness of his empire, began a great palace complex at Persepolis. Added to by suceeding emperors, the palace complex was erected on a huge terrace cut from the rocks of the "Mountain of Mercy" overlooking the plain to the south. The most famous of the structures, probably an audience hall, is today

---

[3]Asimov, Isaac, *Asimov's Guide to the Bible, Vol I, The Old Testament,* New York, Doubleday, 1968.

known as the Hall of the 100 Columns. The artistic sophistication of the structures and their relief sculpture illuminates the power and glory of the Persian Empire, while the sheer scale of the huge terraces indicates its vast resources.

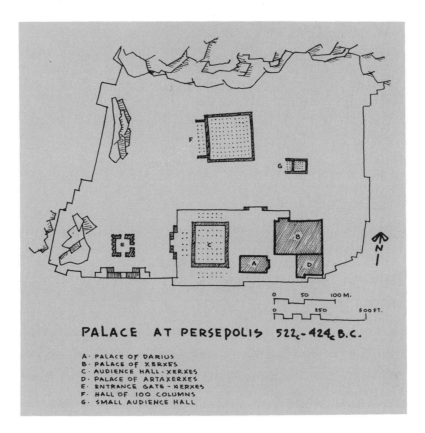

PALACE AT PERSEPOLIS 522.-424 B.C.

A· PALACE OF DARIUS
B· PALACE OF XERXES
C· AUDIENCE HALL-XERXES
D· PALACE OF ARTAXERXES
E· ENTRANCE GATE-XERXES
F· HALL OF 100 COLUMNS
G· SMALL AUDIENCE HALL

FIGURE 21

In truly Oriental fashion, the Persian emperors were lovers of luxury and beauty. Wherever he might travel, from his Lydian capital at Sardis in the West to his Far-Eastern satrapies, the emperor could assure himself, despite the heat and relative dryness of the countryside, of a watered, cool, shaded retreat from the harshness of the semidesert. These private gardens were each walled, shadowed with shade and fruit trees, and well-watered. The traditional pattern for these private retreats is reflected in a Persian carpet. An ornate pavilion occupied the center, as an island surrounded by an artificial pond, and branching into the original Persian, later Islamic, four rivers of paradise.

The private gardens, as well as the great hunting parks, laboriously planted wherever Persian dominance held sway, must have been almost completely man-made. The physiography of Persia dictated this answer to the creation of "the good life." Most of Persia was then, and is now, semidesert. Water supplies were hard-won at great expenditure of energy.

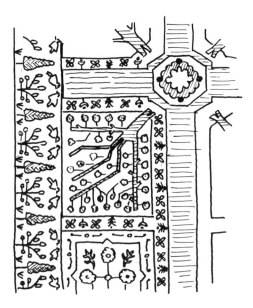

## PORTION OF A PERSIAN CARPET

### FIGURE 22

Figure 23 gives an indication of the massive energy required to produce the luxury of gardens in a desert land. The *qanat*, or horizontal well, comprised the key to the process. Snow and rainfall in the mountains failed to produce a constant surface stream flow on the high plains at the foot of the hills. But some early well-digger must have observed a certain constancy in the depth of water in his vertically excavated well. Apparently on the theory that horizontal wells were easier dug than vertical ones, the *qanat*, or horizontal water-tunnel became common practice. Such tunnels often extended many miles, from the main shaft at the foot of the mountain to the point at which the gently sloping tunnel reached the surface. From thence, the never-failing water supply fed into surface channels and pools to provide abundant water for orchards, gardens, parks, and fields of crops.[4]

Some such system as this must have made possible the great parks and hunting preserves of the Persian empire, since Richard Frye[5] reports some of the *qanats* to have been as long as 48 kilometers (30 miles).

As early as the seventh century B.C. Assyrian kings were known to have constructed extensive royal parks (see Fig. 19). These parks were usually the king's hunting grounds, and also places for feasts, assemblies, and audiences. Figure 24 shows in miniature a

[4]Wilbur, Donald N. *Persian Gardens and Pavilions*, Rutland, Vt., Tuttle, 1962.

[5]Frye, Richard N. *Iran*, New York, Holt, Rinehart and Winston, 1953.

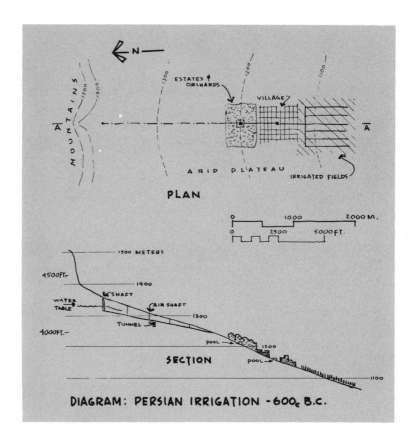

FIGURE 23

FIGURE 24

little of how one of Darius' hunting parks must have appeared. The palms shown are probably those Pliny the Elder, Roman statesman and naturalist, called "Royal" because they had been reserved by Persian kings for their own use. The winged figure above the charioteer's head symbolized Ahura Mazda, the Zoroastrian god worshipped by Darius.

The manner of planting the royal parks may be illustrated by the report of Lysander, the Spartan, who visited Cyrus at Sardis (Lydian capital of the Persian empire). Lysander admired the regularity of the way the trees were planted: "how straight the rows of them were and how elegantly all the rows formed angles with one another."[6] He may have referred to a great park owned by Cyrus at Celaenae, and extending above the town on both banks of the Maeander River. Here Cyrus used to hunt on horseback for exercise. The park was so large he could within it review 130,000 troops.

Further evidence of the luxury in which the Persian Emperors lived is found in the Old Testament book of Esther, which describes a great feast held by King Ahasuerus (Xerxes) in the garden of his palace at Susa. The feast for the nobles and all the people lasted for 180 days.

While the Persian Empire flourished, the Greeks were busily building cities, establishing commercial colonies among the Aegean Islands, on the coast of Asia Minor, in the Bosporus (cf. Lygos, a Greek village on the Golden Horn as early as 700 B.C. See Fig. 49).

The earliest Greeks were Acheans, who apparently migrated into the Peloponnesus during the fourteenth and thirteenth centuries, B.C. After them came Aeolians and Ionians, preceding the Dorians, who arrived about 1000 B.C. What had these early Greeks found when they landed on the Greek peninsula?

The climate of Greece is (and was then) mesothermal, the coldest month above 0°C (32°F), and below 18°C (65°F); the warmest month above 10°C (50°F). Greece has a dry summer season, and the climate in general is similar to Southern California.

Most of Greece is mountainous, cut by small, rapid rivers, with limited fertile soils, but relatively rich in minerals, especially marble and limestone.

The ancient Greeks upon arrival found a lean land, divided by mountains, often impassable, with meager soil and water, without navigable rivers, and with few forests. Discomforts were great; the land was surrounded by stormy seas. Herodotus, Greece's first historian (c484–c425 B.C.) wrote: "Hellas has always had poverty as her companion."

During the Homeric period (800–700 B.C.), the time of the great heroes, Aeneas, Achilles, Agamemnon (King of Mycenae, leader of the Greeks in the Trojan War), Homer speaks constantly of heroes eating meat. By Periclean times (443–429 B.C.) beef herds appear to have declined almost to the vanishing point. At her highest cultural peak, then, only on days of high festival was meat available. In fact, the usual Greek diet of two meals a day of barley and other grain dishes was so austere that Persian invaders complained of it.

[6]Wright, Richardson, *The Story of Gardening*, New York, Dodd, Mead, 1935, p. 38.

Thus, topography, climate, and a mix of peoples combined to produce on the Greek peninsula and the Aegean Islands a high-level culture characterized by:

1.   City-States: a country of isolated valleys, with detached communities.
2.   Trade and colonialism: meager food resources, and a maritime country (no part of Greece is much more than 48 kilometers [30 miles] from the sea) forced the Greeks to become sailors, traders, and colonizers.
3.   The steady climate and the meager diet caused the Greeks to be hard workers, enduring of hardship, and apparently led to a desire for outdoor, public life. Note for example, that most Greek architecture was outdoor architecture (agoras, gymnasia, theatres, temples).
4.   As in other early cultures, the earliest rulers were kings (cf. Agamemnon of Mycenae). But the nature of the country successively produced aristocracies, forms of democracy, and eventually dictators (tyrants).
5.   In contrast to Egypt, Babylonia, Assyria, and Persia, Greece continued as separate city states. Such unity as existed was in terms of religion and the periodic Olympic games. The Delian league (of much later time) with Athens heading it, was the closest Greece came to Empire.

Greece has had influence on western man far out of proportion to her size. The Attic Peninsula, plus the islands of the Aegean Sea, comprises a land area little over 50,000 square miles, little larger than the present state of Ohio (40,740 square miles), smaller than the land area of the New England States (66,624 square miles).

Yet, "let your fingers do the walking" through the yellow pages of the *telephone* book, to call a *mechanic,* who can repair the *electrical* system of your *automobile,* and you have used four words of Greek derivation. Over half of the English language derives from Greek and Latin, everyday speech of these early cultures. A large proportion of the language of science (most of the section headings in the Geologic Timetable, Appendix A, come from the Greek) was common in the verbal intercourse of the Greek philosophers. So, too, has American culture been influenced by Greek concepts of what is fine, what is beautiful. Not too many years ago a courthouse was not a courthouse unless it looked like a Greek Temple; a bank was not a bank if it had not a Greek facade. In many modern upper-middle-class subdivisions are an astonishing number of "Colonial" houses, indirect descendants of the Greek megaron house.

Of importance to us as physical land-planners are some of the tangible, measurable, Greek institutions. One of the most widely known philosophical concepts of the Greeks, later expressed by a Latin who had probably studied in an Athenian Lyceum (school) is: *"Mens sana in corpore sano,"* or, "A sound mind in a sound body." Note in the Asia Minor coastal town, Priene (Fig. 25) the cultural, spiritual, political, and commercial institutions, which were typical wherever Greeks settled. What town of today (then called *polis,* not a place, but a coherent community of people, who must be capable of meeting together and dealing with problems face-to-face) has, within its 26 to 28 hectares (65–70 acres) and a population between 5,000 and 10,000, all this?

4 churches (temples)
1 open air theatre
a city council chamber
a civic center and shopping center (agora)
a gymnasium capable of seating the entire population

Athens, the premier Greek city, in Periclean times—495–420 B.C.—had a total population of 290,000 persons. Perhaps 20 cities of the time had more than 10,000

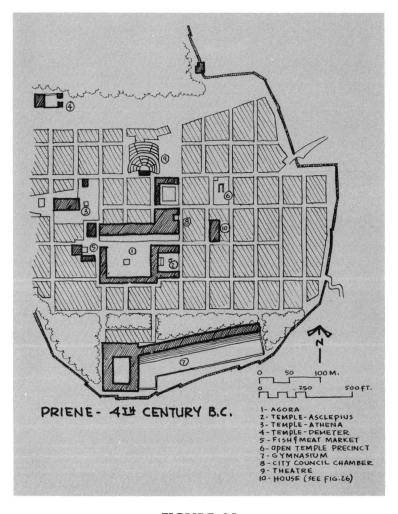

PRIENE - 4ᵗʰ CENTURY B.C.

1- AGORA
2- TEMPLE-ASCLEPIUS
3- TEMPLE-ATHENA
4- TEMPLE-DEMETER
5- FISH & MEAT MARKET
6- OPEN TEMPLE PRECINCT
7- GYMNASIUM
8- CITY COUNCIL CHAMBER
9- THEATRE
10- HOUSE (SEE FIG.26)

FIGURE 25

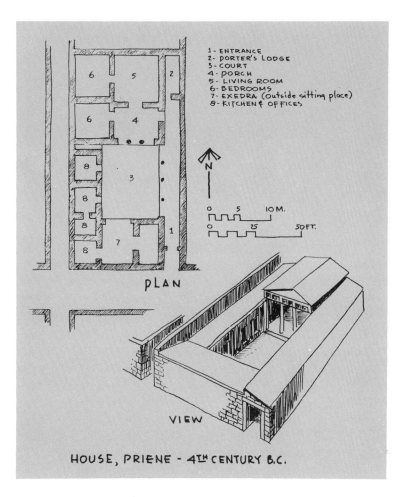

1 - ENTRANCE
2 - PORTER'S LODGE
3 - COURT
4 - PORCH
5 - LIVING ROOM
6 - BEDROOMS
7 - EXEDRA (outside sitting place)
8 - KITCHEN & OFFICES

PLAN

VIEW

HOUSE, PRIENE - 4ᵀᴴ CENTURY B.C.

FIGURE 26

people. Cities such as Priene were tight little islands not requiring parks and tree-lined streets. If a resident felt the need to breathe country air, he had only to step outside the city wall.

Greeks were essentially urbanites, anyway, but not given to ostentation. If one were a citizen (a very lofty status), he considered himself at least the equal of every other citizen. It was unnecessary to get ahead of one's neighbors by building a bigger, more elaborate mansion. Houses were therefore simple, functional, and inward-oriented (see Fig. 26). Common walls were the rule, much living took place in the central court, with the porch and family sitting room oriented to the south to take full advantage of the winter sun. Heating was by charcoal-fired braziers. The exedra apparently was the "summer" living room, located on the shady side of the court.

The home was strictly a family place. Women generally kept to the house and its courtyard, while men spent their days engaged in public life at the gymnasium, the theatre, the temples, or arguing politics in the agora. In colonial towns the agora served as the focal point of civic activity.

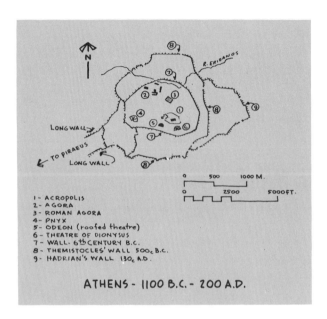

FIGURE 27

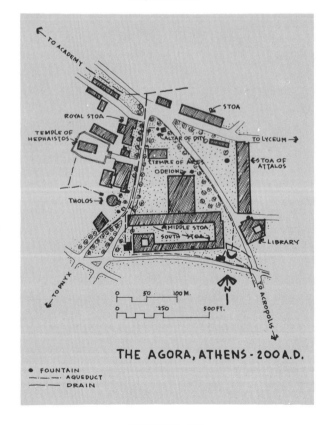

FIGURE 28

In the largest cities a wider variety of social activities existed. In addition to gymnasia and the market place, Athens provided both open-air and roofed theatres, libraries, open-air schools of philosophy and numerous clubs and societies. The city evolved from this way of life.

The agora at Athens illustrates the variety of life (see Figs. 27 and 28). Though the plan shows its conformation in Roman times, this organization was the culmination of well over 1,300 years of continuous occupation, change and development on the same site.

Note, in contrast to the relatively simple, geometric organization of planned towns such as Priene and Miletus, the Athenian Agora must be classed as an "organically grown" space. The Altar of Pity (a sort of place of sanctuary for thieves and runaways) and the Tholos (a temple to minor gods called *phosphoroi*—light-bearers) had been in place in 500 B.C., as well as the temple to Hephaistos (god of fire and iron-working). The space had been occupied for generations by various shopping arcades, but only achieved the state shown in the figure under Imperial Rome.

The two large fountains on the south supplied the agora with drinking water. The overflow from these led down northward in two stone channels provided with dipping basins beside the main traffic arteries. One of the channels watered a sacred grove of laurel and olive surrounding the Altar of Pity. After the Persian wars plane trees were planted to shade the main walks. Black and white poplars grew in spots dampened by the overflow from the fountains and drains.[7]

In general effect, the central space must have appeared to the Athenians much the same as some of the more-casually developed New England town commons, except that with urban foot traffic as heavy as it must have been to the shops and to dramatic performances in the Odeion, there was probably no village "green." The Mediterranean climate is not especially conducive to lush turf in any case.

So, although the Greek culture gave us the public park, athletic field, and college campus (journalists still refer occasionally to campuses as "the groves of academe"), we have not yet excavated, in our search for our past, any truly Greek "gardens" as such.

However, despite the leanness of their land, the Greeks must have known gardens. Homer's Odyssey, the fifth Book, describes an early Greek garden:

> In it flourish tall trees; pears and pomegranates and apples full of fruit, also sweet fig and bounteous olives . . . Here, too, a fertile vineyard has been planted . . . beyond the last row of trees, well laid garden plots have been arranged, blooming all the year with flowers. And there are two springs; one leads through the garden while the other dives beneath the threshold of the great court to gush out beside the stately palace; from it the citizens draw their water.[8]

[7]*Garden Lore of Ancient Athens*, Courtesy of the American School of Classical Studies at Athens, 1963.

[8]*Ibid.*

Athens, even in its greatest period, had built aqueducts to distribute water supplies, but these were meager at best, and sufficient only to supply public fountains as those in the agora.

While the philosophers conducted their schools (academies or lyceums) in groves outside the city walls, the Greeks knew little of garden luxury inside the city walls. Some citizens of wealth owned suburban farms and orchards (which idea of rustic villas the Romans readily adopted). After the threat of Persia had been eliminated, Greeks traveled extensively in Asia Minor and other Persian possessions, thus learning Persian garden lore. In later centuries, a Greek like Theophrastus (287+ B.C.) could love his garden so well that he left it in his will to 11 friends as a sacred possession. Epicurus (died 270 B.C.), described by Pliny the Elder as "that connoisseur in the enjoyment of a life of ease," was the first to lay out a garden in Athens, conducting therein his "epicurean" school of philosophy.[9]

It would appear, therefore, that the legacy left us by the Greeks, although it included much of science, and most especially a love of learning, as well as the Olympian tradition of outdoor, vigorous exercise, excluded gardening on any great scale. We shall have to leave it to Alexander (Macedonian, not Greek) to Hellenize (read easternize) the Greek world, amalgamating the puritanic austerity of Greek culture with the pleasure-loving culture of Persia and Egypt.

[9]*Ibid.*

# 6       The Age of Alexander
## (350–200 B.C.)

Strange as it may seem, Alexander, the son of Philip of Macedon, the king of an obscure kingdom north and east of Greece, by virtue of an insatiable greed for power, gave his name to one of the most magnificent, ostentatious ages of man's cultural development.

In 336 B.C. when Philip died suddenly, his son Alexander assumed the reins of the kingdom of Macedon. Thenceforward, he drove himself, his generals and his armies to control over the eastern Mediterranean, Asia Minor, Egypt, the Persian highlands, and lands as far north and east as present Afghanistan and western Pakistan. All of this territorial control he accomplished in what today is considered a short life-span. Born in 356 B.C., Alexander the Great became king of Macedon in 336 B.C., and died at the age of 33 in 323 B.C. at Babylon, the center of his newly founded empire.

It seems appropriate, at this stage of the study of man's environmental control, to review. Back in 825 B.C., just before the Homeric Age, the Greeks were just discovering the advantage of bronze over stone weapons. Babylonians have not yet seen their own far-famed Hanging Gardens. The Assyrians are a power, in their twin cities of Nineveh and Nimrud, up north along the Tigris. Memphis is the liveliest city port on the Nile, while the Phoenicians, in the eastern end of the Mediterranean, have just become a maritime power, but have not yet founded Rome's great early rival, Carthage (See Fig. 12).

In 375 B.C., just before Alexander appears (see Fig. 29), Greece controls the eastern Mediterranean, and Phoenicia has established Carthage in the western end. Persia is the great power to the east, and Egypt still maintains its identity. Greek Athens, Corinth, and Syracuse are important cities, matched in size and glory only by Phoenician Carthage, Egyptian Memphis, and durable, but by now Persian, Babylon.

Onto this stage strode Alexander, the Macedonian, afterwards known as "The Great." The stage, of course, had been set by Alexander's father, Philip, but it was Alexander who took advantage of the actors and props already set. It must be noted that the Persians, eastward from the Mediterranean, had been for centuries the Greek *bête noire*. Commercial and political rivals from the time of the Athenian league, but now with its armies made up principally of Greek mercenaries (Greece, a small, poor country, apparently had, as its most important export, Greek hoplites), Alexander (correctly, it turned out) saw the great empire focused on Sardis, Babylon, and Persepolis as ripe for conquest.

As Alexander's star so briefly flashed across the skies of history, he almost opened up the Far East, as represented by India. Only a sit-down strike on the part of his armies prevented a proposed march on the Ganges.

Thus did Alexander the Great Hellenize the then known world of the Eastern Mediterranean. Greek governance, language, and traditions by the time of Alexander's untimely death dominated not only the lands surrounding the eastern two-thirds of the Mediterranean, but the Alexandrian Empire extended as far east as the Indus River valley, encompassing both Greek City-States, and the former Persian Empire (See Fig. 20).

Alexander's political governance of his empire included the rather wise philosophy of encouraging local religion and custom, just as Darius before him, a conception later used to good effect by the Roman Catholic church as it established primacy in the Medieval world of Western Europe. Thus, during his military conquests of the East, Alexander's generals were established as military governors in the various subdued provinces as the Macedonian-Greek armies raced on to new conquest.

The generals rapidly, especially after the death of their supreme commander, assumed the trappings of Asiatic potentates.

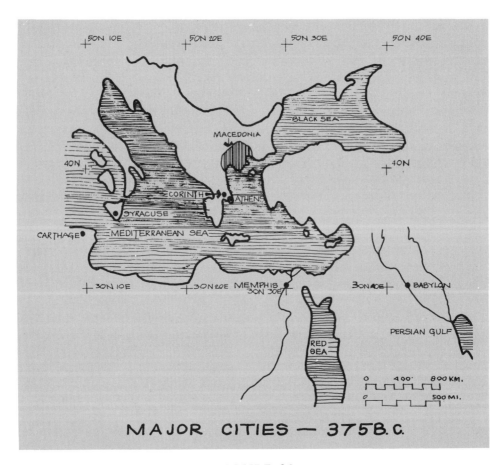

FIGURE 29

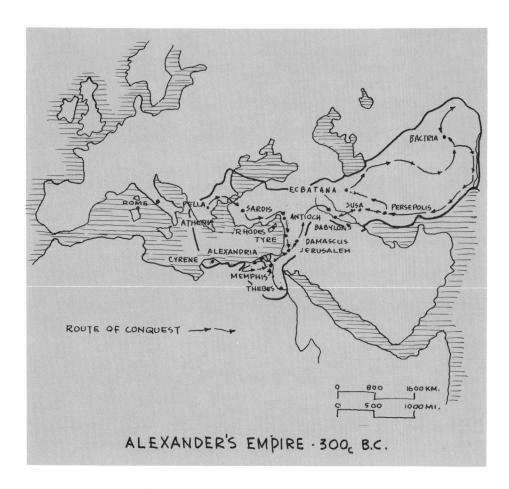

ALEXANDER'S EMPIRE · 300c B.C.

FIGURE 30

For example, Seleucus Nicator, one of Alexander's generals, founded for himself a new imperial city, Seleucia, just north of Babylon, on the Euphrates. Soter I, another general, became the first in the long dynasty of the Ptolemies, Greek Pharaohs of Egypt, accepted as the God-Kings of that land which consistently refused to Hellenize its art forms, language, and traditions.

A century later, the urban geography of the eastern Mediterranean appeared as in Figure 30. Athens, formerly the greatest, most sought out center of cultural thought, was by this time reduced to a rather provincial town of little over 30,000 people. Yet Alexandria, founded by the great one himself, rapidly exerted its influence to become the greatest city of the then known world. In fact, the other name for the Hellenistic age (that of the dominance of Greek language and culture over the "western world") was the "Alexandrian Age," after the city itself.

You will note that by 200 B.C. Rome had also become a major city, but its cultural dominance waits for yet another age. Of importance here are the form, scale, and character of this glorious capital, politically the capital of Egypt, but culturally capital of

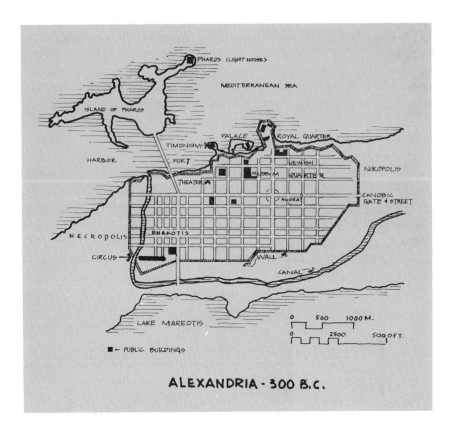

FIGURE 31

the known world. Alexandria's form exemplifies the highest level of Greek urban planning, using lessons learned and practiced for centuries by the Greeks in establishing their far-flung series of commercial colonies. The gridiron pattern, well established in such towns as Priene and Miletus, was naturally repeated here (See Fig. 31).

However, there were basic differences in the pattern, clearly expressing not the essentially Greek democratic pattern of a citizen-ruled town such as Priene but a seat of Eastern (Persian) absolute monarchy. Note, for example, the great east-west ceremonial avenue traversing the city from end to end, crossed by a second major ceremonial street. These major thoroughfares, according to Triggs,[1] were each 31 meters (100 feet) wide. (Contrast these with the 7-meter [23-foot] width of the major streets of Priene, Fig. 25.)

Exemplifying the cosmopolitan character of the city was its division into quarters. Northward, near the port and harbor, was the *regia*, or royal quarter, containing the palaces of the Ptolemies. Eastward was the Jewish quarter, where even then lived lawyers, scholars, and merchants from Jerusalem. The southwest quarter, the site of an earlier Egyptian fishing village, remained essentially Egyptian, and was named (after the village) Rhakotis.

[1]Triggs, Inigo, *Town Planning*, London, Methuen, 1909.

Greek institutions dominated, of course. The theatre, temples, and at least one, possibly two, agoras had prominent positions. The commercial agora is thought to have been near the landward terminus of the great bridge connecting the city with its harbor-protecting island of Pharos. A second agora, principally devoted to political and religious uses, probably was located at the junction of the two crossing main avenues.

Greek sculpture and architecture expressed the visual character of the city. But Alexandria's great contribution to history was its magnificent university, contained in the "museum." Its libraries gathered together over 490,000 scrolls, thus preserving and enriching the Greek heritage for later use by Rome and its successors.

As the world's cultural mecca, Alexandria gathered unto itself the greatest thinkers of its era. Poets and prose writers such as the poet Theocritus of Syracuse and the satirist Lucian worked, wrote, and thought here. Archimedes, another Syracusan, was thought to have discovered some of his most important mechanical theories here. Eratosthenes, a geometrician and astronomer, here determined the radius of the earth by comparing the angle of the sun's rays at noon on the longest day of the year in Alexandria with the angle on the same day at a location far up the Nile on the equator.

Alexandrian trade with other major ports, had its impact too. Navigators from Alexandria expanded the bounds of the known world as they learned of such remote areas as the North Sea, not again to be seriously considered until western Europe felt the impact of Viking raiders.

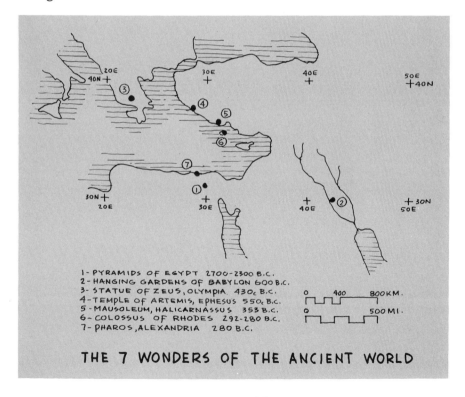

1- PYRAMIDS OF EGYPT 2700-2300 B.C.
2- HANGING GARDENS OF BABYLON 600 B.C.
3- STATUE OF ZEUS, OLYMPIA 430c B.C.
4- TEMPLE OF ARTEMIS, EPHESUS 550c B.C.
5- MAUSOLEUM, HALICARNASSUS 353 B.C.
6- COLOSSUS OF RHODES 292-280 B.C.
7- PHAROS, ALEXANDRIA 280 B.C.

THE 7 WONDERS OF THE ANCIENT WORLD

FIGURE 32

Alexandria, as a major seaport, because of its well-protected harbor, became known otherwise for its colossal lighthouse, some 134 meters (440 feet) in height, on Pharos island. In fact, the Pharos lighthouse became the seventh wonder of the ancient world.

Apparently, in the Hellenistic world originated the Chamber-of-Commerce syndrome, which insists that, no matter in what city we live, we have some feature that is the first, the biggest, or the most, anywhere in the world.

Figure 32 locates the Seven Wonders of the Ancient World. Why seven? Probably because the number 7 has ever been a magic number. All have since been destroyed, except curiously enough, the earliest, the great Pyramids of Gizeh. But all have loomed large in the imaginations of men, as monuments to man's genius for attempting, and, more often than not, successfully achieving feats considered impossible by sceptics and doubters.

The Hellenistic world represents to us the culmination, up to this point in time, of man's forward progress toward control over his destiny and toward control over his physical environment. True, abject poverty and slavery was the condition of the largest percentage of people. True, Hero, an Alexandrian mechanician, had invented a steam engine, but applied it only to open and close temple doors.

But the Ptolemaic dynasties of Egypt and the Seleucid dynasties of Syria and Persia molded the world of that day into a wide unity of trade and learning, and made it possible for Rome, as it overshadowed the Mediterranean World, to absorb Hellenistic (Greek) culture, thus preserving it as a still vital part of our own present-day culture.

# 7  The Seven Hills of Rome
## (753 B.C.–300 A.D.)

Workmen in 1874 A.D. digging the foundations for the treasury building on the Via Settembre in Rome, to reach solid, undisturbed ground, dug through 12.5 meters (41 feet) of the debris of ancient Rome.[1] This 1,100-year storehouse of physical evidence available to archeologists has given us reasonably accurate record of one of the world's great empires.

Rome, a tiny, barbaric village at the end of the Greek Homeric age, came to dominate the known world of the early centuries of the Christian era. First she was a rude hamlet, lorded over by a tribal chieftain, next an expanding agrarian republic, third, a struggling minor military power, reluctantly seeking "overseas" expansion, fourth, a glittering empire known best for the aphorism "All roads lead to Rome," and last, during decline, almost a myth.

We can only touch lightly on the major import of the Romans and their remarkable institutions. We will, then, in the next few pages, examine Rome and her significance as she grew lustily, produced innovations and ideas still significant, and as she declined while the moving finger of time inexorably delineated her demise.

By 323 B.C. (see Fig. 33), the tiny republic of Rome had already consolidated a collection of villages on the hills south of the Tiber, done away with kingship (about 450 B.C.), and had absorbed the Etruscan civilization to the north. Alexander, secure in his empirical ambitions, could safely ignore the tiny, still semibarbaric Latin state.

The Romans, basically farmers, had not yet visions of making the Mediterranean Sea a Roman lake. The Hellenes dominated the eastern end, while Carthage controlled the western shores of the Sea.[2]

The Samnite Wars of the third century B.C. permitted Rome to absorb the Grecian cities of Southern Italy. The Punic Wars, during which time Rome gained final supremacy over the ancient Phoenician maritime culture of Carthage, next faced Rome with the task of administering a Mediterranean commercial and political empire of rapidly expanding proportions.

By the time Julius Caesar of Gallic War fame (see Fig. 34) had arrived on the scene, the Mediterranean could be called *Mare Nostrum* (Our Sea) by Rome. Her commercial enterprise, made necessary by military conquest, extended as far as relations with the Han Dynasty of China (Fig. 35).

---

[1]Reported to John Ferris, *Saturday Review*, August 14, 1971, p. 4, by Professor Rudolfo Lanciani, Italian archeologist.

[2]McEvedy, Colin, *Penguin Atlas of Ancient History*, Baltimore, Md., Penguin, 1967, p. 59.

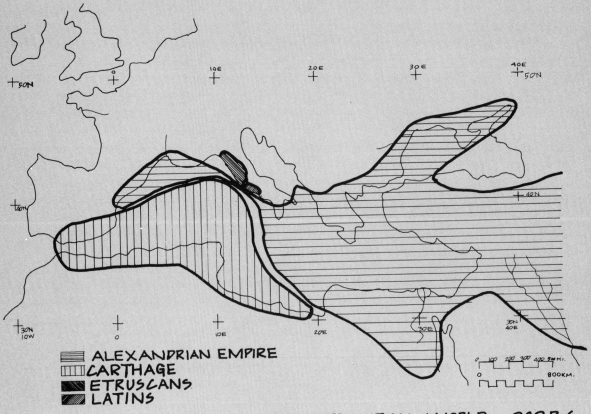

ALEXANDRIAN EMPIRE
CARTHAGE
ETRUSCANS
LATINS

FIGURE 33                    MEDITERRANEAN  WORLD — 323 B.C.

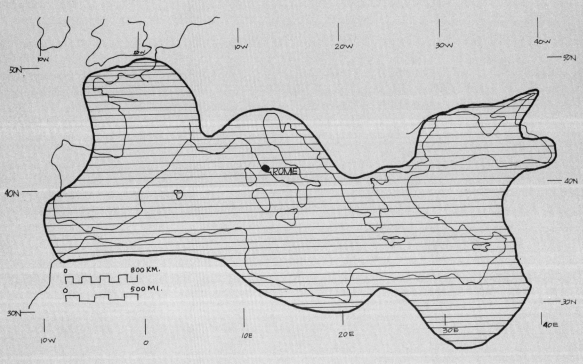

FIGURE 34                    JULIUS  CAESARS  WORLD

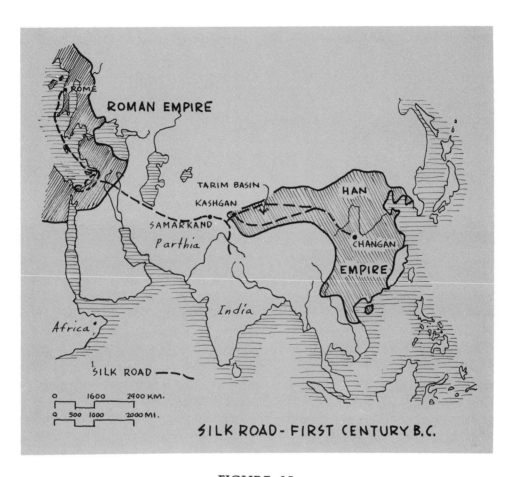

FIGURE 35

In fact, records indicate that during the height of the silk trade, the Roman exchequer came dangerously close to bankruptcy, silk fabrics becoming a major luxury item and a medium of exchange. Grapes and clover were introduced into the eastern empire of Wa Tsi (Han Emperor) while Rome absorbed oriental silk production.

Rome's position as a "world" power forced on her a complex system of military and political governance. As Rome expanded throughout Italy, the Mediterranean area, and north to Britain, she inevitably impressed on conquered regions the imprint of her administrative skill.

The understanding of the Romans, in selecting town sites and in planning, is evident today throughout that world once under *Pax Romana* (the peace of Rome) (Figs. 34 and 36).

In Italy and in the western provinces street plans still indicate their Roman origins. Florence, Turin, Ostia, and Aosta in Italy, Trier and Cologne in Germany, Barcelona in Spain, Gloucester and Lincoln in Great Britain, Timgad and Leptis Magna in North Africa, all give evidence of Roman rule.

The checkerboard-pattern of streets, found wherever Romans traveled, had a long and checkered history.

The earliest type was the *castrum*, as Ostia (see Fig. 37) founded 338 B.C. The town originally was a small garrison of perhaps 300 families guarding the exposed coastline. Ostia's later growth out of the rectangular grid pattern of the castrum is proof of her importance as Rome's port on the Mediterranean at the Tiber's mouth.

Later, as Rome absorbed Greece and her institutions, the Hippodamean plan (named for Hippodamus of Miletus), became the common pattern of provincial towns. Aosta (Augusta Praetoria, 23 B.C.), in the alpine foothills in the northwest corner of Italy, represents the Greek plan.

The odd and asymmetrical siting of the town gates suggests, however, a third influence. Anyone who has studied Latin is familiar with Julius Caesar's accounts of his conquest of Gaul: *"Omnia Gallia in tres partes divisa est."* Rome's legions could march 12 to 20 miles in a day and still have time to establish a fortified (with perimeter ditch and rampart) camp each night. Upon subduing a piece of territory, they established

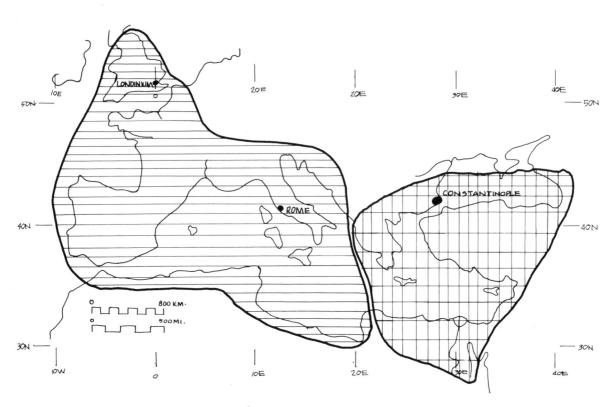

EASTERN & WESTERN EMPIRES — 300c A.D.

FIGURE 36

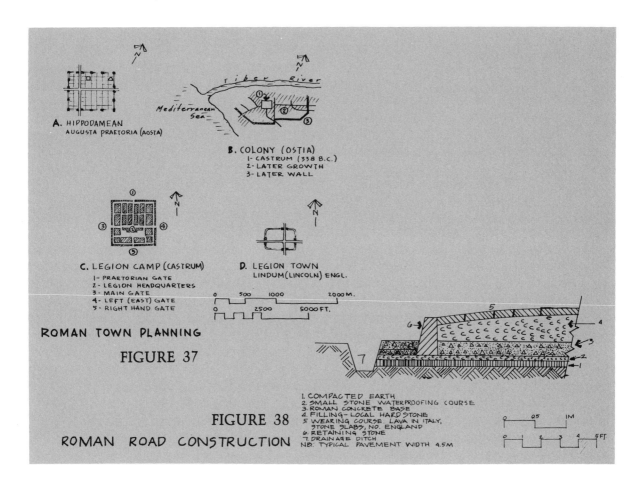

A. HIPPODAMEAN
AUGUSTA PRAETORIA (AOSTA)

B. COLONY (OSTIA)
1- CASTRUM (338 B.C.)
2- LATER GROWTH
3- LATER WALL

C. LEGION CAMP (CASTRUM)
1- PRAETORIAN GATE
2- LEGION HEADQUARTERS
3- MAIN GATE
4- LEFT (EAST) GATE
5- RIGHT HAND GATE

D. LEGION TOWN
LINDUM (LINCOLN) ENGL.

ROMAN TOWN PLANNING

FIGURE 37

FIGURE 38

ROMAN ROAD CONSTRUCTION

1. COMPACTED EARTH
2. SMALL STONE WATERPROOFING COURSE
3. ROMAN CONCRETE BASE
4. FILLING- LOCAL HARD STONE
5. WEARING COURSE: LAVA IN ITALY, STONE SLABS, NO. ENGLAND
6. RETAINING STONE
7. DRAINAGE DITCH
N.B. TYPICAL PAVEMENT WIDTH 4.5 M

permanent legionary camps, each, wherever located, constructed on a nearly identical pattern. These garrisoned forts frequently became military, then civil government centers. Legionnaires, after completing their 20 years of military service, could settle where they wished. Often they chose these fortified towns and were immediately on familiar ground.

This unified system of establishing towns and controlling territory was made more efficient by the impressive system of Roman roads. Roman military engineering surpassed anything the world had seen up to that time. Coupled with well-engineered bridges and tunnels, the Roman highway system extended throughout the empire, permitting communication that was extremely swift for its day. Sections of some of these roads may be viewed today, so well were they built (see Fig. 38).

Thus, by virtue of a highly organized system accompanied by efficiency in logistics and administration, Rome, with quite astonishing rapidity, became, as the earlier republic gave way to empire, the dominant city-dynasty of the first five centuries A.D.

Rome, the stellar attraction of its world, left us a number of major legacies. She adopted Greek architecture and was strongly influenced by its glories. But, by adapting and expanding on Greek sculptural ideas while applying her own engineering skills, the Roman Empire produced a unique institution.

Her codified laws, based on a long history of civil litigation, still persist as the legal structure of many European countries.

The Latin language, modified over centuries, is the basis of our own, and, in more or less pure form, comprises that large body of tongues known as "Romance languages."

But it is in the field of civil engineering that Rome's most important legacy persists. Land subdivision began with the Etruscans, the early Latins' near neighbors, as part of religious rites pertaining to the land. Etruscan surveyors laid out land in easily divisible rectangles. Later Roman law stated firmly that only property that was measured and with fixed boundaries was truly property.[3] In many areas of northern Italy, aerial photographs reveal ancient Roman rectilinear land-use patterns.

Strangely, though, the city of Rome itself was bewildering in its confusion of places and directions. Perhaps by reason of its being so early founded, perhaps because it became a mecca for so many so quickly; in any case Rome, like Athens before her, exhibits the pattern of an "organically grown" community (cf. Fig. 39 and 40 with Fig. 27.)

Traditionally a consolidation of a number of small villages on the hills east of the Tiber, by the end of the fourth century B.C. Rome was already a major city when it was sacked and burned by Gauls from over the Alps. In fact, it was this disaster which prompted Servius Tullius to build what is still recognizable as the "Servian Wall."

The necessity to establish a forum, a place of public assembly, during the republic, probably caused great argument and debate. But final choice of location was in the valley between the Capitoline and Palatine hills. This choice (the land being swampy) led to the construction of a great storm drain, still visible today as the cloaca maxima.

Thus began the tradition of Roman public works. Other cities of more remote ancestry had such public institutions as streets, drains, water supply, parks. But none had them on the superhuman scale so evident in Rome (see Fig. 41).

At this point, while discussing Imperial Rome, it seems appropriate to discuss the matter of scale. Hans Blumenfeld[4] has made it clear that, in spatial design for people, there are four kinds of human scale, defined in terms of visual form. (In terms of social content, "human scale" may be defined as a group in which every person knows every other person by face, voice, and name).

The basic concept is: the person must be visible. Further refinement of the concept has to do with the eye and its normal angle of sharp perception, 27°. Thus, we can determine the maxima and minima. Physiological optics reveals the smallest discernible angle in vision is one minute. Thus, one cannot discern an object at a distance greater than 3,450 times its size. M. Maertens, a German architect, in 1877, determined that a person can be concisely identified as a specific individual at a distance

[3]Lavedan, Pierre, *L'Histoire d'Urbanisme*, Vol. I, Paris, Henri Laurens, 1966, p. 357.

[4]Blumenfeld, Hans, "Scale In Civic Design," *Town Planning Review*, Vol. 14, No. 1 (April 1953).

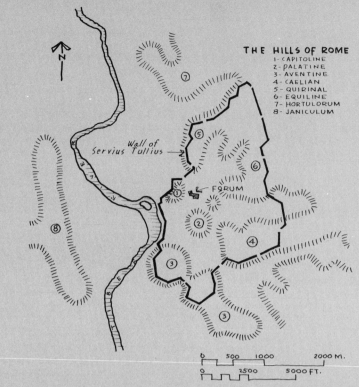

THE HILLS OF ROME
1- CAPITOLINE
2- PALATINE
3- AVENTINE
4- CAELIAN
5- QUIRINAL
6- EQUILINE
7- HORTULORUM
8- JANICULUM

Wall of
Servius Tullius

FORUM

0 500 1000 2000 M.
0 2500 5000 FT.

ROME 378ᴄ B.C.

FIGURE 39

FIGURE 40

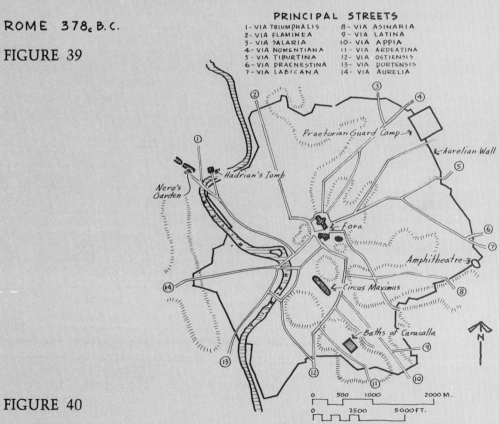

PRINCIPAL STREETS
1- VIA TRIUMPHALIS      8- VIA ASINARIA
2- VIA FLAMINEA         9- VIA LATINA
3- VIA SALARIA         10- VIA APPIA
4- VIA NOMENTIANA      11- VIA ARDEATINA
5- VIA TIBURTINA       12- VIA OSTIENSIS
6- VIA DRAENESTINA     13- VIA PORTENSIS
7- VIA LABICANA        14- VIA AURELIA

Praetorian Guard Camp

Aurelian Wall

Hadrian's Tomb

Nero's
Garden

Fora

Amphitheatre

Circus Maximus

Baths of Caracalla

0 500 1000 2000 M.
0 2500 5000 FT.

IMPERIAL ROME, 200ᴄ A.D.

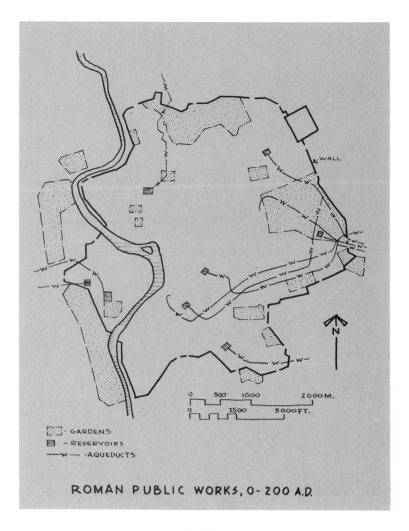

ROMAN PUBLIC WORKS, 0-200 A.D.

FIGURE 41

no greater than 21 to 24 meters (70 to 80 feet). He relates this distance to the width of the nasal bone, the smallest part of the human body indispensable for identification.

The five scales of spaces may be defined as follows:

1. Intimate human scale: Spaces, within which individual facial expression is recognizable, or spaces with maximum horizontal dimension of 15 meters (48 feet), and vertical heights of 6 meters (21 feet).
2. Human scale: Spaces of maximum horizontal dimensions of 22 meters (72 feet), with vertical dimensions of 9 to 10 meters (29 to 30 feet).
3. Public human scale: This involves spaces of public nature, intended for use by fairly large groups. Palladio, an Italian architect

(1518–1580 A.D.) wrote: "Piazze ought to be made of such size as the multitude of the citizens require, that it [sic] may not be too small for their convenience and use, or that, through the small number of people, they may not seem uninhabited." In a plaza, surrounding buildings, to be impressive, should be seen at a distance not more than three times their horizontal dimension. In the most successful plazas of history, the dimension, 137 meters (450 feet) appears most frequently and proportion rarely exceeds 1:3 (the ratio between short and long sides; the short side being 1, the long side 3 times that).

4. Superhuman scale: This is the monumental scale, described by the dramatist Pierre Corneille as "the scale of gods and kings." (See Figs. 43, 44, 46.)

5. Extrahuman scale: A scale, not at all related to the human individual, but to that of nature—mountains, plains, seas. It is the scale of our contemporary super-highways, great power dams, airports, and massive bridges spanning bays and harbors.

In Imperial Rome, we are first made aware of the planning results of the shift in Roman government from republic to empire. The Forum Romanum, for centuries the place of public assembly, apparently evolved, through a series of independent spatial-need decisions over time, as indicated by its plan (see Fig. 42). (Fig. 43 identifies the "superhuman" scale of the space.)

The rostrum (originally the prow, or "beak" of a captured enemy war vessel) became the speaker's stand, and a prime purpose of the space itself was for public assembly. Over time, of course, shopping, political, and religious functions gravitated here, the focal point of the city. But, not only did the forum represent the focus of city life, it also constituted, in Roman minds, the center of the then known world. The expression "all roads lead to Rome" was apt, in its day, for, located near the rostrum (Fig. 42) was the Mileum Aureum, the golden milestone, from which distances were calculated in miles[5] to the limits of the empire.

Compare the Forum Romanum with the Imperial Roman Fora, a progressive series of the "bigger and better," where it would appear that each of the emperors tried to outdo his predecessors. Julius Caesar ruled as dictator until his untimely demise on the Ides of March, 44 B.C. Augustus, the first emperor, reigned from 27 B.C. to 14 A.D.

Nerva's forum somehow does not fit the pattern. But it should be remembered he was not a military commander who had the backing of the Roman Legions. He was a distinguished lawyer, over 60 at the time of his ascension, and considered by the politicians as "safe." This may explain why his forum is so niggardly in terms of scale. However, he saved himself by adopting as his son and heir one of the great army

[5]The Roman mile, or 1,000 paces of a legionnaire.

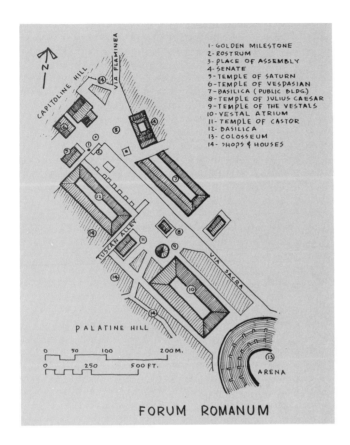

1- GOLDEN MILESTONE
2- ROSTRUM
3- PLACE OF ASSEMBLY
4- SENATE
5- TEMPLE OF SATURN
6- TEMPLE OF VESPASIAN
7- BASILICA (PUBLIC BLDG.)
8- TEMPLE OF JULIUS CAESAR
9- TEMPLE OF THE VESTALS
10- VESTAL ATRIUM
11- TEMPLE OF CASTOR
12- BASILICA
13- COLOSSEUM
14- SHOPS & HOUSES

FORUM ROMANUM

FIGURE 42

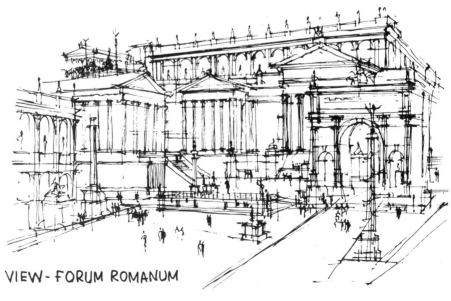

VIEW- FORUM ROMANUM

FIGURE 43

commanders, Trajan (98–117 A.D.). Trajan's military conquests had been extremely profitable, since they included Dacia, a province on the Danube containing important gold mines. Trajan's forum was the grandest of them all, and, as had become customary, included within the complex a temple (see view of a portion of Trajan's temple forecourt, Fig. 45) for the worship of his person as a god.

As did the Roman road system, and the commonality of town planning throughout the empire, the imperial fora expressed clearly the truly impressive Roman insistence on form and order. A major impression one gains from a study of Imperial Rome is that the Romans, perhaps because of their superb skill in using concrete, and probably because their civic institutions required spaces for huge crowds, used the superhuman scale in their public institutions.

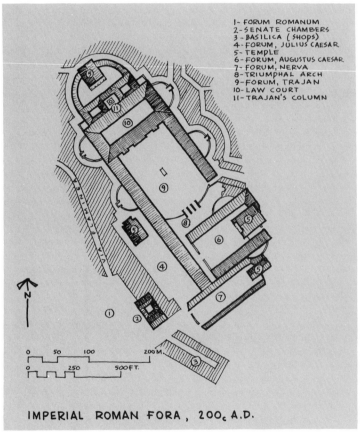

1- FORUM ROMANUM
2- SENATE CHAMBERS
3- BASILICA (SHOPS)
4- FORUM, JULIUS CAESAR
5- TEMPLE
6- FORUM, AUGUSTUS CAESAR
7- FORUM, NERVA
8- TRIUMPHAL ARCH
9- FORUM, TRAJAN
10- LAW COURT
11- TRAJAN'S COLUMN

IMPERIAL ROMAN FORA, 200 A.D.

FIGURE 44

FIGURE 45

TRAJAN'S COLUMN FROM TEMPLE COURT

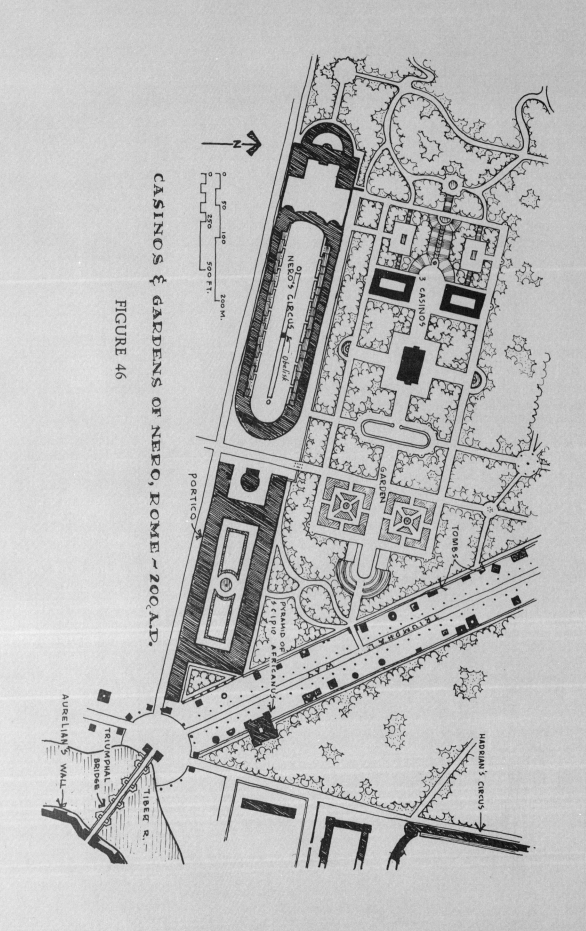

CASINOS & GARDENS OF NERO, ROME ~ 200 A.D.

FIGURE 46

As well, Roman emperors, as gods and imperial monarchs, displayed, as public figures, the superhuman in the scale of their gardens (see Fig. 46). Nero, emperor from 54–68 A.D. erected a pleasure palace on the west bank of the Tiber, which provided public entertainment (the circus and portico, the latter probably filled with shops), as well as a delectable "private" paradise for the emperor and his large retinue of servants and sycophants. We are fortunate to have a reasonably complete record of these imperial gardens, since the site chosen by Nero in later times became the location of the Vatican, and St. Peter's basilica, for which Michelango was principal architect in the sixteenth century. Of interest in tracing the threads of tradition, let it be noted that an obelisk, transported from the Egyptian Nile to Rome and raised as a symbol of Roman conquest on the spina (central divider) of Nero's circus, stands today as the focal point of Bernini's grand elliptical plaza before St. Peter's Cathedral.[6]

While the stones speak to us of the past, our knowledge of the exact forms, colors, and textures of Nero's gardens is lost, in view of the ephemeral character of plant materials.

Fortunately for us, but, of course, unfortunately for the dwellers therein, a Graeco-Roman city, Pompeii, fell prey, in 79 A.D., to the powerful forces of nature. In that year, Mt. Vesuvius (having warned an unaware populace in 63 A.D. of its coming devastation by causing a destructive earthquake) "blew its top," almost instantaneously burying Pompeii under an average depth of 7 meters (23 feet) of lava and ash. We thus have an almost complete record of the houses and gardens of that pleasure town.

Well-to-do Romans lived on a lavish scale, in sharp contrast to the Greeks before them. Compare, for example, the house of Loreius Tiburtinus, in Pompeii (Fig. 47) with that of a similarly placed Greek in Priene (Fig. 26).

Loreius Tiburtinus was a descendant of a noble Roman family that had moved to Pompeii perhaps as early as the time of Sulla (Lucius Cornelius Sulla, Roman dictator 138–78 B.C.).[7] Tiburtinus' palatial home was one of the largest dwellings on the via dell' Abbondanza, near the Amphitheatre.

The portal, flanked on either side by shops, contained two seats outside for clients. The atrium, in process of being redecorated at the time of the eruption, contained a marble impluvium. Beyond, the peristyle and its adjacent chambers resembled a suburban villa, with the major difference that, being in the crowded city, it was self-contained and inward-looking. At the rear of the house, a spacious portico, with its sunken water channel, overlooked a spacious garden, containing pear, chestnut, pomegranate and fig trees (Pliny the Younger praised Pompeian figs as the tastiest in the Italian peninsula). Another canal formed the axis of the garden. Displayed along it were statuettes of animals and the Muses, as well as a small temple. Flanking the canal were covered walks. These garden features call to mind the Egyptian nobleman's estate (Fig. 14) as well as the sixteenth-century Italian villa (Figs. 70 and 71).

Of course, there was not an unbroken thread of tradition from Egypt through Greece, to Rome, and on through the period of the Renaissance. As far as European culture is

[6]Letarouilly, Paul, *Vatican I, The Basilica of St. Peter*, London, Alec Tiranti, 1953.

[7]Maiuri, Amedeo, *Pompeii*, Novara, Italy, Instituto Geografico de Agostini, 1951.

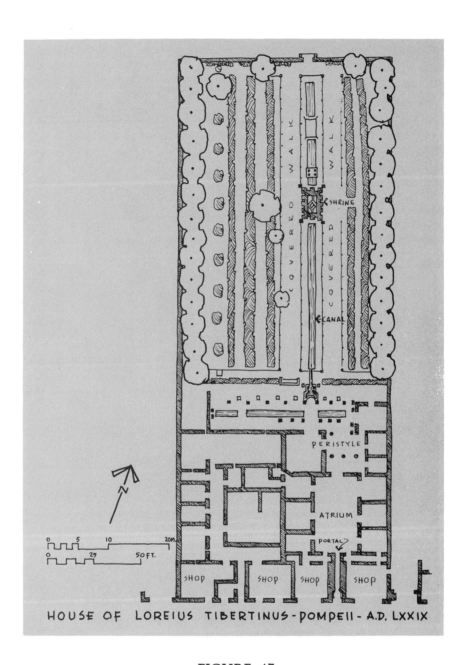

FIGURE 47

concerned, evidence indicates that the classic traditions of Rome became lost during the succeeding era known as the Dark Ages, but were later revived.

In fact, it appears that much of the Renaissance and later interest in classic forms was rediscovered, as fifteenth-century Italian literati rekindled an all-consuming interest in classic art and literature.

One of the more fascinating literary studies that began in the sixteenth century and persisted into the twentieth dealt with careful examination of, and conjecture about, the Villas of Pliny the Younger.[8]

An architecture student in 1927 found it possible, from careful examination of similar Roman architecture (including that of Pompeii), and Pliny's description of his Laurentine Villa, to produce a reasonably accurate plan of this villa on the Italian shore of the Tyrrhenian Sea at Laurentum, south and west of Rome (see Fig. 48).

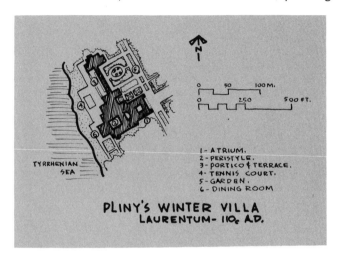

FIGURE 48

Pliny's letters, in translation or in the original Latin, fortunately remain available to us as his legacy to our time, as he astutely considered and put to good use the environmental advantages of site.

The Laurentine Villa (Fig. 48), being only 17 Roman miles from Rome, had the advantage of accessibility. His villa at Laurentum was to Pliny what a second home or vacation cottage is to today's weary executive.

The villa itself, while on the shore, and therefore exposed to Mediterranean storms, Pliny arranged to protect with glazed windows and deep overhanging eaves. Room arrangements were protected from storm while being located for the best sea views. Other rooms served as sunlit retreats in cold periods, while still others offered shade in summer. While the grounds were attractively arranged, they served as well for exercise grounds (cf. tennis court).

Pliny knew which plants would thrive near the seashore, as well as those which, because of exposure to sea spray, would not survive. This sensitivity to habitat runs through all Pliny's letters—those describing the Laurentine Villa as well as another he owned near Florence, which we know as his Tuscan Villa.

---

[8]Caius Plinius Caecilius Secundus, an orator and statesman who lived from about 62 A.D. to about 113 A.D. In the year 100 A.D., he became a Roman Consul, and died in his consular province of Pontus-Bythnia, the southern shore of the Black Sea. The son of Caius Plinius Secundus (Pliny the Elder), a thoroughgoing naturalist, the younger Pliny is best known for his numerous letters, probably written for publication. Helen H. Tanzer's *The Villas of Pliny the Younger,* New York, Columbia University Press, 1924 contains copies of these letters, in the original Latin and in English translation. They are remarkable for their keen perception of natural process.

We find in his enthusiastic description of a well-loved country home a sensitive awareness of the forces of nature, and great skill in adapting site conditions to the creation of a very comfortable country seat. Pliny came by his awareness from his father, Pliny the Elder (23–79 A.D.). Pliny the Elder's great work had been an encyclopedia of natural history ("*Historia naturalis*"), divided into 37 books. The compendium deals with the nature of the physical universe—geography, anthropology, zoology, botany, and mineralogy.

Both Plinys, Elder and Younger, being recognized scholars, probably had access to the monumental work of Vitruvius (late first century B.C.; early first century A.D.), architect for emperor Augustus. Vitruvius' "*De Architectura*" in 10 volumes, discussed city planning, architecture, and engineering.

Thus these three individuals, the two Plinys and Vitruvius, among other serious investigators of the nature of the physical world, prepared the foundation for the Renaissance world that was to follow.

Before that "rebirth" was to occur, however, an Empire would dissolve, other cultures become dominant, and the light of knowledge be kept glowing by a few dedicated individuals.

# 8

# The Golden Gate
## (The Byzantine Empire, 327–1453)

The inscription engraved on the Golden Gate in Constantinople's outer wall, built by Theodosius (379–395 A.D.) reads, "He who built this gate of gold will bring to you an age of gold."

This prophecy, in fact, was quite true. The Eastern Roman Empire at this time was worth $600 million. Ten percent of this wealth was contained within the city.

The Byzantine Empire (so named after the earlier city Byzantium on the Golden Horn), kept alive the Hellenized culture of the Romans until it could return to Western Europe through Venice toward the end of the so-called "Dark Ages" and at the beginning of the Renaissance.

Originally (about 700 B.C.) a tiny fishing village named Lygos; in Greek times, a colonial trading center, by the end of the second (Roman) century A.D., Byzantium occupied a land area on the point of 168 hectares,[1] (415 acres). The city wall, built during the time of Septimius Severus (Roman Emperor, 193–211 A.D.), was later (during the reign of Constantine—324–337 A.D.) moved farther west (see Fig. 49).

During his reign, pressures from the west induced Constantine to move the capital of the Roman empire to a new capital city on the Bosporus. Finding there seven hills,[2] Constantine egocentrically called his "new Rome" after himself.

The hub of the city was a golden milestone, located in the Augusteon, the probable location of the agora of the former Greek city. The Augusteon was so named after a monumental statue to Augustus Caesar located there.

Having divided the city into 14 districts (as Rome before it had been) Constantine proceeded to cover his new city with handsome monuments, and had shipped there works of art from all over the empire.

The imperial capital achieved such success that Theodosius II (Emperor 379–395 A.D.) had to push back the wall again, at which time he built magnificent new gates, including the Golden Gate, whose inscription is quoted above.

During its golden age, Constantinople-Byzantium apparently was a magnificent example of the planner's art. A major triumphal way led west, out of the Augusteon, through a whole series of fora (note the insistence, at least in the early centuries, on Roman ways) toward the Theodosian city gates.

[1]Hectare: Combined Greek-Latin word, *hecto* (Greek) plus *are* (Latin). One hectare equals 10,000 square meters.

[2]Lavedan, Pierre, *L'Histoire d'Urbanisme*, Vol. I; *Antiquites*, Paris, Henry Laurens, 1959.

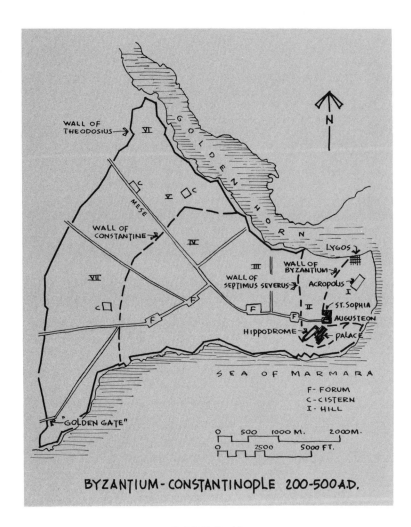

BYZANTIUM-CONSTANTINOPLE 200-500A.D.

FIGURE 49

The topography of Constantinople discouraged a rectilinear plan. However, it presents less a picture of "organic" growth, than Rome, and, in fact, presages the radial plans of Renaissance Rome, and, later still, those of Paris, Versailles, and Washington, D.C.

The multiple distribution of fora (in contrast to their concentration in Rome), implies the districting of the city into quarters, each with its own function.

We know that the various trades, whether by chance or by law, tended to be grouped. At Athens, for instance, "Ceramika" revealed a local grouping of potters. Both in the near and far east, reservation of certain streets to specialized activities has existed for millennia.[2]

Societally, Byzantium was a cosmopolitan city. Here there lived Greeks, Egyptians, Romans, Alexandrians, and Lebanese. The city, as a center of commerce, attracted skills from all over: Jewish glassmakers, Spanish cattle-breeders, Moorish silversmiths, Armenian stone-cutters, and Persian weavers. The high cultural level is illustrated by the predominant commerce of the city, in luxury goods and *objets d'art*.

By the time of Justinian (Emperor, 527–565 A.D.), who completed the original Hagia Sophia in 542, the emperor was an eastern monarch, having done away with the consulate and senate (though the Roman Senate house still stood at the east end of the Augusteon—see Fig. 49).

Byzantium had, at this time, a population exceeding 700,000. Life was easy, with free wine, bread, oil, and free public physicians and hospitals, not to mention the almost daily races at the hippodrome between the two factions, the Greens and the Blues. The Greens were known as the radical faction, mostly artisans and merchants, while the Blues were conservative farmers and landowners.

Harold Lamb describes the city during its greatest glory:

> As you sail in from the Propontis (Sea of Marmara) there is a public bathing place on the left. There the Emperor made a park [see Fig. 50] always open to those who wish to rest, or those who anchor as they sail by. Sunrise floods it with light, and evening fills it with pleasant, shade. The sea flows quietly around this court, like a river. The park itself gleams with marble colonnades. . . .[3]

The plan of the imperial palace complex (Fig. 50) illustrates fairly clearly the significance of Byzantine civilization at its peak. Note the exuberant Byzantine (semioriental) forms, yet controlled (the careful axial treatment) by Roman engineering skills.

The elaborate gardens express both Persian and Roman influences. The Hippodrome, Senate house, and baths are pure Roman, while the original Hagia Sophia, (later elaborated and enlarged) expresses the overlay of Christianity on the Roman pagan culture.

The importance (to us) of the Eastern Empire as exemplified by Constantinople includes:

1. The maintenance of a secular imperial system.
2. The retention and fusion with oriental cultures of a great commercial and industrial empire such as Rome had been.
3. The preservation of oriental and classical civilizations, melded with Christianity:
   a. Oriental despotism.
   b. Centralization of government.
   c. Continuation of political tradition (especially Justinian's codification of law).

[3]Lamb, Harold, *Constantinople, Birth of an Empire,* Copyright © Harold Lamb, 1957, Alfred A. Knopf, Inc., p. 109.

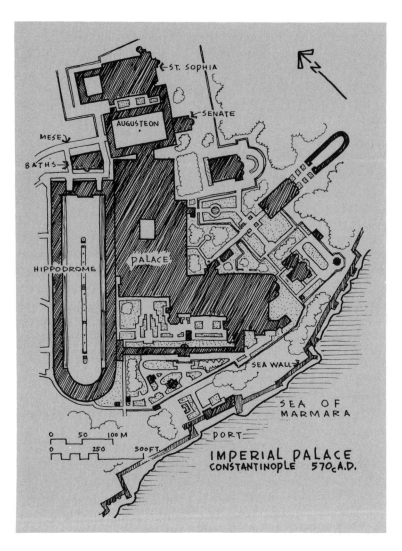

FIGURE 50

d. An oriental love of luxury and display (cf. later Venice).
e. Center of trade between East and West (until Portuguese mariners discovered the Good Hope route around Africa).
f. Maintenance of Greek learning and language.
g. Eventual transfer of oriental learning to Europe.

In summary, Byzantine society, with its sharp contrasts between oriental luxury, cruelty, and blood sports, and Graeco-Roman intellectualism, helped to produce the foundations of the Renaissance and humanism.

While Constantinople-Byzantium kept aflame the light of classical knowledge, during the so-called Dark Ages (see Chapter 9), another important culture came to dominate the southern half of the Mediterranean. Islam, based on the religious tenets of its prophet, Mohammed (540–632 A.D.) spread its influence over former Persia, among the peoples of North Africa, and into Spain (see Fig. 51; also Chapter 10).

A century later, Charlemagne, out of Aix-la-Chapelle, had himself crowned in the Papal State as Emperor of the Holy Roman Empire, in reality a relatively minor kingship; his rule extending over semibarbaric knights and peasants, while the highly cultured citizenry of Byzantium pursued a hedonistic life style.

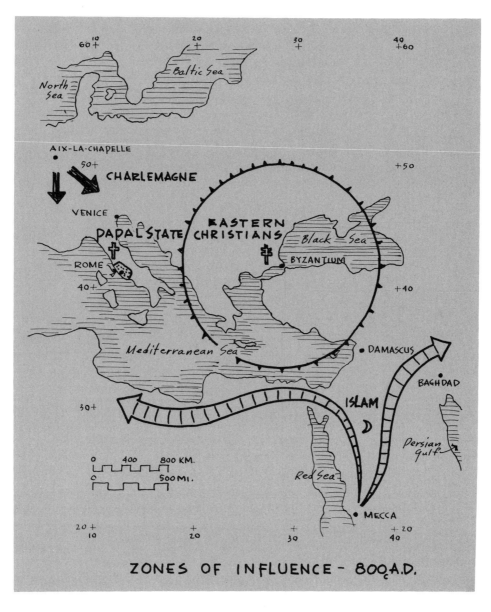

FIGURE 51

# 9

# *Le Moyen Age* *
## (Europe, 500–1300)

The term "Dark Ages" is often applied to the period in European history between the dissolution of the Western Roman Empire (500), and the rise of the Renaissance in Italy (1300). Such, however, with the possible exception of the early centuries, was not the case.

The Middle Ages constituted, in fact, a period of transition, one of ferment, and the era in which the Age of Exploration leading to the Modern World was distilled. Study of the text and illustrations contained in this chapter reveals a period in history rich in reexamination of old ideas, adaptation of old techniques to novel situations, and an era of quest for new ways.

The early part of the period marked a shift in government away from the Roman imperial system, under which the citizens were taxed to produce revenues, expended by the emperor in civil administration and military control.

The new form of administrative governance took the feudal form, in which the peasantry tithed to support local rulers (feudal barons). The barons, in turn, swore fealty to the local king, promising to support him in militry conquest. The "new" system involved total fusion of economic and political obligation in a reciprocal relationship of land-tenant and overlord.[1] By 500 A.D., European political boundaries were confused, and the entire region had broken up into a series of relatively small baronies and kingdoms.

While the secular world thus changed, the Roman Catholic Church began its wide-ranging missionary work in Europe. The establishment of missionary colonies throughout Europe led, by necessity, to the establishment of the monastic orders. Thus developed an institution which provided rest for the weary traveler[2] reaching the end of his day exhausted by the hard physical labor of moving overland on muddy trails.

The monasteries (see Fig. 53) were self-contained communities. Not only did they mean retreat from the world on the part of the monks; they also kept knowledge alive through their exquisite and painstaking copying of ancient scrolls and manuscripts.

---

*The Middle Ages.

[1]McEvedy, Colin, *The Penguin Atlas of Medieval History*, Baltimore, Md., Penguin, 1961.

[2]The word "travel" comes from a French-modified Latin word, *travail*, which today signifies "trouble."

The monks' haven usually contained within its enclave a hospital, ministering to the body as well as the spirit. Note, in Figure 53, that within the extensive walled compounds, most of man's physical needs were met from what could be produced from the forest, the field, or the fishpond.

In fact, so successful was the monastic system that many of the orders became wealthy enough that it was necessary for the church to pass through several internal reformations in the period, as well as eventually becoming an important factor in the external (protestant) reformation.

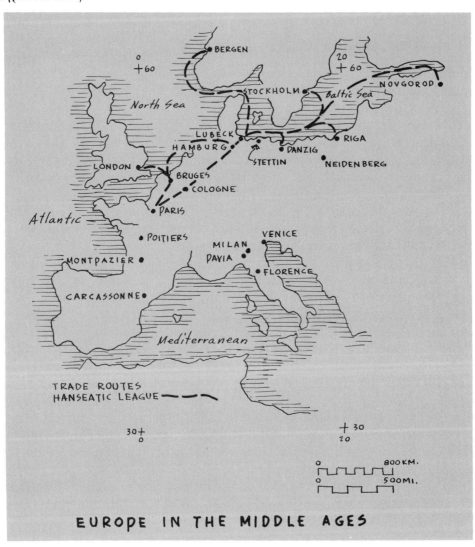

FIGURE 52

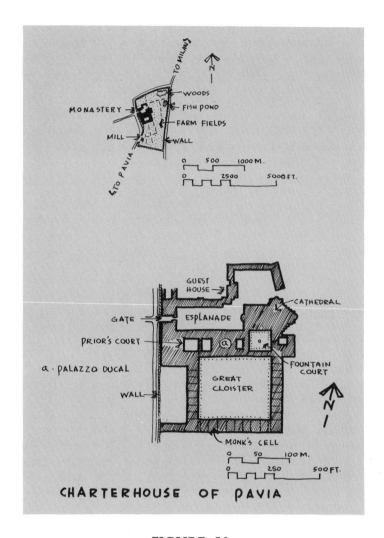

FIGURE 53

Certosa di Pavia, as illustrated, shows a late medieval monastic cloister yet demonstrating the concept. Figure 53 shows the immediate land-holdings of the order, a self-sufficient community. Figure 54 implies, by its scale and complexity, the relative wealth of the monastic orders toward the end of the period. Compare, for example, the scale of the great cloister with that of the public square in Venice (Piazza San Marco, Fig. 63).

Figure 54 represents in greater detail the relationship between the rather severe, ascetic, and reclusive life of the individual monk and the rather splendid and almost baroque quality expressed in the elaborate Fountain Cloister, located next to the Cathedral, but directly accessible to the library, the refectory (dining room), vestry, chapel, and cathedral.

Contained elsewhere in the building complex (see "a," Fig. 53) but strategically adjacent to the priory itself, was a sumptuous suite known as the Palazzo Ducal. This series of rooms was apparently provided especially as a spiritual retreat for local secular princes. Thus was the prior able to keep, as representative of the Papal State, his finger on the pulse of politics and commerce in his spiritual domain.

"The Church militant," in the Middle Ages, was a phrase more literal than figurative. The church, through the Papal State, warred with the rising secular states. Minor (often self-styled) princes warred with each other for territorial gain. Norse pressures from Scandinavia were at times severe. And there was, for at least a century, the holy war against the Saracen.

Until the advent of gunpowder and the cannon as weapons of war in the fourteenth century, the mailed knight was the principal instrument of attack; the castle, with its topographically strategic position, or its wide, deep moat (in the lowlands), the principal instrument of defense.

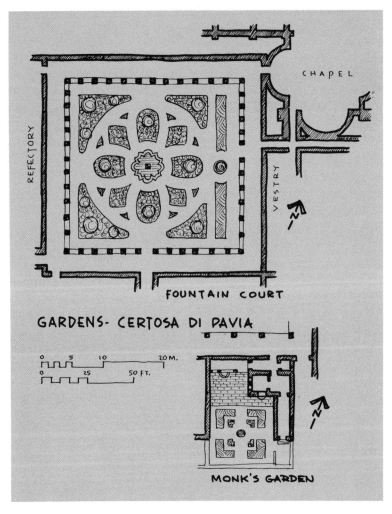

FIGURE 54

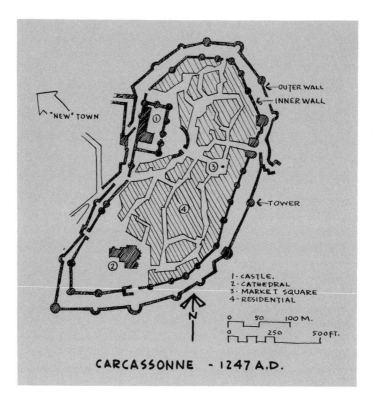

FIGURE 55

Carcassonne, in Southern France (see Fig. 55), built early in the thirteenth century by Louis IX, represents the end of an era. More than a castle, probably because of its strategic importance for defense against possible incursions from moslem Spain, and perhaps, too, in defense of France against the aggressive Italian City-States, Carcassonne illustrates the ultimate in medieval defensive works. Restored by the architect Viollet-le-Duc (1814–1879) in the nineteenth century, this last of the castles still attracts tourists and is well worth a visit.

The castle keep, the final defense, dominated the town at one end, (representing secular might), while the cathedral, at the other, indicated spiritual authority. The market square indicates the growth of trade.

By this time in the Middle Ages, castles and walled towns were already proving too confining, and consequently Carcassonne rapidly became the "old town" while a new, larger city, grew up outside the walls to the northwest.

The thirteenth century brought with it major shifts, from isolated, self-contained enclaves, to interdependent cities, growing nations, extensive trade and many of the municipal institutions known today. Greater use of horse (and oxen) power made possible more extensive farming, and thus more adequate food supplies. Though the diet of the common people was still frugal, trade brought, by the thirteenth century, increased supplies of protein. The monasteries still controlled the production of spiritous alcoholic beverages, and beer was the common drink. Municipal police already had to place regulations on public drinking. In view of population increases, wood supplies became scarce, and frequent disastrous fires in cities caused the eventual introduction of brick and tile into Europe (probably from Islamic Spain). Coal was coming into wide use (sources were England and the Saar) as an industrial fuel, but was not yet widely used for house heating.

Road building and maintenance now was recognized as a municipal responsibility, though in rural areas the rule was that the adjacent landwoner had that task, which was usually neglected. In any case, the old Roman roads had been created primarily for foot traffic, and horse-drawn vehicles now dominated. City streets (see Figs. 56 and 57), early

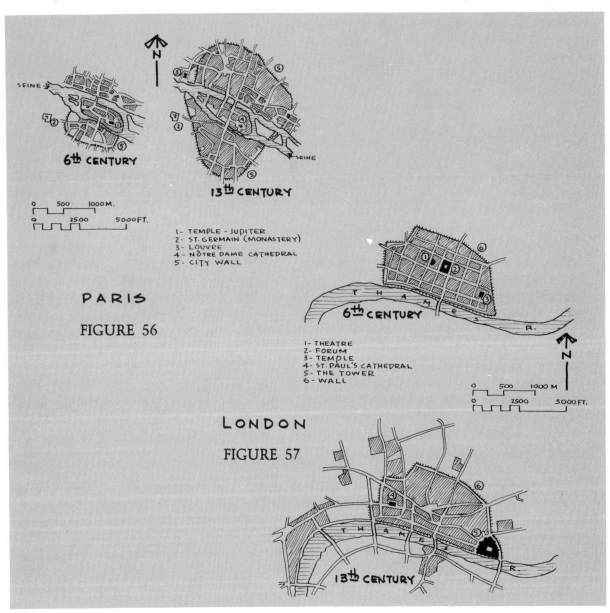

6<sup>th</sup> CENTURY

13<sup>th</sup> CENTURY

0   500   1000 M.
0   2500   5000 FT.

1- TEMPLE - JUPITER
2- ST. GERMAIN (MONASTERY)
3- LOUVRE
4- NOTRE DAME CATHEDRAL
5- CITY WALL

PARIS

FIGURE 56

6<sup>th</sup> CENTURY

1- THEATRE
2- FORUM
3- TEMPLE
4- ST. PAUL'S CATHEDRAL
5- THE TOWER
6- WALL

0   500   1000 M
0   2500   5000 FT.

LONDON

FIGURE 57

13<sup>th</sup> CENTURY

in the period, laid out without planning, consistently followed the irregular (today called "medieval") pattern. Little attempt was made to light them, or except for important places even to pave them. Refuse was thrown into the streets, and drainage was usually inadequate.

Yet, in the Middle Ages, the urban institution begun by Ur 5,300 years earlier continued to flourish. The changes in size, form, and complexity, though not abrupt, were nonetheless remarkable.

Consider the "tale of two cities." While Paris (Fig. 56), originally a prehistoric island village, expanded on both left and right banks as a tightly packed, walled, urban complex with its typical medieval institutions (church and castle dominant), London (Fig. 57) gradually evolved from a Roman Castrum (sixth century and earlier) by the accretion of villages without the walls.

Both the Louvre, as a donjon or keep, and the famed Tower of London were strategically placed at the downstream end of the city. In the case of Paris, the tower may have had, as purpose, protection against Viking raids, while London's Tower probably protected the populace from remembered incursions by barbaric Saxons. In both cases, the walled fortresses provided protection for a burgeoning international trade. Early made possible by the Hanseatic League (see Fig. 52) which for generations controlled the processing and distribution of herring, caught in the north Atlantic Ocean and North Sea, the established trade routes gradually carried a wide variety of goods, from wool and woolen cloth from the north of the British Isles, to Florentine fabrics and Venetian glassware. The wide extent of trade produced a wealthy class of merchants and tradesmen, so that the social structure of the period began to take on the complexities of today's society.

Water, by the thirteenth century, was extensively in use for power, as mechanization of crafts grew. Industrial use of power included hammer and crushing mills, tanning, fulling[3] and sawmills. This mechanization included applications to metallurgy, thus permitting an increase in size and quality of wrought iron objects, and even to the production of metal castings.[4]

These increases in manufacturing tended to accelerate the rise of cities, as those who formerly had been tied to the land now drifted toward urban centers, where the demand for labor was great, and where the money supply tended to gravitate.

By the end of the period population concentrations were so great that local water-pollution problems became recognized, thus reintroducing piped-in water supplies, as opposed to use of local wells.

One of the consequences of the rise in population, the concentration of people in cities, and the rise of national governments (monarchies), was in the thirteenth century, a rash of "new towns."

These, in contrast to the irregular, apparently haphazard form of older, established communities (see London and Paris), took form as regularized, planned towns (cf. colonial towns of the Romans and Greeks before them).

---

[3]"Fulling" is the thickening of cloth by moistening, heating, and pressing.

[4] Singer, Holmyard, Hall, *A History of Technology, Vol. II*, New York, Oxford University Press, 1957.

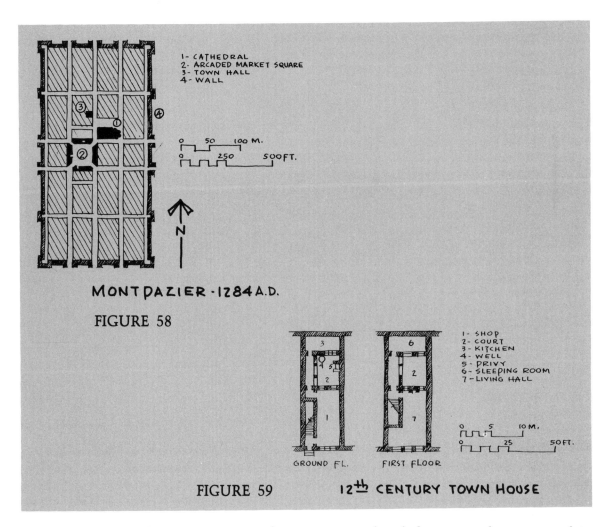

1- CATHEDRAL
2- ARCADED MARKET SQUARE
3- TOWN HALL
4- WALL

MONTPAZIER · 1284 A.D.

FIGURE 58

1- SHOP
2- COURT
3- KITCHEN
4- WELL
5- PRIVY
6- SLEEPING ROOM
7- LIVING HALL

GROUND FL.        FIRST FLOOR

FIGURE 59          12ᵗʰ CENTURY TOWN HOUSE

Montpazier, in France, represents but one example of the many that appeared in Europe during this expansionist era. Though yet needing defensive walls or the feeling of security engendered by a nearby castle (cf. Neidenberg, built by Teutonic knights), these colonies represented something new and different (regularized city blocks), and yet old (cf. Roman Castrum towns).

At Montpazier, an old form reappears in the market square, which was arcaded in the manner of the Roman basilica or the Greek stoa but lacked the grace of these earlier peristyle forms, since the arcading took the form of heavy gothic arches. In this connection, refer again to the cloisters of Certosa di Pavia, for another example of the continuing tradition of the internal-looking peristyle form of classic Greece and Rome.

Even in the houses of the period, the interior courtyard (see Fig. 59) was carried north from the Mediterranean, but used merely as an interior natural-light source. Imagine night-lighting of the commoner's home in the middle ages. The sole source might have been the open hearth, or, at best, a bit of rag dipped in liquid fat. Beeswax candles were only for the wealthy.

Though cities were increasing in size and importance and though personal wealth was possible, the average citizen lived a less spacious life than did a Greek citizen. Compare the relatively cramped quarters shown in Figure 59, with the home of a Greek citizen of Priene (Fig. 26, Chapter 5).

MEDIEVAL HOUSES-NORMANDY

FIGURE 60

Figure 60 illustrates the outward appearance of some average European homes of the middle ages, to us romantic versions of the idea "house." "French Provincial," though not today as "popular" as "Georgian Colonial," still provides reasonably ready real estate sales in middle-class subdivisions.

One of the most fascinating civic forms that theorists have "discovered" to have evolved in the Middle Ages is that of the public open place or plaza. Actually, however, the name itself is much more ancient. The English word "place" (Spanish "plaza"), as it refers to an open space or square in a city or town, derives from the Latin *platea*—a street, area, or courtyard. *Platea*, in turn was adopted by the Latins from the Greek *plateia*—a street. Properly, *plateia* derived from *platys*–flat, broad.

The characteristic shape of the medieval public open space indicates its evolutionary origins. Examination of the plans of medieval London and Paris shows the typically evolved irregular street pattern, as developed over time. The open spaces at street junctions consequently took these irregular shapes.

Theorists have, from study of numerous examples of these medieval "squares," derived the form as determined by the way in which the approaches to the place were terminated (see Fig. 61A).

Compare this kind of nonaxial approach with the typical form of the Renaissance plaza of the sixteenth and seventeenth centuries; it was strictly axial and focused on an important public building (see Fig. 61B).

To complicate matters, Figure 61C reproduces the Greek agora (Fig. 25). Examine, again, the Athenian agora (Fig. 28), as well as the Forum Romanum (Fig. 42). These much earlier public places exhibit the characteristic form of the "medieval square" (Fig. 61A).

The key seems to be that these spaces evolved over time. The Agora at Athens

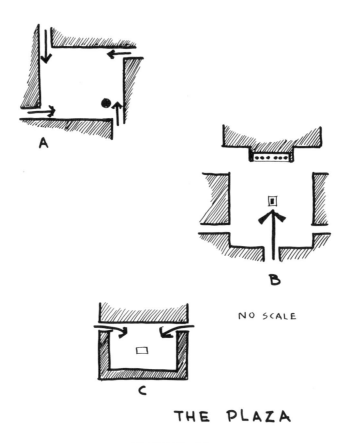

THE PLAZA

FIGURE 61

changed form as new needs were met over a period of 1,000 years. The Republican Forum in Rome has a history of at least half that long. It may be significant that of the Imperial Roman fora each was built to honor a single individual and each was created within one lifetime (Fig. 44). Similarly, the agora of the planned Greek colony exhibits nonevolution but creation to meet an immediate need.

The examples of medieval piazzas shown in Figures 62 and 63 illustrate the characteristic of the theoretical medieval square in terms of the termini of views on the approaches. You will note that the Piazza della Signoria evolved over at least a century, while the Piazza San Marco evolved over 800 years. Both piazzas are considered Renaissance squares simply because of later (fifteenth and sixteenth century) attempts to provide unity, using classic Roman or Greek porticos (the arcades of San Marco, the loggia in Signoria). In fact, however, their basic forms evolved to their present state prior to 1400. This, in addition to their nonaxial spatial relationships, places them within the Middle Ages.

While a basic frame of reference of this document is the evolution of the garden as an environmental need, we cannot claim very much in the way of its evolution during the Middle Ages.

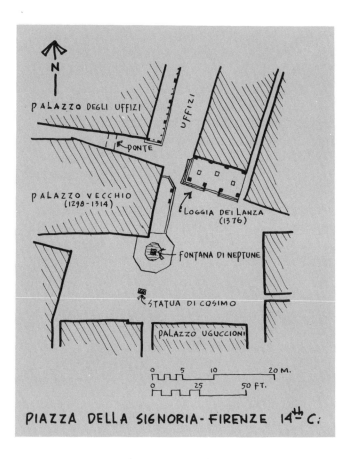

FIGURE 62

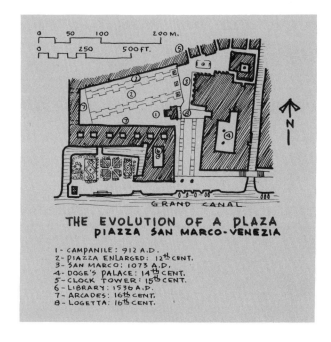

FIGURE 63

The literature of the period is full of romance and fantasy. Romantic writings, both of the period (cf. *Sir Gawain and the Green Knight*)[5] and of the much-later Victorian period, are full of tales of King Arthur and his knights of the round table. These knights, according to the tales, were noblemen of the highest degree, each seeking his own Holy Grail. Each, on a quest, carried with him a guerdon, perhaps a wisp of the scarf of his lady fair. According to the stories, the noble knights never did anything more than chastely kiss the hands of their ladies, or perhaps go so far as to stroll with them in the castle garden or *plaisance.*

In fact, these pleasure gardens, when one considers the nature of castles, built wholly for defense, were relatively meager attempts. During a siege, all the townspeople had to be accommodated within the castle keep. Where, then, could there be space for gardens?

There is limited factual knowledge of medieval gardens. What is available consists mainly of pictures included in illuminated manuscripts or lists of plants, often called "herbals." In view of space limitations, most medieval gardens contained only medicinal herbs, vegetables, and a few fruit trees. Monastic gardens provide the most frequent reference. These were simple, usually square, with square, raised beds (see Monks' Garden, Fig. 54) and normally contained mostly medicinal herbs. Very few flowers were grown, generally limited to the rose, lily, violet, and marigold.

Needless to say, as one views the period as a whole, when monasteries, castles, whole towns were by necessity inward-looking and strongly defended against the outside world, the common character of the medieval garden was that of a walled-in, enclosed, inward space—a retreat from the world.

[5]Gerould, Gordon Hall, ed., *Beowulf and Sir Gawain and the Green Knight*, New York, Ronald, 1935.

# 10 The Moors in Spain
## (632–1400)

Gardening as an art form received its greatest impetus in Europe at the end of the Middle Ages through Western European contacts with Islam in Spain and North Africa.

Nero had his "Golden Palace" in Rome, Pliny the Younger describes artfully created gardens surrounding his villas but, with the exception of Pliny's letters, the physical forms of gardens were almost literally buried under the rubble of wars and counter-wars from the dissolution of the Roman empire to the rise of the Italian city-state.

However, during the period in which Western Europe spent all her energies breaking out of feudalism into monarchism, a high level of culture flourished in the arid lands to the west, south, and east of the Mediterranean Sea.

The cultural antecedents of the gardens of the Moorish Caliphs in Spain may be found in what is now the Iraqi plateau, between Turkey on the west and Pakistan on the east, and between the Caspian Sea on the north and the Arabian gulf on the south. As in Egypt, and significantly, throughout the Arabic world, the country is dry over much of the year.

Historically, the Medes first appeared in the territory about 800 B.C., in contact with the Assyrians. By 500 B.C. Cyrus of Persia had subdued both the Medes and Assyrians. The Persians then ruled the lands east of the Mediterranean until conquered by Alexander in about 330 B.C. Thereafter, Persian and Greek attitudes blended into Hellenism.

Beneath this thin veneer of political history lay a deep-seated environmental awareness. Throughout Aryan Persia, and later Semitic Islam (as well as Hebrew Palestine), deeply ingrained into the nature of the peoples was that instinctive yearning for coolness, shade, and visual seclusion during periods of rest, and an inherent passion on the part of a high culture for protection from a harsh desert or semidesert environment.

As a matter of fact, the root word for the English "Paradise" is, in old Avestan (ancient Iranian-Indo-European language preceding Persian) *pairidaeza*, meaning "an enclosure" from *"pairi,"* "around."

Genesis 2:8–14 describes the Garden of Eden thus: "And the Lord God planted a garden in Eden, in the *east*; . . . And out of the ground the Lord God made to grow every tree that is pleasant to the sight and good for food, . . . A river flowed out of Eden to water the garden, and there it divided and became four rivers."[1]

---

[1] *Holy Bible, Revised Standard Version*, New York, Nelson, 1962. Emphasis by the author.

Donald L. Wilbur, during a study-tour of Persian gardens, describes his experience: ". . . toiling up the long dusty road from Baghdad to Teheran in the scalding heat of summer I soon learned to seek shelter in *gardens* along the way, sometimes alongside a teahouse *pool, banked around with potted plants, and sometimes along a rushing rivulet within a fragrant orchard. Almost at once the identification of the garden with paradise,* made by the Persians, seemed natural and appropriate."[2]

As Islam, following 632 A.D., came to dominate Persia and quickly spread westward to Spain, the Koran became for the Moslems (Moors, Saracens) The Book.

In Mohammedanism, five of the seven paradises are gardens. The Koran declares: ". . . for him who dreadeth the tribunal of his Lord are prepared two *gardens, planted with shade trees.* In each of them shall be two fountains flowing."[3] Although Figure 64 represents an eighteenth-century garden, it is directly descended from many like it from centuries past.

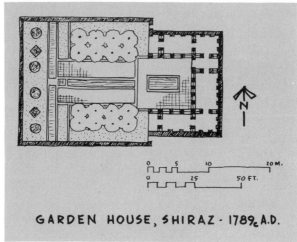

GARDEN HOUSE, SHIRAZ - 1789₄ A.D.

FIGURE 64

To assure continuity of the historic thread through these chronicles, it is necessary to establish the relationships that existed between the highly cultured, literate Arab world, and the yet semi-barbaric states of Europe. Commercial contacts apparently were maintained between the two worlds, even at the height of feeling engendered during the crusades.

Let us then, imagine ourselves to be Leonardo Fibonacci, from Pisa, in Italy, living for a time in Cairo, in 1200, as a representative of a commercial house. He might have described in glowing terms the daily life of this, one of the greatest cities of the Arab world (population of 2 million) thus:

[2]Wilbur, Donald L., *Persian Gardens and Pavilions*, Rutland, Vt., Tuttle, 1962, p. 13. Emphasis by the author.

[3]Wright, Richardson, *The Story of Gardening*, New York, Dodd, Mead, 1935, p. 121.

In the early morning, the Arab visits the *hammam* or bath house. He bathes himself in the pool there, shaves, and puts on clean clothes, in preparation for the Muezzin's call to prayer. He bows, then kneels on his prayer rug, facing toward Mecca, and prays to Allah.

Your typical Arab gentleman (really quite cultured, you must know; not at all the monstrous beast we used to think him during the battles for Jerusalem) is very well educated. Over half the people here can read and write.

Incidentally, here is something we can use. It will, I think, revolutionize our accounting procedures. The numbering system I am about to describe will make it possible for our accountants to throw away the abacuses they now use (the adding machine we got from the Greeks), and be able to add and subtract columns of figures. I hear this numbering system was recently invented by a Moroccan genius.

The "picture" for each numeral from one to nine contains the appropriate numbers of angles (the Moroccan must have had access to an ancient Euclidean geometry text). He has also added a cipher, or zero, a circle, representing nothing, or no angles. The word "cipher" comes from the Arabic *sifr*, meaning "empty," or zero.

Graphically, the system looks like this:[4]

$$\Lambda Z \exists 4 5 6 7 8 9 0$$

Your wife will be interested, because Cairo's women live so differently from ours at home, in the way Arabic wives spend their time. Arabic ladies (no, despite what you may have heard, the Saracen is not necessarily polygamous) live in a secluded apartment. Servant girls may be seen by visitors, but never the lady of the house. She seldom goes out, but does not seem to mind. The "harem," or women's quarters, looks out onto a pleasant interior garden court, where fountains splash, and the lady may receive visits from friends.

Once a week, the wives visit the *hammam*, which is a sort of beauty parlor. All the ladies of the neighborhood arrive at dawn, and spend the day together. They are served a cold lunch at

---

[4]According to Mrs. Abdelkri Boujibar, director of the Museum of Morocco, as reported to Charles McHarry, *Chicago Tribune-New York Times* Syndicate.

noon, and are then served a new drink, called coffee which is an interesting brew. I think you'd like it, even though it is different.

The routine of the *hammam* includes a steam bath, massage, pedicure and a facial. Then they (the ladies) have their hair washed, and apply a henna rinse (to bring out highlights), have their nails varnished red, and apply kohl, or (in Arabic *alkuhl*), a powder with which they paint their eyelids. This powder is very fine in texture and highly refined, by techniques of which we are not yet capable.[5]

This is the most amazing country I've ever visited. Before I return to Pisa, remind me to bring back drawings of some of the things I have seen. For instance, these people use wind for power, in the form of a sort of windmill. They have methods of dying cloth you wouldn't believe, the colors are so much richer and clearer than ours. From somewhere in the mysterious east, they have imported a worm which (you'll never believe this) spins fine fibers, from which the Arabs manufacture a cloth of a smoothness that is unbelievably fine.

Well, I had best cease this rambling, as I must make a good repast now, as tomorrow Ramadan, the Mohammedan month of fasting, begins. Perhaps the next time I write, I will have more and even wilder tales to tell.

*Leonardo Fibonacci*[6]

The establishment of Mohammedanism coalesced the Arabic peoples into an Empire that, at its height, spread across North Africa, the Middle East, to India. Its farthest penetration into Western Europe was halted by Charles Martel at Poitiers, in France, in 732. However, for some 800 years Arabic Emirates occupied Spain, introducing into that peninsula Moorish customs, architecture, and cultural attitudes.

Contemporary description says that, during the height of Moorish power in Spain, there were as many as 50,000 sumptuous villas in the valley of the Guadalquivir, which waters the region of Andalucia, in the south of Spain. Cities of the valley which still retain some of the Moorish character include Sevilla and Cordova.

During the latter centuries of Moorish occupation, pressures from the Christian (Washington Irving named them "Gothic") forces from the North increased. The last remaining stronghold of the Moors (1200–1400+) was at Granada, in the southern part of Andalucia. Granada lies south of the Guadalquivir, on the Darro, a minor tributary, and northwest of the Sierra Nevada.

South of the city lie two relatively high promontories, upon which Al Ahmar

---

[5] "*Al kuhl*" became "alcohol," meaning highly refined spirits.

[6] Leonardo Fibonacci actually existed; the events, materials, and technologies he describes are real, though the letter is a figment of the author's imagination.

(1238–1358) and his successors built the Fortress Alhambra (so named for the red brick used), and, above the fort, a pleasant retreat, the Generalife.

Both overlooked Granada, but also had magnificent views to the South toward the perpetual snows of the Sierra Nevada, towering to heights exceeding 3,353 meters (11,000 feet).

Before describing the fortress and its delightful gardens, let us read Washington Irving's graphic description of the region to "get the feel" for the environment:

> Many are apt to picture Spain in their imaginations as a soft southern region decked out with all the luxuriant charms of voluptuous Italy. On the contrary, though there are exceptions in some of the maritime provinces, yet, for the greater part, it is a stern, melancholy country, with rugged mountains and long, naked, sweeping plains, destitute of trees and invariably silent and lonesome, partaking of the savage and solitary character of Africa. What adds to the silence and loneliness is the absence of singing birds, a natural consequence of the want of groves and hedges. . . . Thus the country, the habits, the very looks of the people have something of the Arabian character.
>
> The ancient kingdom of Granada . . . is one of the most mountainous regions of Spain. Vast sierras or chains of mountains, destitute of shrub or tree, and mottled with variegated marbles and granites, elevate their sunburned summits against a deep blue sky, yet in their rugged bosoms lie engulfed the most verdant and fertile valleys, where the desert and the garden strive for mastery, and the very rock, as it were, compelled to yield the fig, the orange, and the citron, and to blossom with the myrtle and the rose.
>
> The Alhambra [see Fig. 65] is an ancient fortress or castellated palace of the Moorish kings of Granada, where they held dominion over this their boasted terrestrial paradise, and made their last stand for empire in Spain. The palace occupies but a portion of the fortress, the walls of which, studded with towers, stretch irregularly round the whole crest of a lofty hill that overlooks the city . . .
>
> In the time of the Moors, the fortress was capable of containing an army of forty thousand men within its precincts, and served occasionally as a stronghold of the sovereigns against their rebellious subjects. After the kingdom had passed into the hands of the Christians, the Alhambra continued a royal demesne, and was occasionally inhabited by the Castillian monarchs.[7]

[7]Irving, Washington, *The Alhambra, Tales of a Traveler*, Copyright © The Macmillan Co., New York, 1925. Irving lived in the Alhambra for three months in 1829.

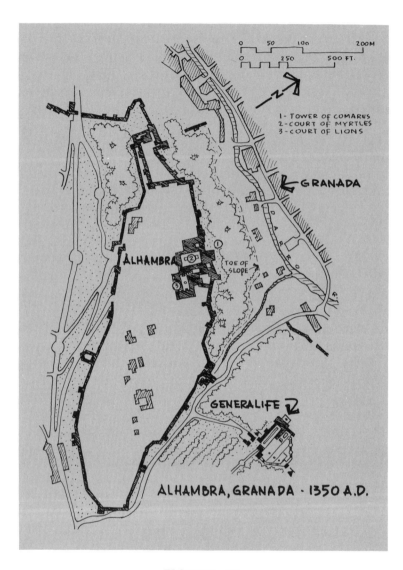

FIGURE 65

Contained within the palace itself, are a number of apartments, including several interior courts that exquisitely reflect the characteristics of the "earthly paradise" previously discussed.

Two of these are illustrated here (see Fig. 66)—the Court of the Myrtles and the Court of the Lions. The Spanish Christian conquerors renamed the Court of the Myrtles "The Court of the Alberca" (pool), because of the immense basin, or fishpool, bordered (in Washington Irving's time) by hedges of roses. Evidently, roses proved too difficult to maintain in later years which may explain why in this century the two hedges are of myrtle.

Adjacent to the Court of the Myrtles to the east are the Royal Baths, illustrating the elaborate tile paving characteristic of Moorish design.[8]

At the north end of the larger court is the Tower of Comares, the dominating feature of the fortress, which contained, on its ground floor, a ceremonial hall, where receptions for visiting dignitaries took place, thus acquiring the name "Hall of the Ambassadors."

Another peristyled court, but done with the exquisite delicacy of the Moors, whose columns contrast sharply to the relative heaviness of Greek and Roman columns, is the Court of the Lions, so named from the elaborate central fountain supported by 12 lions. This fountain is rather an anomaly in view of the Mohammedan prohibition against

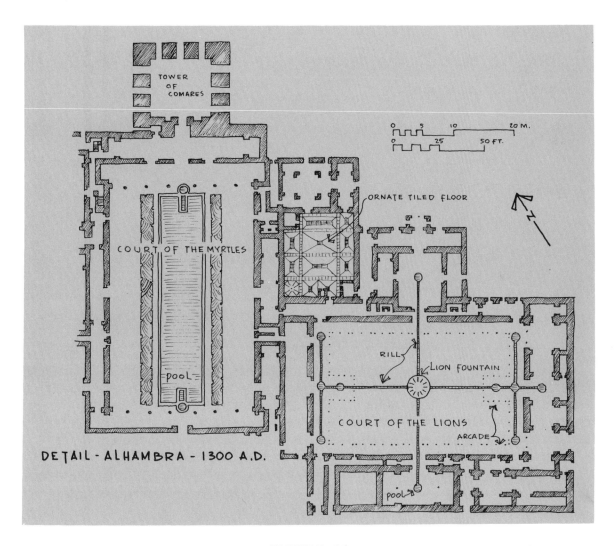

FIGURE 66

[8]Sordo, Enrique, *Moorish Spain, Cordoba Seville Granada*, New York, Crown, 1963, p. 175.

representations of living things. The explanation for this departure from the Islamic norm seems to be that the lion fountain was of Byzantine origin, "liberated" by Saracenic troops.

Extending outward from the Lion Fountain's base, in four cardinal directions, are narrow channels in the floor of the court, leading to other pools and fountains in the court as well as in rooms connected to it. These channels, or rills, express the concept of the "four rivers of paradise." In addition, the way in which the water was used, (a whole series of rills, small jets, and splashing fountains), indicates the inbred poetic nature of the Arab. Although the broad mirror pool in the Myrtle Court expresses lavishness, the use of water in the Court of the Lions illustrates the Moorish awareness of the preciousness of water, based on the nomad's long experience with extreme water shortages.

Connected to the Alhambra by a series of paths, and perching on a high hill to the East, is the Generalife, built as an even cooler, airier, retreat than the naturally air-cooled courts of Alhambra itself.

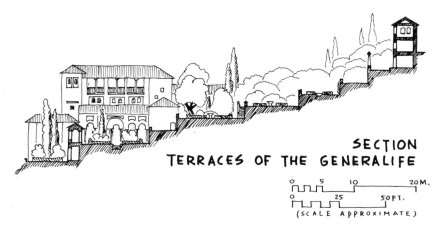

SECTION
TERRACES OF THE GENERALIFE

(SCALE APPROXIMATE)

FIGURE 67

It, too, expresses poetry in water use. Every terrace has its own fountain, each differing from the other. The lowest of the terraces contains a long, narrow pool (the river concept), and even the balustrades of the flights of steps leading diagonally from the highest pavilion downward to the major "casino," are scooped out into rills. Even today, the person descending the stairway can trail his hand in the cooling mountain water.

The terracing of the gardens of the Generalife, and its overlook design (see Fig. 67) presage the later hillside gardens of the Italian Renaissance villas of the fifteenth and sixteenth centuries.

# 11         *L'Uomo Universale** (1200–1700)

> He has painted himself as brave as a French grenadier, as vindictive as a viper, superstitious to the last degree, full of eccentricity and caprice, a pleasant companion among friends, but not susceptible of affectionate attachments; rather loose in sexual relations, a bit of a traitor without being aware of it; slightly tainted with spite and envy, a braggart and vain without suspecting himself to be such; a madcap who firmly believed he was wise, circumspect, and prudent. Fully persuaded he was a hero, he dashed this picture of himself upon the canvas without a thought of composition or reflection, just as his fiery and rapid fancy prompted. We derive from it something of the same pleasure which we feel in contemplating a terrible wild beast who cannot get near enough to hurt us.[1]

Giuseppe Marc'Antonio Baretti[2] thus described Benvenuto Cellini (1500–1571), Italian artist in metals and autobiographer. The characterization typifies the Renaissance man as a total individual with all the human foibles and yet capable of extremely sensitive artistic expression.

Giorgio Vasari (1511–1574) Italian painter, architect, and biographer, wrote of Michelangelo (Michelangelo Buonarroti, Italian painter, sculptor, designer of St. Peter's Rome):

> While the artists . . . were doing their best to imitate and to understand nature bending every faculty to increase that high comprehension sometimes called intelligence . . . the Almighty Creator took pity on their fruitless labor. He resolved to send to earth a spirit capable of supreme expression in all the

*The Universal Man.

[1]From p. 14, *The Life of Benvenuto Cellini*, translated by John Addington Symonds. Permission Liveright Publishers, New York. Copyright © 1931 by Liveright Publishing Corporation.

[2]Italian critic 1719–1789.

arts, one able to give form to painting, perfection to sculpture, and grandeur to architecture. The Almighty Creator also graciously endowed this chosen one with an understanding of philosophy and with the grace of poetry.[3]

Although contemporary designers look with disapproval upon the creations of the Italian fifteenth and sixteenth centuries, most generations between then and now have considered the centuries of *la rinascita* (rebirth) incredibly fertile and fascinating, producing a race of giants who discovered their own individual worth, and proceeded to open the eyes of western Europe to a whole world.

"The Italian Renaissance buildings and gardens . . . were made by the independent and turbulent nobles of the country, proud, ostentatious, competitive, jealous of each other's success, but esthetically appreciative, often excellent artists in their own right, and in any case having command through riches or feudal power of the labor of great numbers of artisans and of the skill of a group of artists of greater attainment than the world has since seen."[4] An understanding of the geography of Italy dictated the forms of the great villas of the Italian Renaissance. While the valleys and plains in summer were unpleasantly hot, even unhealthy, nearby were steep hills, higher, and consequently exposed to cooling breezes, and well supplied with ground and surface waters.

As had Pliny 1,400 years before, the Italian princes, perhaps intuitively, more probably from studies of Roman authors in the original Latin, and surely themselves having observed the ruins of their ancestors' villas, recognized the advantage of site. As avid collectors, these brilliant individualists incorporated into their designs actual classic sculptures, executed generations before in classic times.

The planning of these estates was not necessarily the work of a specific profession. The designer might be architect, sculptor, painter, or hydraulic engineer, as occasion served. Thus, the Italian villa of the Renaissance was of unified design, just as the now-famous paintings and magnificent sculptures of the period were unified wholes in themselves. As early as the fourteenth century, Boccaccio, an early humanist, could describe Tuscan villas of importance and beauty.

The rise of humanism in Tuscany was inevitable. For many reasons, some geographic, some political, some "accidents of nature," Florence (less specifically, the province of Tuscany) saw the birth of the Italian Renaissance in arts and letters (see Fig. 68).

Tuscany (Italian *Toscana*), early in medieval times a margravate[5], later (during the eleventh century) a Lombard[6] duchy, in the twelfth and thirteenth centuries subdivided into small republics and reunited under the Medici Dukes of Florence (Firenze).

---

[3]From the book *Lives of the Painters, Sculptors, and Architects* by Giorgio Vasari. Ed. by Wm. Gaunt. Trans. by A. B. Hinds. Everyman's Library Edition. Published by E. P. Dutton & Co., Inc., and used with their permission.

[4]Hubbard, Henry Vincent and Kimball, Theodora, *An Introduction to the Study of Landscape Design*, Hubbard Educational Trust, 1959, p. 39.

[5]A margravate was a German feudal holding.

[6]The Lombards were Teutons who invaded Italy in 568 A.D., settling in the Po valley, north and east of Tuscany.

FIGURE 68

Even earlier, the Romans had recognized the strategic location of Florence on the Arno
River, on the overland route to Gaul, and had therefore established there one of their
garrison towns. Important and powerful Romans recognized the bracing qualities of the
climate in the hills near Florence. Geography dictated that Florence, during the Middle
Ages, located as it was on the ancient Roman Cassian Way, should become a center of
trade in silks, tapestries, and jewelry, bringing overpowering wealth.

By accident of birth, Dante, poet and student of classic philosophy in the thirteenth
century, was a Florentine. He wrote in the local dialect (Tuscan), which eventually
became the speech of the entire peninsula. Prior speech patterns had been so fragmented
that most formal communication had to be in Latin. Giovanni Boccaccio, fourteenth-
century author of *The Decameron*, clearly delineating man as "human" was, too, a
Tuscan.

Perhaps of most significance to this narrative, Florence saw, in the late medieval
period, the rise of the merchant prince. The city, as a center of trade, made it possible for

individuals to amass large amounts of capital. Civic-minded capitalists such as Cosimo de Medici used the perquisites of their powerful positions intelligently to foster esthetic achievement, as well as civic improvement.

Under the aegis of the Medici family, the public square (Piazza Signoria, location of the Palazzo Vecchio) was improved by the addition of the Loggia (see Fig. 62).

Cosimo commissioned Brunelleschi to design a foundling home adjacent to the church of the Santissima Annunziata. The piazza before it is recognized today as the first of the "Renaissance Squares" (see Fig. 69).

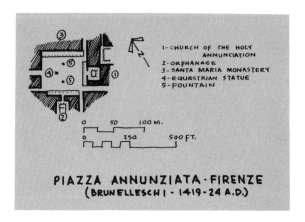

**FIGURE 69**

Cosimo de Medici, scion of a powerful family, whose progeny later (for example, Catherine de Medici) was instrumental in spreading the Renaissance to the rest of Europe, in addition to conducting an eminently successful mercantile and banking empire, was fascinated with classic thought. His palace in Florence became filled with original Greek and Roman sculpture, his library with Greek and Roman manuscripts or copies thereof, and he gathered around him the best of the artists, poets, philosophers, and writers of his day.

Pressured as he must have been with business and civic affairs, and oppressed by the heat of the summer airs in the city, Cosimo entrusted Michelozzo Michelozzi with the design of a country villa at Fiesole, in the hills east of Florence. It was to serve the purposes so well-defined in the letters of Pliny the Younger (cf. Pliny's Tuscan Villa) and, significantly, was erected in a similar setting.

Built on a hillside, overlooking a peaceful valley filled with olive orchards and vineyards, cooled by the local summer breezes, the Villa Medici set a "new" style in country estates. Surprisingly enough, the villa was extremely modest in scale (cf. Fig. 70 with 71) and simple in design.

However, it set a style which persisted into the early years of our century. Stylistically, it paid more than passing homage to classic thought. Its siting and plan, although unique to its setting, was strongly influenced by the architectural theories of the day. Leon Battista Alberti, a contemporary and familiar of Brunelleschi and Michelozzi, published, in about 1450, his *de re Aedificata*. In it, he reiterated principles

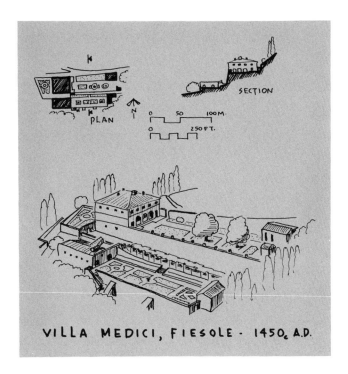

VILLA MEDICI, FIESOLE - 1450, A.D.

FIGURE 70

of building and site selection gleaned trom studies of the 10 voiumes of *De architectura*, by Marcus Vitruvius Pollio, late first-century B.C. and early first-century A.D. (Roman writer on architecture, engineer, architect for Augustus). Vitruvius, in his 10 volumes discussed city-planning, building materials, temples and Greek order, public and private buildings, interior decoration, water works, chronometric instruments, construction, and military machinery.

From this compendium, Alberti derived theories of site planning considered valid today:

1. Consider a site on solid ground, well-drained.
2. Consider orientation of the site to horizontal and vertical angles of the sun.
3. Consider relation of site to prevailing winds, to provide cooling breezes in summer and protection from cold winter winds.
4. Determine adequacy of water supply.
5. Use local materials, so that the structures fit the environment.

Michelozzi's villa, designed as a retreat (cf. Pliny) from the pressures of Florentine business and social life, became, for Lorenzo de Medici, Cosimo's grandson, the setting for his "Platonic Academy."

This "academy" (shades of Plato, Socrates, and Aristotle) became an informal gathering of some of the finest minds of the day. The group assembled for good food, good wine, and stimulating discussion on any given day might include: Marsilio Ficino, a platonic philosopher; Giovanni Pico della Mirandola, humanist; Poliziano, Medici family tutor; and Giorgio Vasari, painter, architect, biographer. Vasari described the villa (Fig. 70) as a: "magnificent and honored palace, founded in the steepness of the slope at huge expense but not without utility."

Perhaps the greatest significance of the Villa Medici, as it set the pattern for the remainder of the period, is in its deep-rooted indications that gardening had again (as with the classic Romans) become a "fine art."

Lorenzo's philosophic retreat expressed an awareness that house and garden belong together as a unit; that this unity may have a clearly defined purpose, such as an atmosphere of welcome; and that the garden, on a slope, may look out on the world.

The Villa Medici at Fiesole, in Tuscany, established a pattern. The second stage in its evolution maintained the unity of house and grounds, but elaborated upon that principle (see Appendix B under Three Eras of Garden Design).

In phase 1, the early Renaissance, though water was featured in the "Philosopher's Garden," it was used sparingly in small, axially located, quiet pools or fountains.

However, Alphonso V, King of Spain, had in the early fifteenth century, resided in Naples. It was there he introduced the Moorish poetic use of water in his palace grounds. This intriguing usage of water as a design element was developed to its fullest extent by Italian architects and hydraulic engineers at the Villa d'Este, at Tivoli, outside Rome.

Cardinal Ippolito d'Este became governor of Tivoli[7] in 1549. He chose to build his villa on a hill overlooking the town because of the lovely views toward the Sabine mountains.

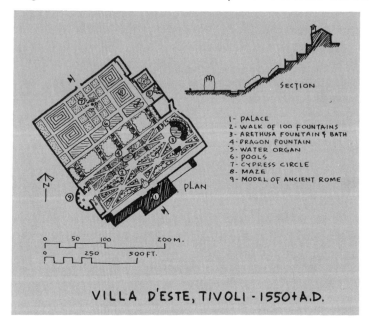

FIGURE 71

[7]Ancient Tibur, 26 kilometers (16 miles) northeast of Rome.

His designers (Pirro Ligorio, architect, and Orazio Olivieri, hydraulic engineer) made full use of the river Anio, pouring its waters over the hill by conducting it through the gardens to mark the cross paths effectively (see Walk of the Hundred Fountains, Fig. 71).

Cardinal Ippolito's villa was no philosopher's garden. The palace (an astonishingly severe, plain barracks) was built to accommodate 250 people. The gardens (see Fig. 71), by their very scale and variety are intended to astonish, amuse, and delight. Identified on Figure 71 are a few of the variations introduced into the overall theme, to provide the visitor with maximum pleasure while unmistakably awing him with the ostensible wealth and power of the owner. Here, on the Walk of the Hundred Fountains, he is overwhelmed by sheer numbers of jets, sprays, and trickles of water devices. The Arethusa Fountain contains a large elliptical basin about 15 by 23 meters (50 feet by 75 feet) in dimension, into which gushes a large waterfall. Behind the waterfall is a cave-like passageway for the refreshment of its cool darkness. At the opposite end of the same level, approached along the walk of the fountains, stands a miniature replica of ancient Rome, as visualized by the architect. In this sculptured area are included water tricks, for the amusement of whoever watched the sudden shock and surprise on the face of the innocent victim. Concealed operators could observe the approach of the intended dupe, twist a valve, and drench the stroller either from above, from an apparently innocuous piece of sculpture, or even upward from the pavement itself. On the lowest level of the gardens lay four huge ponds of quiet, mirror-like quality, each one larger than the "fishpond" in the Alhambra, and fed through a cascade, which was supplied through the exhaust from the water organ, producing organ sounds whenever the water was turned on. Water organs were apparently popular devices, as John Evelyn[8] describes a similar water organ in the Quirinal gardens of Cardinal d'Este on Monte Cavallo, in Rome.

Also, during its early years, according to contemporary engravings, there were four mazes (see Fig. 72): devices for the delight of garden visitors, which have apparently fascinated people since the time of the Egyptians. The maze was, during the Middle Ages, incorporated as part of the floor pattern in the naves of great cathedrals (as at Amiens), where penitents would, on their knees, follow the pattern from beginning to end, while murmuring their pleas for absolution.

While the Villa d'Este at Tivoli illustrates the lavish use of water, made possible by an ample supply (the River Anio), the Villa Lante, at Bagnaia, of the same period, exemplifies, on a smaller scale, and perhaps with greater harmony, a water garden made possible with only a modest supply of water.

Bagnaia, a little town about 6 kilometers (3.8 miles) from Viterbo, and governed by Roman cardinals (as Tivoli), became, as of about 1560, the country villa of Bishop Gian Francesco Gambara. Later, the estate came to the Lante family, who owned it up to our time. The design is attributed to Vignola (Giacomo Barozzi 1507–1573).

Lante expresses more clearly than any other the marriage of casino and garden to produce the essence of the term "villa," and further establishes the theoretical three

---

[8]English diarist, 1620–1706.

MAZE - VILLA D'ESTE - 16th CENTURY          FIGURE 72

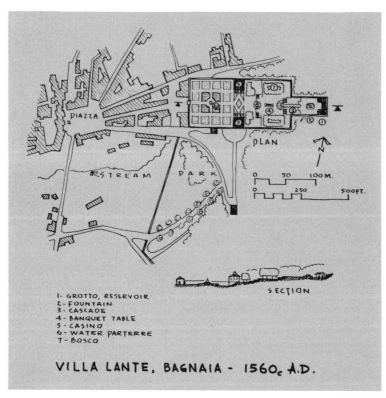

1 - GROTTO, RESERVOIR
2 - FOUNTAIN
3 - CASCADE
4 - BANQUET TABLE
5 - CASINO
6 - WATER PARTERRE
7 - BOSCO

VILLA LANTE, BAGNAIA - 1560c A.D.          FIGURE 73

principal parts of the Italian garden: the *bosco*, or grove; level, well-defined terraces; and a parterre, or garden of figured ground-pattern.

The villa plan, as shown, with its associated walled "park," (cf. Sorensen[9]) dominates the town. The garden and twin casinos, dedicated to the secular pleasures of a prince of the Papal States, occupies nearly as much area as the village, whose piazza relates to the main gate at the bottom of Bishop Gambara's garden. The large, central square of the parterre is a huge tank with a centrally located circular fountain approached by four bridges over the tank's water surface. Surrounding the tank are a whole series of smaller, square, colorful flower beds basking in the brilliant Italian sunshine.

In contrast to the water features of Villa d'Este, which are organized on a series of minor cross-axes, Vignola has here arranged the garden axis to correspond exactly with the hydraulic axis. The water supply is nowhere near as lavish as at d'Este, but, placed upon the principal axis and as the unifying element, consists of a whole series of rills, cascades, and stepped fountains, strategically arranged at the locations of changes in grade. Everything—steps, paths, borders, even the twin casinos—depends on the central theme of the water axis, the key design element in the gardens. Shady twin *boscos* (man-made miniature forests) contrast sharply with the brilliantly sunlit open paths making it possible for the stroller to be delighted with the intricate water play. Even the banquet table on the second terrace has its own central water channel, upon which were floated some of the lighter dishes to titillate the jaded appetites of the diners.

This period, then, in garden design, sincerely reflects the spirit of its time. Still a single, harmonious, unified composition, its total composition illustrates a relatively stable period. Gone is the philosopher's garden (Medici at Fiesole), arranged for the foregathering of intellectuals engaged in serious discussion of man, his pagan origins, and his present identity. Now man seems to know who and what he is, drawn back to Mother Church, but permitting himself, with wealth, to enjoy thoroughly the secular pleasures of the ostentatious display of affluence.

Some historians regard the previous period (1503–1573) as being baroque. However, in view of the rather careful consideration given to interrelation of all the parts of the gardens (as at d'Este and Lante) to a single, unified idea, as opposed to the gradual decline in order characteristic of the seventeenth century, known as the Baroque era, the term "baroque" will be used for the period 1573 to 1775. In the present context, "baroque" is defined as a situation in which the basic use of form tends to violate the principle of fitness to a particular environment, as well as denying the specific characteristics of the materials used.

Isola Bella, originally a small, relatively flat island (basically a large rock of schist rising out of the depths of mountain-girt Lago Maggiore at the bottom of the Italian Alps) was entirely rebuilt into a fantastic fairyland, expressing clearly and forcibly man's arrogant dominance over nature. The major feature of the garden consists of ten terraces. The five upper ones make it seem possible that the architect had in mind some account of Babylonian hanging gardens.[10]

[9]Sorensen, C. Th., *The Origin of Garden Art*, Copenhagen, The Danish Architectural Press, 1963, p. 19.

[10]Gothein, Marie Luis, *A History of Garden Art, Vol. II*, New York, Dutton, 1928.

Count Vitalione, the owner, attracted by the idea of surmounting almost overwhelming difficulties, had built here, between 1632 and 1670, a castle with gardens behind, which, though never completed, still floats like a mighty battleship upon the surface of the lake. Though in the lower Alps, the deep lake valley creates a microclimate making possible exuberant, semitropic gardens.

The gardens, no longer a single entity, impossible to view all at one time (except in the views one gets from the approaches across the lake), are pyramided at the climax into a series of flower-laden level terraces filled with soil, containing an astonishing variety of waterworks, sculptures, obelisks, statuary, and even a garden wholly devoted to citrus fruits (later to be called "orangeries"). Hospitality (meaning, in most cases, "come over to my house to see what I've accomplished with my wealth") itself here became a gesture. Cardinal Scipio Borghese had inscribed above the gate to his baroque gardens, built in the same period near Frascati, a paragraph expressing the spirit of the age: "Whoever thou art, now be a free man and fear not the fetters of the law. Go where thou wilt, pluck what thou wilt, depart when thou wilt. Here is all for the stranger more than for the one who owns. In the golden age that promises security to all men, the master of the house will have no iron laws. Then let him who evilly and of set purpose shall betray the golden rule of hospitality beware lest the angry steward burn the tokens of friendship." A posturing statement, it indicates adherence to a philosophy that the great baroque estate was a showplace, a window for display.

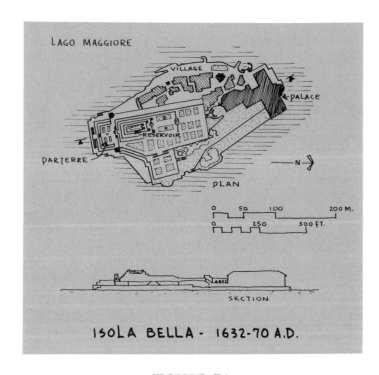

FIGURE 74

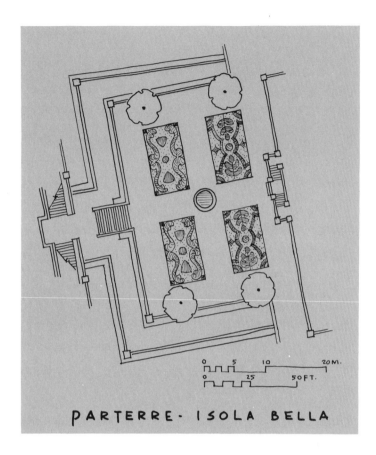

PARTERRE · ISOLA BELLA

FIGURE 75

The baroque character of Isola Bella is everywhere expressed. Perhaps the clearest expression of its effulgence is the terrace at the south end of the island (see Fig. 75).

The terrace is enclosed with marble balustrades and contains vases and statuary. Its baroque significance is expressed in the profusion of colorful flowers, carefully but extravagantly disposed in artfully contrived geometric forms, designed to be viewed as a flat plane from above. This small, architectonic garden gives a foretaste of the French *parterre de broderie,*[11] so carefully delineated by Boyceau (early 1600s) in his *Traité du Jardinage,* and so often employed in French garden art.

[11]*Parterre* is French for "on the ground;" *broderie,* for "embroidered."

# 12 "L'Etat C'Est Moi"*
### (France, 1200–1715)

It has been said, with truth, that Louis XIV, while responsible for shaping Versailles, was himself shaped by it into the most brilliant of the absolute monarchs of this age of monarchies.

The culmination of the Renaissance in France occurred in May 1664 when Louis XIV entertained his court at his recently completed palace and pleasuregrounds of Versailles with a week of uninterrupted festival. For this festival, Jean Baptiste Poquelin (better known by his pseudonym, Molière) produced four plays, in some of which the King himself took part.

The Renaissance in France developed on an entirely different plane than in Italy. For geographic, cultural, and political reasons, the "age of enlightenment" developed more conservatively, and yet reached national scale and brilliance unseen before or since.[1]

Geographically, the area the world now calls France, lies north and west of the Alpine barrier separating it from the earlier center of the Renaissance, Italy. Lying north of the 43rd parallel of north latitude (see Fig. 76), and exposed on the west to Atlantic winds and currents, its low-lying topography places it in a moderate marine climate, having mild winters but lacking the strong Mediterranean sunshine.

Culturally, feudalism persisted in France far beyond the period of political change which had earlier evolved in Italy.

Because France was a part of a tremendous land mass, maritime commerce developed much more slowly and later than in its neighbor to the south.

At the time of the greatest flowering of Italian intellectual thought, France was still involved in a confused series of military conflicts, including the so-called Hundred Years' War, a major conflict between the feudal monarchs and nobles of France and their neighbors across the English Channel.

As elsewhere, geography, cultural background, climate, and topography dictated the timing and form of cultural evolution. The French were conservative. This conservatism is illustrated by the persistence of castles and moats long after the monarchy had become absolute, with the kingdom's borders the first line of defense. French climate, Atlantic rather than Mediterranean in origin, and therefore cooler and damper, caused a

---

*"I am the State." Louis XIV before the French Parliament, April 13, 1655.

[1]Although the Mogul conquerors of India (1526–1875) built such architectural marvels as the Taj Mahal, stunning in its sheer size, Versailles, epitomizing French Renaissance culture, far outshown the Mogul Empire at its height.

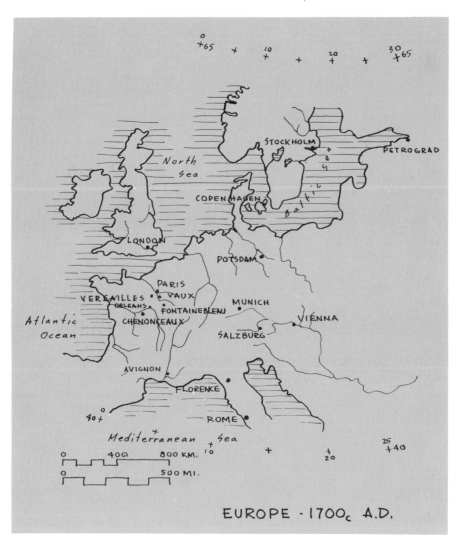

FIGURE 76

delight in use of color in garden design. The topography of the parts of France where the monarchs owned extensive lands seemed to require large, flat sheets of water, rather than the trickling cascades, impressive jets, or gushing torrents of the Italians.

As indicated in the chronological chart (see Appendix B) France early came under monarchal control, in contrast to the independence of city-states in Italy. Kingship itself had the effect, due perhaps to the huge retinues of courtiers and servants required, of vastly increasing the scale of garden development in France, when compared to the scale in the Italian villas.

French chateau design from the sixteenth through the eighteenth centuries had strong Italian undertones since Italian garden designers, along with artists with other skills, were brought to France beginning with Francis I. Both Catherine and Marie de Medici were queens of France, and brought regal command to bear during their reigns.

Fontainebleau illustrates clearly the ways in which the French, intrigued by Renaissance Italy, adapted the forms of the Italians, but modified them to meet the demands of their own climate, topography, political structure, and temperament. Originally a hunting seat of French feudal noblemen, Fontainebleau lay in the midst of a great wood, some 56 kilometers (35 miles) south of Paris, on flat marshy, ground. During his reign (1515–1547) Francis I built here a fine castle, embracing a number of courts, grouped in no sort of order. Surrounding most of the buildings lay a wide canal, or moat, reflecting the traditional defense mechanism used so effectively in French river valleys in feudal times.

The nearby marsh was converted into a gigantic pond bordering the castle on one side (see Fig. 77). On the west edge of the pond, an avenue of four rows of trees, between protective walls, led to an entrance gate or pavilion to the north. West of the entrance

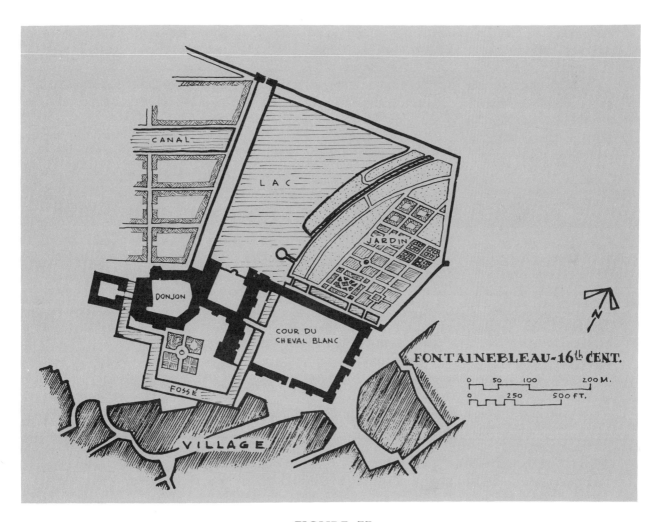

FIGURE 77

avenue lay fruit gardens, a canal, and meadows. East of the pond lay a garden called *Le Jardin des Pins* (The Pine Garden) containing not only evergreen plantations, but formal beds laid out in box,[2] probably containing the vegetable gardens. On the south side of the castle keep, inside the moat, were laid out gardens, four-square in design, containing box, flowers, and varicolored earths. The central feature was a statue known as Diana of Versailles.

After the time of Francis I, the palace and gardens passed though a whole series of modifications. Catherine de Medici expanded the gardens. Henry IV built to the west of the palace a grand canal, 1,200 meters long, (3,937 feet), 40 meters wide (131 feet), upon which boats sailed for the pleasure of Henry's guests. This long series of innovations continued until, at the time of Louis XIV, the grounds near the palace appeared as in Figure 78. The palace itself had, over the years, expanded into a rabbit warren of courts, rooms, and passages to accommodate the vastly increased retinues necessary to support the elaborate court of Louis, the Sun King. Marie de Medici's reasonably modest gardens elaborated in form and extent, to feed the ever more jaded appetite of the court for novelty, under the watchful eye of André Le Nôtre, the world's greatest garden geometrist.

Le Nôtre had already, by 1656, made his reputation, having glamorized the gardens at Fontainebleau and the Tuileries for Louis XIV. But both were strong-willed, and, although we do not know the exact basis for the tiff, for a time Le Nôtre was out of favor with Louis. During these days away from the court, André Le Nôtre kept busy. He had already completely redesigned Chantilly for the Great Condé, and had thus firmly fixed in his mind, through having seen them created, those innovations from which Le Nôtre's name cannot be separated.

How Le Nôtre continued to reinforce his reputation and to achieve world-wide fame, makes a fascinating anecdote. The story really began during the reign of Louis XIII. The chief residence of the French kings at that time was in Paris at the expanded Louvre, with its extensive gardens known as the Tuileries. Louis XIII's chief gardener, Monsieur Le Nôtre, had his son, André, working in the gardens. But Le Nôtre *père* insisted that Le Nôtre *fils* be educated as an artist. Working with such painters as Simon Vouet, Charles Le Brun, and others, André developed skills as painter and draftsman to add to his learned vocation of gardener. Having visited French gardens and toured Italy, he early began to conceive ideas of his own for improvements in the relatively (to him) unsophisticated gardens of French royalty.

It transpired, then, that Le Nôtre, in 1656, during his banishment from the court, suddenly had the opportunity to put all his ideas to the test; to create, as it were, the ideal physical expression of the grand idea. Nicolas Fouquet, in his important post as Louis' Finance Minister, felt he needed a chateau worthy of his lofty social status.

Having purchased sufficient ground near Melun, 48 kilometers (30 miles) from Paris, Fouquet gathered to him the architect Louis Le Vau, the gardener Le Nôtre, and the painter-sculptor Le Brun. The three succeeded in creating a truly classic example of

---

[2]*Buxus sempervirens.*

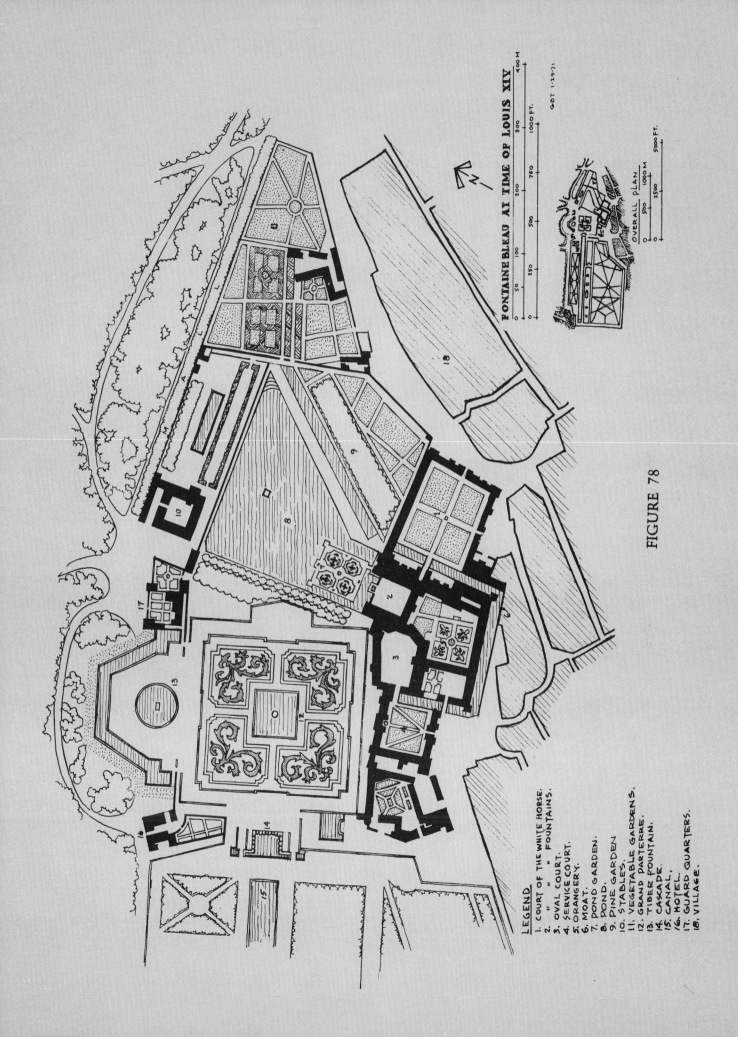

LEGEND
1. COURT OF THE WHITE HORSE.
2. " " " FOUNTAINS.
3. OVAL COURT.
4. SERVICE COURT.
5. ORANGERY.
6. MOAT.
7. POND GARDEN.
8. POND.
9. PINE GARDEN.
10. STABLES.
11. VEGETABLE GARDENS.
12. GRAND PARTERRE.
13. TIBER FOUNTAIN.
14. CASCADE.
15. CANAL.
16. HOTEL.
17. GUARD QUARTERS.
18. VILLAGE.

FONTAINEBLEAU AT TIME OF LOUIS XIV

OVERALL PLAN

FIGURE 78

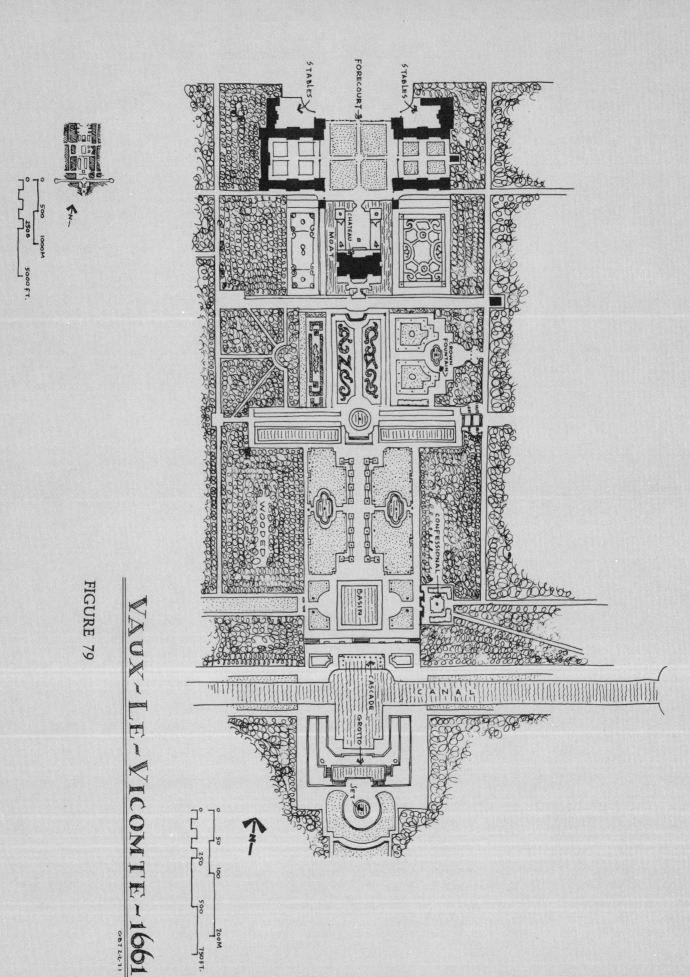

VAUX~LE~VICOMTE~1661

FIGURE 79

French Renaissance design. Here was virgin land except for three small villages that were purchased and destroyed. Here the artists could start afresh, with no necessity of adapting to already-existing buildings and spaces, as had been the case at Fontainebleau and other previous works.

Scale had to be somewhat reduced (see Fig. 79). After all, Fouquet was only mortal, only the King's Finance Minister, not the King himself. Nevertheless, the scale was magnificent enough, the forms architectural and elaborate enough to delight the eye of the most blasé courtier, surfeited as he might be with towering, powdered periwigs, intricately embroidered silks and satins, and yawn as he might at the latest *parterre de broderie.*

Take note of the conservatism mentioned earlier. The moat still persists as a comfortable reminder of the past, even though it is purely decorative. Here, the strong major axis reflects that of the Italian villa. The variety in use of water is also consistently Italian, but here it is brought together in vast, flat sheets, reflecting the flat, watery ground of this part of France.

The garden-plan innovations conceived by Le Nôtre here included, in broad scale, a wide variety of forms and patterns, but, in Italian fashion, were arranged to present a unified whole. The natural waterways Le Nôtre gathered together to form moats and grand canals. Through the forest (or park), the gardener laid out radiating avenues to extend the formalized nearby grounds of the chateau. The entire composition, providing views of nearly unlimited extent, formed a design intended for show, display, and delight for Nicolas Fouquet's guests. This need, on Fouquet's part, to show off his wealth and power proved his undoing. His grievous political error in 1661 was in exhibiting to the court a chateau and gardens more impressive than any of those belonging to King Louis XIV.

Work completed on his new, magnificent country place, Fouquet opened it to his friends with a week of festival in midsummer. However, *Louis* had not been invited. Naturally, the court buzzed with tales of the magnificence of Fouquet's new country chateau, and of the fabulous entertainment, including dancing, plays, mock naval battles, and fireworks, that regaled the guests for a whole week. Naturally, too, Louis himself soon became aware of the gossip. Nothing would do but that Fouquet should put on another fete, with Louis the principal guest.

Two weeks later, Fouquet was imprisoned (something having to do with his financial manipulations). Le Brun, Le Vau, and Le Nôtre were on their way to Versailles to begin the designs for a chateau so far outreaching Vaux that no place should ever match it. And that is how a misguided courtier and leading government official aroused the jealousy of an absolute monarch, resulting in the most fantastic garden the world has yet seen.

Vaux-le-Vicomte at Melun represents the last of the large French Renaissance gardens designed to be viewed as a unit. The sunlit parterres, featuring sculptural display and dominated by elaborate fountains, could be viewed as a whole from the raised terrace on the south facade of the chateau. Just as in the baroque phase of the Italian Renaissance, the "high" French Renaissance rapidly gave way to multiplication of scale and multiplicity of garden elements so well illustrated at Versailles.

Of Louis XIV's Versailles, in 1685, Madame de Sévigné wrote to her daughter, Madame de Grignan: "This kind of regal splendor is unique in the world."[3]

Louis himself, while establishing his position as the predominant figure of the many splendors of Versailles and holding tight the reins of government, diverted himself with the building of his palace, and in frequent consultation with Le Nôtre, designing the palace's immense grounds.

One-and-a-half hour's carriage ride from the Louvre (the traditional seat of French royalty) lay a huge forest some 5 kilometers (3 miles) broad, beloved as a hunting preserve by Henry IV, and used often for the same sport by succeeding kings. In 1631–1634 Louis XIII rebuilt Henry IV's shooting box (hunting lodge) as a rather small Italianate villa.

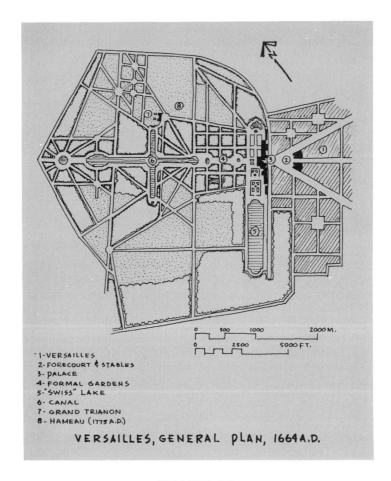

1-VERSAILLES
2-FORECOURT & STABLES
3-PALACE
4-FORMAL GARDENS
5-"SWISS" LAKE
6-CANAL
7-GRAND TRIANON
8-HAMEAU (1775 A.D.)

VERSAILLES, GENERAL PLAN, 1664 A.D.

FIGURE 80

[3]Mauricheau-Beaupre, Charles, *Versailles*, Monaco, Documents d'Art, 1948.

Beginning in 1661, and occupying thousands of laborers (including, at times, large segments of the French army), the time and energy of hundreds of skilled artisans and craftsmen, and taking 25 years to achieve its present form, the hunting lodge was transformed, the forest regimented, the town transformed from a sleepy village to a bedroom town for court hangers-on, and a great ceremonial avenue constructed to connect Louis' pleasure grounds with France's chief city, Paris. Le Nôtre, Le Vau, and Le Brun taxed their artistic skills to the utmost and must have been themselves awed with their temerity in taking on so vast a project (see Figs. 80 and 81).

Keep in mind that the entire length of the main axis of Vaux would fit on the axis of Versailles between the palace and the beginning of Versailles' grand canal, and that from the palace to the end of Fontainebleau's canal equals the Versailles distance from the palace to its canal cross-axis.

Of course, Versailles had to be huge in scale. Louis, by creating it, was himself transformed into the most brilliant, sought-after, and fawned-over monarch the world had known. Whenever and wherever Louis walked in his gardens, he was followed by perhaps two thousand sycophants seeking some personal goal. Versailles rapidly became the mecca, not only of every French courtier, but that of the ambassadors of all of Europe.

Le Nôtre's gardens took on variety and scale previously unknown. During periods of festival, vast cutting gardens were robbed of their bloom to decorate the paths. Wherever Louis went, portable pumps operated the fountains, which otherwise lay calm. Even today, the vast scale and widespread character of the waterworks make it impossible to play the fountains except on special occasions.

It cannot come as a surprise that the impact of Versailles' gardens penetrated most parts of Europe. Cardinal Richelieu, Louis XIII's Prime Minister had, long years before, made France an international power. Louis XIV, ruling France from 1661 until his death in 1715, took unto himself the stupendous task of making all state decisions. Under his personal aegis, the court of France quickly became known throughout Europe as the most brilliant the world had known. With a Brobdingnagian ruler shaping the larger-than-life palace and pleasure gardens of Versailles, and himself being formed thereby, it is no wonder Louis XIV, could, with justification, reiterate L'état c'est moi, or that visitors from all nations gave Louis the appellation Le Roi Soleil (the Sun King).

It is small wonder that the Margrave of Baden-Durlach (one of many German princelings) should, in 1715, the year of Louis' death, found a new residence near Baden and Wurttemburg in Southwest Germany. Karlsruhe (see Fig. 82) emulates Versailles in that all its roads and pathways focus on the palace, just as the pathways and highways of Versailles focused on Louis' bedchamber (without central heating, palaces tended to be cold, drafty places in winter. Apparently, it was common practice for Louis to conduct the business of state from his pillared, canopied, and curtained bed, in the royal bedchamber located on the axis of the palace.).

Nor is it any surprise that the Palace of Herrenhausen became the royal residence of Duke John Frederick. Herrenhausen lay 2 kilometers (1½ miles) from Hanover, connected to the city by a beautiful avenue of linden trees believed to have been laid out by Le Nôtre, as well as the superb gardens.

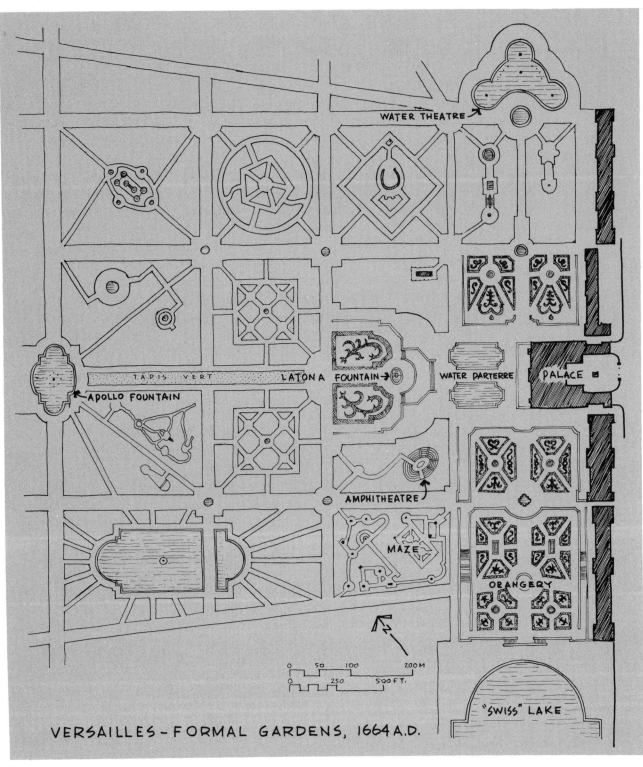

FIGURE 81

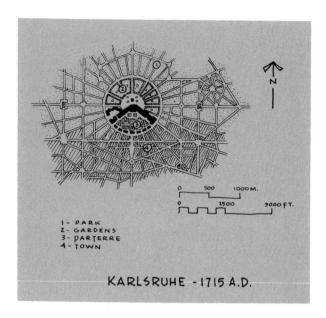

1 - PARK
2 - GARDENS
3 - PARTERRE
4 - TOWN

KARLSRUHE - 1715 A.D.

FIGURE 82

The list of European gardens whose plans may be traced directly to Versailles is virtually endless. Hellbrun, near Salzburg; Nymphenburg, near Munich; Sans-Souci at Potsdam; and Schönbrunn, near Vienna comprise but a few of the imitators of Le Nôtre's classic style. Hampton Court, a royal English seat since before Elizabeth I, during the eighteenth century had "crow's foot" *allées* (radial paths) extended outward for a distance from the palace facade.

The expression of the grand, expansive style penetrated to Poland, Russia (Petrograd, since 1924 Leningrad) and into the Scandinavian countries. Ironically enough, the style returned, as well, to Italy, the place of its birth, in the form of the regal gardens at Caserta, near Naples.

And, also ironically, when George Washington needed a plan for the capital city of the new founded federation of states, he called on Pierre L'Enfant, a military engineer born in France, to lay out the city. L'Enfant's plan shows remarkable resemblance to the gardens of Versailles, but it is significant that the major axis focuses on the capital, while the minor axis has the White House as a terminus. The mall corresponds to Le Nôtre's *tapis vert* (green carpet), the reflecting lagoon to the grand canal, and the diagonal street pattern, with streets intersecting at *ronds points*, is pure Le Nôtre. The horns of the taxicabs, if one has a vivid imagination, may even sound as the beaters' horns, driving the deer onto the forest *allées* for the "sport of kings."

# 13

# Tight Little Island
## (England, 1200–1750)

Non-English-speaking people the world over use English as a second language. Its contemporary usage in diplomatic circles and its increasing importance as the international scientific language, indicate the far-reaching influence of this "tight little island." The fiercely independent English spirit, which forced King John to sign the Magna Carta at Runnymede in June 1215, proved a first step toward eventual dissolution of the historic concept of the Divine Right of Kings.

Well before Elizabeth I (1533–1603), in whose reign (1558–1603) the Renaissance began in England, English ships had begun the vigorous exploration and world trade which eventually made Great Britain a nation "on which the sun never sets." The island seat of empire became a major world power despite geographic fact. England contains less land area than her seventeenth-century colony, New England.[1]

Geographic location, topography, and climate had their own influences on the islands. All of England lies north of the 50th parallel, north latitude. That parallel, as it crosses the Western Hemisphere, first touches land north of Gander, Newfoundland, passes within 240 kilometers (150 miles) of the southern reaches of Hudson's Bay, continues west to Winnipeg, Manitoba, and reaches the Pacific ocean well north of Vancouver, British Columbia. The fortuitous circumstance, however, of oceanic currents gives England her mesothermal climate,[2] similar to that of the Pacific Northwest. Topographically, England has no "young" mountains (such as the western hemisphere's Rocky Mountains), but generally exhibits rolling, gently undulating countryside, composing a series of relatively small-scale visual terrain units.

Thus, England, with her individual spirit, her unique geographic and climatic position, had a Renaissance similar in forms to that of France and Italy, yet quite different in visual character. As with France, the English Renaissance had its origins in the feudal system, which, while comparable to that of Europe, took a different form in England, and for some of the same reasons as in France, occurred later.

---

[1]England: 130,347 sq. km. (50,327 sq. mi.)
New England: 172,515 sq. km. (66,608 sq. mi.).

[2]Average yearly temperature between 17°C and 35°C (32°F to 65°F).

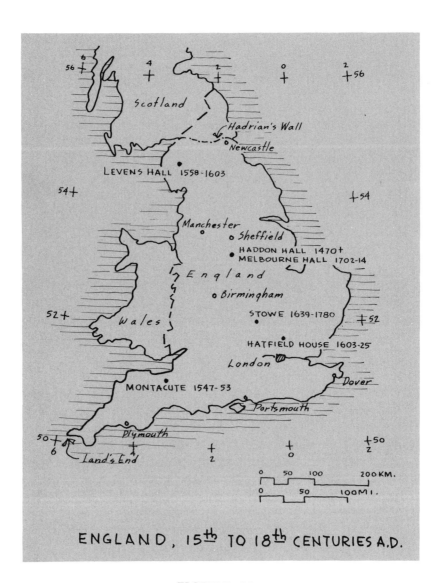

FIGURE 83

Although often ruling his land holdings with an iron hand, the British Lord of the Manor, at least as early as the thirteenth century, recognized the right of the peasantry to profit from its own labor (see Fig. 84). Manorial estates, quite large in size and often many in number (as owned by single individuals), early developed agricultural practices permitting the peasants to work their own designated strips of farmland, providing them with at least a small amount of economic freedom.

The manor-house system in the English Renaissance pattern persisted for generations longer here than elsewhere. Many of the manor estates have remained to the present in

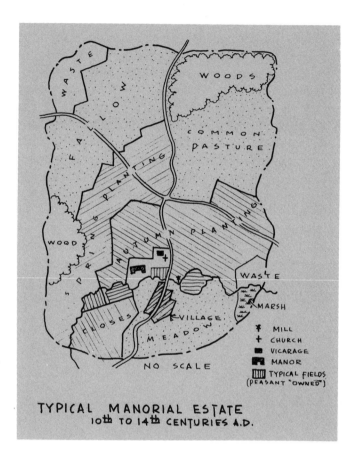

**FIGURE 84**

the hands of direct descendants of original feudal lords. The genealogical records of large numbers of these "first families" remain and are often proudly displayed in the form of coats of arms, proudly hung on baronial walls (and with surprising frequency on the living-room walls of homes in the democratic United States).

While large land-holdings, early established in the years following the Norman conquest, tended to remain the basic pattern in the British Isles, the crag-mounted, or moated castle, apparently had an early demise, in contrast to what we have already observed in France.

Agriculture in England until well into the sixteenth century remained a major revenue source. The island nation early found herself deficient in nonrenewable resources. For this reason, if for no other, the manor estates retained a simplicity and functionality, even at the height of the Renaissance.

"Conservative" and "insular" describe the English character in some minds. The Englishman, with his fiercely independent spirit, certainly did things in his own way. Yet, as he traveled on the continent for business or pleasure, he saw much he considered "good design," and adapted it to the English environment in his own way.

English gardens from 1450 to the mid-eighteenth century, express two garden-planning systems. On one hand, English gentry, strong conservators of the land, held fast to practicality. On the other hand, European garden concepts inevitably crept into their plans. As one examines the historic development of a few typical English gardens, these contrasts become apparent.

Haddon Hall (Fig. 85) as early as 1470 exhibits several of the typically English garden-planning forms not found in earlier French or Italian designs. The forecourt here, as well as at Montacute, Levens Hall, and Hatfield House, is an entrance green, or lawn, rather than a gravel paved court. While the terracing of the immediate grounds of the "castle" reminds us of Italy, their shape tends to be square, rather than oblong (see also Montacute, Levens Hall). The middle terrace at Haddon Hall (2 in Fig. 85) is laid out in small, square beds, later elaborated (see Knot garden, Hatfield House, Fig. 86) into intricately woven, "knotted" patterns in box, rosemary, or even colored earths.

Another typically English garden innovation appeared early at Montacute (Fig. 85). The gardens, instead of lying on the main axis through the house, frequently lay in the direction we already know in France and Italy as the cross axis. Levens Hall (Fig. 85) and Hatfield House (Fig. 86) show this contrast.

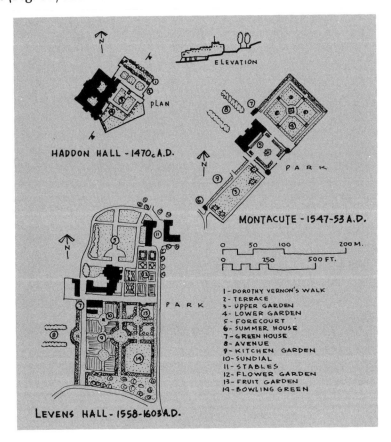

FIGURE 85

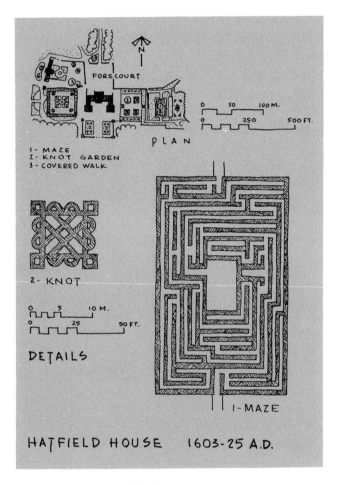

FIGURE 86

Perhaps the most typically English garden innovation of Renaissance times was the "forthright," a straight path often wide enough to accommodate four people walking abreast, extending directly out from the house, or parallel to one facade. Dorothy Vernon's Walk at Haddon Hall, may be the earliest example, but the forthright appears also at Levens Hall and Hatfield House.

A further English stylistic form, the mount, although not specifically illustrated here, seems to have occurred in England, but not elsewhere. During the early medieval period, the mount may have served as a watchtower, from which to observe the approach of cowans and eavesdroppers. Yet the hill in the garden remained as a feature long after the necessity for close defense disappeared. At Montacute (Fig. 85) for example, the lower garden has a raised path around its perimeter, reminiscent of the "fire step" of medieval castles, or the palisaded forts of early colonists in the New World (see also Fig. 89.)

Levens Hall (Fig. 85) shows another typically English garden feature, the bowling green. As early as the thirteenth century, the game of bowls had become a popular outdoor pastime. By 1541 royal edict established a fine for playing at bowls elsewhere than at one's home. The game had become so popular that the crown felt it interfered with the earlier important sport of archery. The English longbowmen had, you will remember, established England as a great military power in the battle of Crécy in 1346. Bowls, not being in any way connected with maintaining military skills, was thus considered detrimental to national defense. Of course, the advent of firearms in the fourteenth century, and the building of a strong navy eventually eliminated archery as a military skill, while the game of bowls and the building of bowling greens proliferated.

One last peculiarly English gardening feature deserves mention. Kitchen gardens, as at Levens Hall (Fig. 85) seemed to appear with great frequency as an integral part of the immediate, formalized gardens of the English Renaissance house. Even today, in English new towns, the Englishman insists on at least a postage-stamp sized plot of ground, whether he rents a flat or owns his own plot.

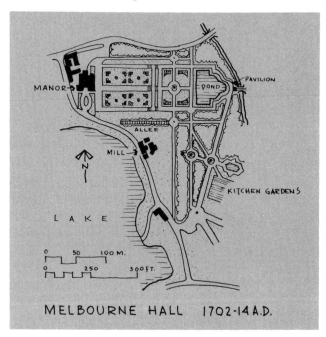

FIGURE 87

English gardens, while expressing the rugged individualism of these northern islanders, were, in the Renaissance era, influenced by the "classic" styles of the European past. The covered walk, reminiscent of the classic peristyle, as well as the medieval cloister, was retained as traditional. The covered walk at Hatfield House (Fig. 86), and the pleached *allée* at Melbourne Hall (Fig. 87), represent this ancient garden form.

The maze as a garden feature, its origins lost in the mists of time, appeared in England as it had elsewhere (see Hatfield House, Fig. 86). So, too, topiary work, the clipping and forcing of plants and shrubs into sculptured forms, appeared throughout England, as it had in Pliny's Roman villas. As well, an architectonic character in the form of stone steps, balustrades, walls, and statuary persisted as a European tradition, though in England considerably softened by the exuberance of England's lush vegetation and by English pragmatism, which led them to be less flamboyant in using stonework, making plant forms serve the same formative purposes.

Melbourne Hall (Fig. 87) perhaps best illustrates the strength of classic Renaissance influence on the English. With its *allées*, meeting at circular *ronds points*, its clipped hedges defining the edges of its paths, and its strict T-square and triangle geometry, Melbourne Hall epitomizes the emulation, even in the uniquely English countryside, of the glory that was France.

So, we see that, even under influences from the rest of Europe as England grew out of her isolation to become a world power, English gardens consistently exhibited a character foreign to what we have observed in Italy and France. English gardens, as illustrated, show *restraint* in scale, and in a significant lack of the exuberance so expressive of the Italian and French designs.

In fact, "foreign" influences of the late-seventeenth century, early in the eighteenth century created an upheaval in garden design. Joseph Addison, writing in *The Spectator*, said, early in the eighteenth century: "I would rather look upon a tree in all its abundance and diffusion of boughs and branches, than when it is cut and trimmed into a mathematical figure; and cannot but fancy that an orchard in flower looks infinitely more delightful than all the little labyrinths of the most finished parterre."[3] Alexander Pope, a poet, contemporary of Addison, and amateur designer of his own garden, could pen, in satiric vein,

> On every side you look, behold the wall.
> Grove nods on grove, each alley has a brother,
> And half the platform just reflects the other.
> The suffering eye inverted nature sees,
> Trees cut to statues, statues thick as trees . . . [4]

[3]Joseph Addison (1672–1719) and Richard Steele (1672–1729) collaborated on two literary periodicals, *The Tatler* and *The Spectator*. Both made significant social commentary and strongly influenced the revolution in English taste in garden design as a revulsion against formalism, and the advocacy of a romanticized version of nature. The quotation is from Batsford, Harry, and Fry, Charles, *Homes and Gardens of England*, New York, Scribner, 1933, p. 41.

[4]Alexander Pope (1688–1744), a contemporary of Addison and Steele, through his poetry, as well as his personal advocacy in his own garden (see Fig. 89) of the Romantic, strongly influenced English taste in gardens. The quotation is from Batsford and Fry, *op. cit.*, p. 41, and is a part of Pope's *Moral Essays*, *Epistle IV*, written to Richard Boyle, Earl of Burlington, *of the use of Riches*.

# 14 Gardens of Illusion
## (The English Landscape School, 1712–1790)

As intimated in the closing paragraphs of the preceding chapter, a revolution in taste occurred in England during the eighteenth century. Many factors influenced changes in approach to garden design. Politically and economically the British had emerged, much to their own surprise, as the most vital, greatest nation in the world.[1] The English soon learned, to their delight, not to copy others, but to create a purely English style to be admired by others.

*Le jardin anglais,* as the new style in gardening became titled in France, has, to us, acquired the name "English Landscape School." Major cultural shifts had much to do with establishing this revolutionary garden art form.

The eighteenth century became an age of enlightenment. The industrial revolution created a newly affluent middle class. The political revolutions of the end of the previous century had produced, in England, a form of nationalism involving the establishment of political parties, notably the Tories (conservative royalists), and Whigs (advocates of constitutional government, civil liberty, religious tolerance, and reform in governmental operations).

Advances in the social sciences provoked deep philosophical discussion of the nature of man, creating the then-new sciences of psychology and sociology. Initial investigations of the buried city of Pompeii almost overnight created archeology as a means of scientific research into man's past. Linnaeus[2], early in the eighteenth century, had developed the binomial system of nomenclature for classifying animals and plants.

Accompanying the enlightenment of science occurred a literary rediscovery of nature as a source of wonder and delight, an inspiration to poets and artists.

In his *La Nouvelle Héloïse* Jean Jacques Rousseau had written: "Nature seems to want to hide her real charms from the eyes of men, who are not sufficiently sensitive to them, and all too often distort them. She avoids populous places, and it is only on the tops of mountains, in the depths of the woods, or on desert islands that she spreads her most ravishing charms. For those who love her, but who cannot travel so far to find her, nothing remains but to do violence to Nature and to force her to take up her abode with them; and this cannot be done without a certain illusion."[3]

[1]Clifford, Derek, *A History of Garden Design*, New York, Praeger, 1963.

[2]Carolus Linnaeus (1707–1778), Swedish botanist and taxonomist, considered the founder of the binomial system of nomenclature and the originator of modern scientific classification of plants and animals.

[3]As quoted in Siren, Osvald, *China and The Gardens of Europe of the Eighteenth Century*, New York, Ronald, 1950, p. 11.

Economics, too, played a major role in the esthetic revolution. Bridgeman and Wise[4] prepared a cost analysis for King George II (1727–1760) revealing excessive labor costs to maintain the formal gardens of previous eras.

Further, among the landed gentry, a gradual change in life style took place. As members of Parliament, landowners seemed to take greater interest in their home estates, perhaps to establish and maintain close relations with their constituencies, rather than fulfilling the former need for establishing personal position in the royal court.

At the same time, the demands of the industrial revolution for raw materials had already decimated the great forests of former centuries, thus, in turn, reducing the numbers of large game animals, especially the stag, the hunting of which had created the great royal parks (cf. Assyria, Persia, and the park at Versailles). Thus, smaller game animals, particularly the wily fox, became the object of the Englishman's hunt, requiring open countryside for this equestrian sport.[5]

Further, explorations of the seventeenth century had opened new vistas on the world. Travelers had rediscovered Italy, with its formerly geometric gardens now overgrown and neglected as intervening centuries had taken their toll, and inexorable nature had clothed their architectonic forms with luxuriant foliage. Seafarers and missionaries (especially the Jesuits) had rediscovered the Orient, and, in particular, China. Discoverers were not all Westerners, either. Chinese visitors to England and the European continent reinforced the cultural exchange.[6] This newly awakened interest in far-eastern countries and peoples disseminated knowledge of China's decorative arts throughout Europe.

Both literary description and the art of landscape painting diffused concepts of artfully contrived "nature" within both the Western and Eastern worlds. Graphic descriptions of the oriental way of gardening (Fig. 88) became widely distributed in England and on the continent, while such European painters as Claude Lorrain (1600–1682, French painter in Italy) and Nicolas Poussin (1594–1665) had provided exciting prospects for producing romantic landscapes in an English countryside ready, in view of the cultural background, for a new and revolutionary form of the gardener's art. The "new" style was introduced, less by professional gardeners than by prominent philosophers and writers.

Anthony Ashley Cooper, Third Earl of Shaftsbury (1671–1713), philosopher, Whig, member of the House of Commons, influenced the change in esthetic thought when he, before Jean Jacques Rousseau, decided that Man, in his original savage state, was "nature's nobleman," and that all else that man has done is corrupt. What he advocated, in effect, returned to the earlier concept of the garden expressing The Garden of Eden, or earthly paradise.

After Shaftsbury came Sir William Temple (1626–1699), statesman, man of letters, and agriculturalist. Temple had traveled abroad considerably, and by 1685 had begun to publish extensively. He became a strong advocate of the Chinese form of gardens, specifically as the English visualized them ("picturesque").

[4]Thomas Bridgeman and Henry Wise, eighteenth-century London nurserymen and garden designers.

[5]Hussey, Christopher, *English Gardens and Landscapes, 1700–1750*, New York, Funk & Wagnalls, 1967.

[6]Siren, *op. cit.*

CHINESE GARDEN
(WOODCUT EARLY 19ᵀᴴ CENTURY)

FIGURE 88

Joseph Addison (1672–1719), essayist, poet, and statesman, had traveled on the continent as part of his cultural education. He recorded his travels from 1699 to 1703 in *Remarks on Italy*. Having achieved literary fame through the publishing of *The Spectator* he was widely read. Therefore, his comment on the "natural look" in planting had the obvious result of turning estate owners away from what was rapidly becoming not only too expensive, but monotonous as well (Italian and French formalism).

Alexander Pope (1688–1744) became the first garden theorist to put the new philosophies in garden design into practice. His garden at Twickenham, after his attacks against formality, became the examplar of the poetic or romantic garden. Here we find, in this small 2-hectare (5-acre) tract, another classic example of a garden in transition. As with Fontainebleau, exhibiting as it did the overlay of Italian garden design on a moated, medieval castle, here, at Twickenham, Pope had brought together ideas from several past cultures, as well as expressing the revolutionary concept of idealized nature.

In Pope's garden plan (Fig. 89) appears the simple, grassy forecourt, even though it here turns its back on the public way and faces the Thames (a much more romantic highway). In execution, the underground passageway became a mystic Italian grotto, with its arches of rough stone and its sound of tinkling waters. The tunnel expressed the Englishman's concept of the Italian's translation of the classic Roman adaptation of the Greek's nature worship as at the awesome cave of the Oracle of Delphi. As one passed through the tunnel (grotto), the eye was led inexorably to a round, domed "temple," small, yet similar in proportion to the Temple of the Vestal Virgins standing in the Forum Romanum.

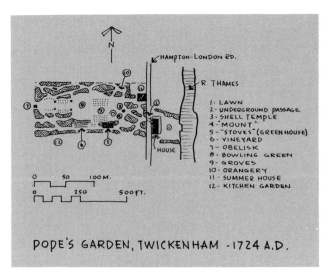

POPE'S GARDEN, TWICKENHAM - 1724 A.D.

FIGURE 89

Next in view appears a mount, apparently an English garden convention, yet from the remote past; a watchtower become a viewing station. To left and right, somewhat hidden yet part of the scheme, appear the "stoves"[7] and "orangery" of French and Italian ancestry. The vineyard appears as an echo of the very remote past, first recorded in Egypt in 2500 B.C., but also an important element in Pliny's Tuscan Villa. To Pope, we suspect, the latter derivation had the greater meaning.

Julius Caesar had seen the obelisk in Egypt, as the Roman Empire expanded with its population demanding greater food supplies. "Liberated" obelisks found their way to Rome in increasing numbers during the ensuing years. To the Englishman on the grand tour of Italy, obelisks apparently represented the tombstone of a dead civilization. To Pope, it appeared only logical to use it to memorialize his mother's tomb, placed at the end of the garden.

The bowling green again echoes the past, and here represents the fierce pride of the Englishman in his own traditions. The groves on the other hand had their Italianate beginning in the *bosco*. The orangery, strangely remote from the greenhouse, in view of the moody English climate, reminds us of Versailles and Fontainebleau. Lastly, as in most English places, the kitchen garden signifies the Englishman's agricultural background. The parts of the gardens were further identified as separate elements, yet pulled together into a unit, by the placement of urns and pieces of statuary (echoes of Greece and Rome) at the juncture of the discrete elements.

Alexander Pope's garden exemplifies the transition in English garden art from European preoccupation with the classic past to romanticized versions of controlled nature in the English Landscape School.

The gardens at Stowe, in Buckinghamshire, not far from London (see Fig. 83 for location) had more influence on garden art of its century than any other English country

---

[7]Stoves were greenhouses.

estate. Its evolution from its early-eighteenth-century appearance as an echo of Le Nôtre's Versailles to its present state as the principal example of the English landscape park, virtually spans the eighteenth century. Alexander Pope called it a "work to wonder at." Laurence Whistler, garden chronicler, said of it: "Bridgeman and Vanbrugh made it; . . . Kent revised it with Brown for understudy; Brown revised it again."[8]

Here at Stowe, we begin to see a strong influence of environment on form. Stowe lies in rolling, arable country at about 122 meters (400 feet) above mean sea level, intersected by shallow valleys, but not so as to give long views. The house had been established on the edge of a south slope. The Temple family (originally sheep farmers) had acquired the extensive land holdings in 1590. Extending from southwest to northeast, north of the house, existed an old Roman road. To the south and east of the house, the village of Stowe, with its church, had access to the Roman road by another east-west lane. Lands north of the Roman road owned by the family contained a "park" (forest) which was used for timber production.

As the family acquired fame and fortune General Sir Richard Temple, a strong Whig, distinguished himself under Marlborough during the wars of Spanish succession. This war led to the final collapse of what had been the Holy Roman Empire. By 1715, Temple had risen to the title Baron (later Viscount) Cobham. The extensive grounds were to take on the "grand manner" as visual evidence of Cobham's position in the world.

Whereas earlier English estates were the product of the culture and tastes of talented amateurs, Stowe was of a scope to demand the services of professionals. Vanbrugh, the architect, remodeled the house, while Bridgeman, the London nurseryman and gardener to Queen Anne, organized the grounds beginning in 1714.

The scheme, at first glance, appears as merely another copy of Versailles. Closer examination reveals that it already begins to intimate the final essence of the English landscape revolution, in which "all nature is a garden." Unquestionably the major axis strikes in clean, French fashion, straight through the house down the south slope to the Octagon Lake, and, in fact, continues south up the next slope towards the town of Buckingham as a double avenue of evenly spaced trees. The parterres are there, the pools, fountains, canals, and bosquets (groves)—all as at Versailles.

But, closer examination begins to reveal innovations. First, Bridgeman introduced the ha-ha wall (Fig. 92). "The device of the ha-ha, which opened the way to true landscape gardening, was not invented by Bridgeman, but he was mainly responsible for its development to enclose the entire 'specific' garden. Its evolution from military engineering can be traced in contemporary allusions or surviving plans, and was evidently gradual."[9] The Bridgeman plan at Stowe clearly indicates the ha-ha's evolution from earlier military fortifications. Both at the rotunda, and south of the temple, extruding from the line of the embankment appear what, in military parlance, would be called bastions.

[8]Green, David, *Gardener to Queen Anne*, London, Oxford University Press, 1956, p. 156. The quotation apparently is taken from Laurence Whistler, *The Imagination of Sir John Vanbrugh and His Fellow Artists*.

[9]Hussey, *op. cit.*, p. 35. Copyright © 1967 by Christopher Hussey. With permission of the publishers, Funk & Wagnalls Publishing Co., Inc.

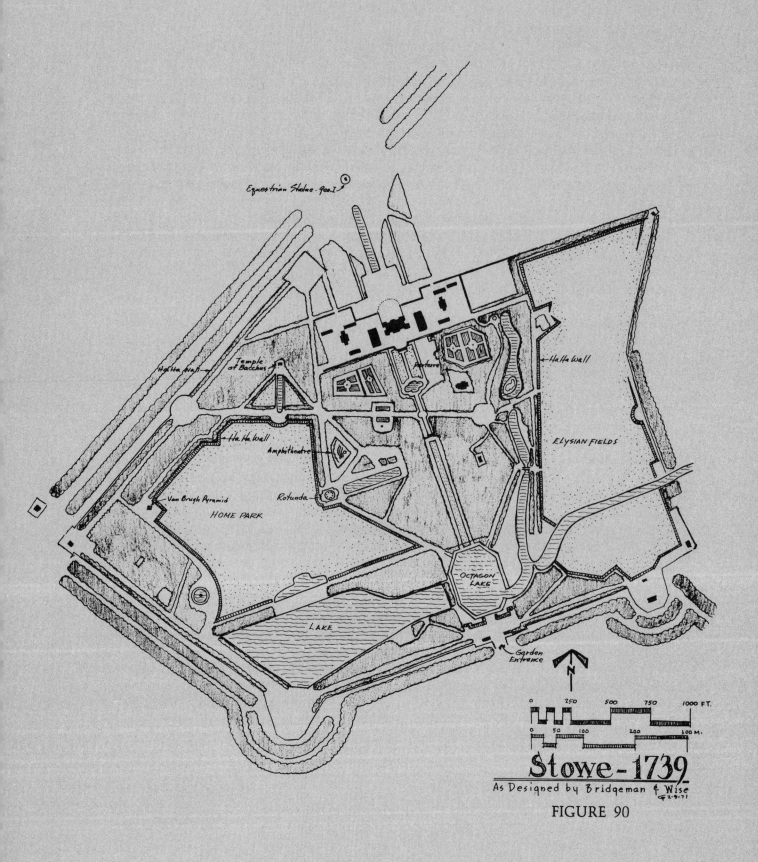

Equestrian Statue. Geo.I

Ha Ha Wall

Temple of Bacchus

Ha Ha Wall

Parterre

Ha Ha Wall

ELYSIAN FIELDS

Amphitheatre

Van Brugh Pyramid

Rotunda

HOME PARK

Octagon Lake

LAKE

Garden Entrance

N

0    250    500    750    1000 FT.

0   50   100        200        300 M.

# Stowe - 1739

As Designed by Bridgeman & Wise

G 2-9-71

FIGURE 90

Lord Cobham's and Bridgeman's second departure from the Versailles tradition occurs in the skewed angle of the cross axis. Earlier, Stowe village had lain, with its church, south and east of the house. Although Lord Cobham may have removed the village, the lane leading from it to the old Roman road remained through Bridgeman's time into that of Sir William Kent, while traces of it even appear in Brown's later modifications.

By 1733, Bridgeman nearing the end of his career, William Kent, failing as painter and sculptor, had begun to achieve fame as architect and garden planner. Italian gardens as he saw them in the eighteenth century were his model. His impressions of Italian villas he gained two centuries after their construction; he saw romantic wildernesses, obliterating any relationship of the parts to the whole. Untrimmed and unkempt, Italian gardens to Kent were a series of pictures, with partially seen glimpses of Italianate or classic structures. This romantic notion of the prior glories of the Renaissance Kent proceeded to interpret in his designs at Stowe, toward the end assisted by Lancelot Brown, chief gardener at Stowe (see Fig. 91).

Kent's designs accepted much of Bridgeman's earlier work, but, in the main, softened and reduced the man-made geometric rigidity in favor of the Italianate models with which he had become enamored.

Untrimmed trees, the garden as a series of pictures, and obliteration of relationship of parts to the whole were his basic themes. In diametric contrast to his predecessor's work, Kent is reported to have worked without level or line. Horace Walpole said of Kent: "He leaped the fence and saw that all nature was a garden."[10]

Strongly influenced by Kent as he labored with him in the gardens at Stowe, Brown (1716–1783) became head kitchen gardener. One of his duties was that of guide to visiting gentry. Thus, soon after Kent's death, Brown emerged as one of the most influential "improvers" of English gardens, and during the third quarter of the eighteenth century, the most influential.

Although widely recognized as an improver, Brown was responsible for seeing destroyed many rather fine historical examples of Renaissance garden forms in England. To the wealthy and famous, he very soon acquired the nickname "Capability," because of his habit, when first viewing a place, of saying that a place had "capabilities of improvement."[11]

Brown thus carried the literary statements of Addison and Pope and the landscape painter's visual descriptions to their logical conclusions. While Bridgeman's work at Stowe, the English version of Versailles, had been softened and made poetic by Kent, Brown literally accepted the tenet of "all nature is a garden." His basic media were wide, rolling fields of turf, mirrors of still water, trees in groves and clumps, and the contrasting or related undulations of light and shade. Color played no part in Brown's designs, as the man-shaped, softened land forms of England became the large idea (see Fig. 93).

---

[10]Clifford, op. cit., p. 132, quotes Horace Walpole, from On Modern Gardening (Written 1770, published 1785).

[11]Clifford, op. cit., p. 157.

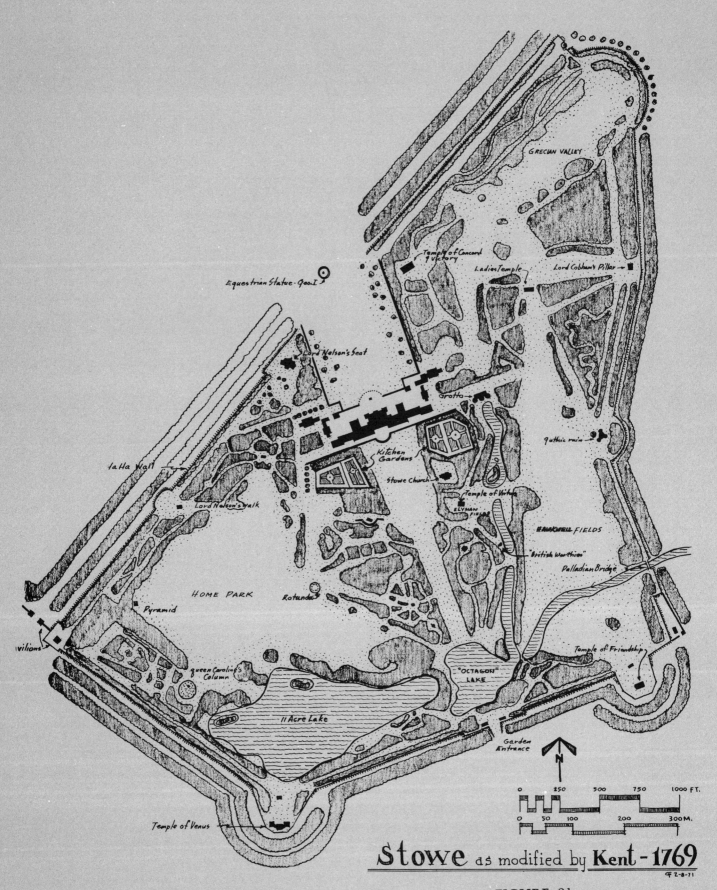

**Grecian Valley**

Temple of Concord & Victory

Ladies Temple

Lord Cobham's Pillar →

Equestrian Statue - Geo.I

Lord Nelson's Seat

Grotto

Gothic ruin

Kitchen Gardens

Stowe Church

Temple of Virtue

ELYSIAN FIELDS

HAWKWELL FIELDS

"British Worthies"

Ha Ha Wall

Lord Nelson's Walk

Palladian Bridge

HOME PARK

Rotunda

Pyramid

"OCTAGON" LAKE

Temple of Friendship

Pavilions

Queen Caroline's Column

11 Acre Lake

Garden Entrance

N

Temple of Venus

0    250    500    750    1000 FT.

0   50  100      200      300 M.

## Stowe as modified by Kent - 1769

G 2-8-71

FIGURE 91

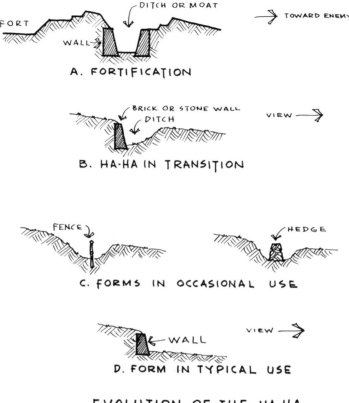

A. FORTIFICATION

B. HA-HA IN TRANSITION

C. FORMS IN OCCASIONAL USE

D. FORM IN TYPICAL USE

EVOLUTION OF THE HA-HA
(NO SCALE)

FIGURE 92

Gone now is geometry. Removed are most of the earlier temples, grottoes, and pyramids. What remains is the classic Palladian mansion in a "pure" setting of artfully created English countryside, to be viewed as a Lorrain or a Poussin might paint them. In fact, the Englishman swelled with pride whenever his home estate was chosen as subject for a "landscape" painting of the period.

Gone, too, was the feeling that the estate's chatelain was "master of all he surveyed" as at Versailles, but was, in effect, the custodian of a portion of an earthly paradise, his own Garden of Eden before the fall. The ha-ha's use, in many instances, permitted the immediate view from the mansion to contain cattle, sheep, or, as pictured by Brown, even groups of native deer. The domesticated or semiwild animals thus appeared to roam free, while the viewers could observe them from the human enclosure. Perhaps this concept can be considered as the first tentative step in a man-dominated world toward recognition of the right of other species to survive in their own habitat. It was unfortunate that population expansion in succeeding generations, along with a blind urge for conquest in the widely expanding industrial revolution, buried this idealized vision until today.

Stowe and the many other English gardens completely redesigned by "Capability" Brown had influence in Europe nearly as extensive as had Versailles a century before.

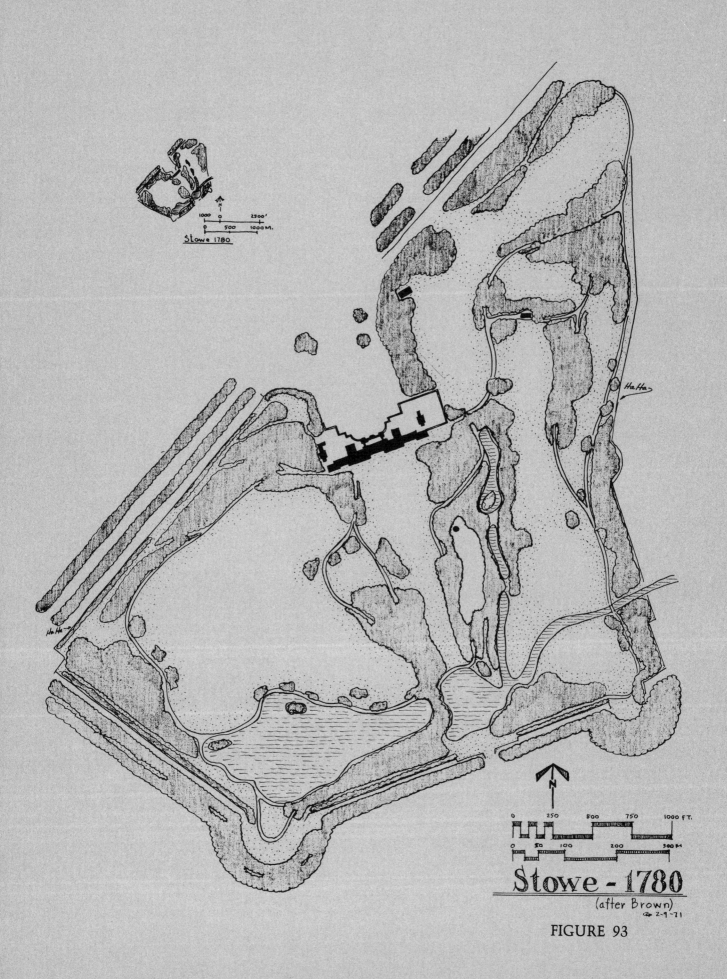

Stowe 1780

1000   500   0   2500'
0   500   1000 M.

Ha Ha

Ha Ha

N

0   250   500   750   1000 FT.
0   50   100   200   300 M.

Stowe - 1780
(after Brown)
2-9-71

FIGURE 93

France, and Italy too, bored with the rigid geometry of Versailles that had dominated the last half of the seventeenth and first half of the eighteenth centuries, adapted with delight what they considered to be the "English garden."

Louis XVI, grandson of Louis XV, an indecisive ruler, preferred the hunting field and his locksmith's shop to the dull routine of coping with the complex social and political conflicts smoldering in France. Five generations removed from his illustrious predecessor, Louis XIV, Versailles to Louis XVI, in its elaborate grandeur, seemed a burden, a stage setting for the court. Marie Antoinette, his queen, thus had little difficulty in persuading the king to create their own version of the English garden in an as-yet-undeveloped portion of the palace grounds.

By 1775 Versailles showed the devastation wrought by time. "All the tall trees have been cleared away, and between them branches are lying about, fountains drying up, and the white bodies of fallen statues sticking up, while here and there one fountain still flows."[12]

Consequently, Marie Antoinette, Louis XVI's queen, created near the Petit Trianon the Hameau (hamlet) a purely French version of what was considered the essence of *le jardin anglais.*

The Petit Trianon had been built for Louis XV as a small retreat, remote from the awesome character of the palace itself. Marie Antoinette enjoyed it so that when she conceived the idea of creating her own private playground, her natural impulse was to build the "English" pleasure grounds nearby.

Immediately adjacent to the chateau were the typical French formal parterres. But beyond was a romantic wilderness, winding through which were the many curvilinear pathways so characteristic (from the French point of view) of the English garden. Deep within the park, past winding streams, lay a lake, and on the banks of the lake, a farm village including a mill, dairy barns, and all the trappings of a stage, set for Marie Antoinette and her maids to play at being farmerettes.

Imitation it may have been, but it was a flattering one to the English. In fact, English garden designers in the new style found themselves in demand. While "Capability" Brown devoted his full time to "improving" the English landscape, others, by now, through apprenticeship, had become relatively proficient and began to "do" English gardens throughout the continent.

One of these devotees of the "new" style was Jacob Moore, who remodelled a portion of the Villa Borghese, just outside the Porta del Populo in Rome. The Borghese family, prominent in Catholic Italy, having produced one Pope (Paul V) and several cardinals, had a fine estate near Frascati. In the early years of the seventeenth century, Cardinal Scipione Borghese established outside the walls of Rome a palace and gardens commensurate with his exalted rank. The nucleus of the villa was a small vineyard outside the Porta Pinciana.

The casino itself went under construction in 1618, designed by Giovanni Vasanzio, a Flemish architect. The typically Renaissance grounds were laid out by Rainaldi and

[12]Gothein, Marie Luis, *A History of Garden Art*, Vol. *II*, New York, Dutton, 1928.

were extended and remodelled by Domenico Sarino, while the waterworks were created by the famous Giovanni Fontana.

But now the wheel turned a complete revolution. Whereas in the sixteenth century, the geometric harmony of house and grounds made so popular by the Italians had reached England, in the latter years of the eighteenth century, the Borgheses hired an Englishman to remodel again, in the latest style, the southwest portion of the extensive grounds.[13]

Here Moore created a Kent-Brown garden, with ruined temples, paths through the forests flowing in Hogarth's "line of beauty," the temple to Aesculepius (Asclepius, legendary Greek god of medicine), seen as opposite terminus to the vista leading to the rounded, cupolaed temple to Diana, the virgin goddess (Greek Artemis).

Thus were the classic myths revisited, not in their original terrifying wild-forest setting, but here, as in England, in a man-made, man-controlled romantic vision of nature made art. In England we had seen a vision of an earlier Italy. Now we see, in the Borghese gardens, a vision of England.

All the while, as England's cultural prominence tended to dominate the European world, a new continent 4,800 kilometers (3,000 miles) across the Atlantic had, since the late-fifteenth century, occupied the dreams and aspirations of kings, emperors, and commoners alike. Exploration and conquest of a new and virgin land will next occupy our attention.

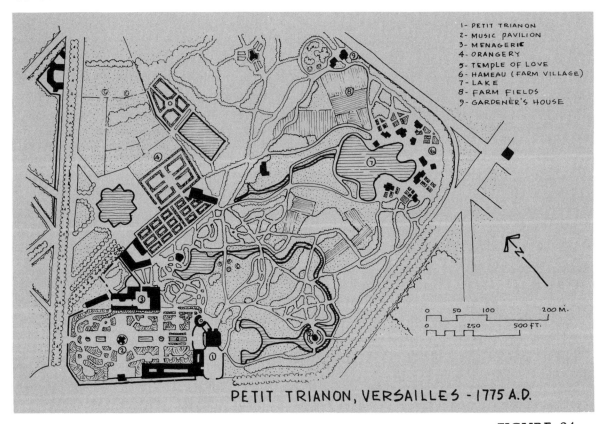

1- PETIT TRIANON
2- MUSIC PAVILION
3- MENAGERIE
4- ORANGERY
5- TEMPLE OF LOVE
6- HAMEAU (FARM VILLAGE)
7- LAKE
8- FARM FIELDS
9- GARDENER'S HOUSE

PETIT TRIANON, VERSAILLES - 1775 A.D.

FIGURE 94

[13]Triggs, Inigo, *The Art of Garden Design in Italy*, London, Longmans, 1906.

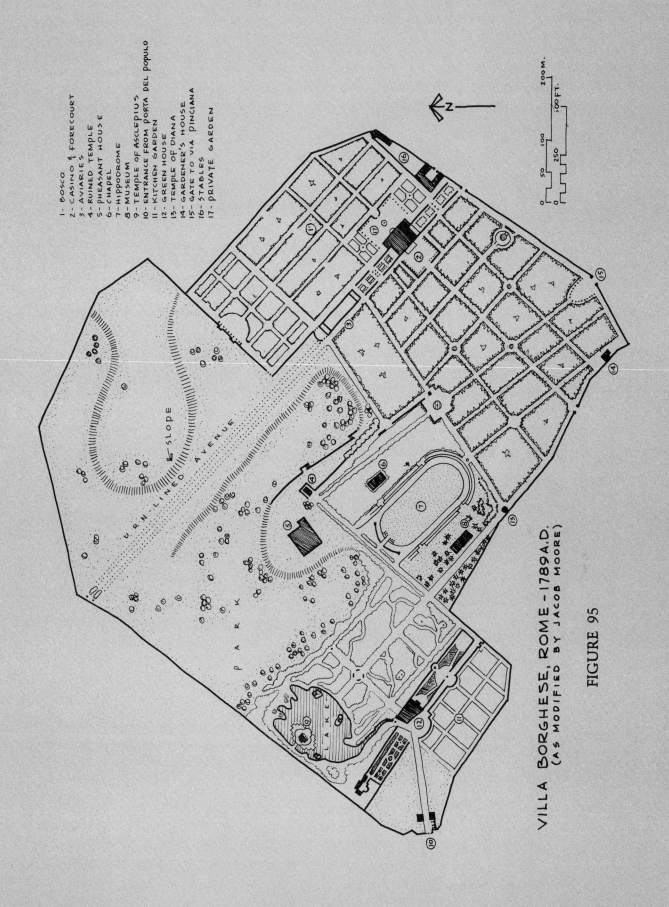

1 - BOSCO
2 - CASINO & FORECOURT
3 - AVIARIES
4 - RUINED TEMPLE
5 - PHEASANT HOUSE
6 - CHAPEL
7 - HIPPODROME
8 - MUSEUM
9 - TEMPLE OF ASCLEPIUS
10 - ENTRANCE FROM PORTA DEL POPULO
11 - KITCHEN GARDEN
12 - GREEN HOUSE
13 - TEMPLE OF DIANA
14 - GARDENER'S HOUSE
15 - GATE TO VIA PINCIANA
16 - STABLES
17 - PRIVATE GARDEN

VILLA BORGHESE, ROME - 1789 A.D.
(AS MODIFIED BY JACOB MOORE)

FIGURE 95

# 15    Conquerors of the Wilderness
## (1492–1800)

The early explorers of the Western Hemisphere (see Appendix B) examined it in much the same fashion as did the fabled blind men discovering an elephant. To one, the elephant felt like a snake, to another, a tree, to a third, a barrel. So it was with the three major powers as they, almost by accident, at first discovered, then explored, and finally established bases for colonial expansion in the "new world."

Spain first discovered an island empire in the Caribbean, then rapidly expanded into Mexico, South America, and the American Southwest (see Fig. 99) lands physiographically much like the Spanish homeland.

The French, on the other hand (perhaps because hardy Breton fishermen had long since returned with huge boatloads of cod from the Grand Banks off New England) penetrated the new continent by way of the frozen north.

The British, relatively late starters in the race for colonial conquest, at first timidly touched on the coasts (perhaps desirous only of retaining mastery of the seas); then, in the dawning years of the seventeenth century, established firm commercial bases on the east coast.

Not until the early years of the nineteenth century did any of them fully realize the magnitude of this new eldorado. What we now see as a major continental land mass containing a great agricultural basin of widely varying climate at its center, flanked by major mountain ranges on the east and west, and threaded throughout with numerous river systems, heavily forested in the eastern half, explorers and early settlers saw only in fragments (see Figs. 96, 97, and 98).

Naturally, during the initial developmental phases of exploitation, the tiny colonies, hardy pioneers though they had to be, transplanted old world technology and ways of life to the opening continent.

The very names of the earliest, and subsequent, settlements, clearly indicate that tradition and memories of their former homes were kept alive. Early Spanish settlements reflect the strong religious structure of Spanish life. Vera Cruz, St. Augustine, Santa Fe, all were named with religious fervor. Canadian cities were given French names, as Montreal (the Royal Mountain), from the strength of the French monarchy. The Dutch, although accepting the American Indian name for the rocky island of Manhattan which they purchased for the traditional $24, named their city after the home place, calling it New Amsterdam. And the English, either royalists or members of recently established protestant sects, tended toward community designa-

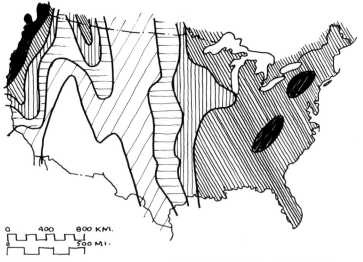

CLIMATIC TYPES
(CONTINENTAL U.S.)

FIGURE 96

- ■ — SUPERHUMID
- ▨ — HUMID
- ▥ — MOIST SUBHUMID
- ▤ — DRY SUBHUMID
- ◺ — SEMI-ARID
- ▢ — ARID

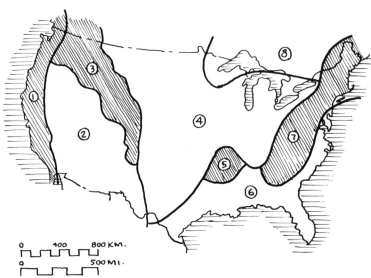

PHYSIOGRAPHY
(CONTINENTAL U.S.)

FIGURE 97

1 - PACIFIC MOUNTAIN SYSTEM
2 - INTERMONTANE PLATEAU
3 - ROCKY MOUNTAIN SYSTEM
4 - INTERIOR PLAINS
5 - INTERIOR HIGHLANDS
6 - ATLANTIC PLAINS
7 - APPACHALIAN HIGHLANDS
8 - LAURENTIAN UPLAND

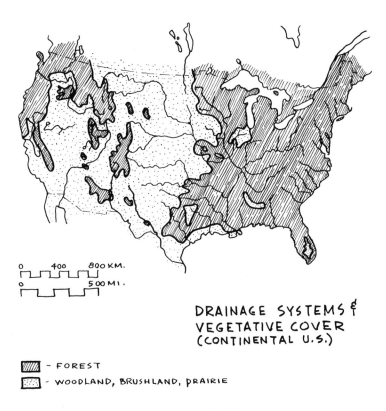

DRAINAGE SYSTEMS &
VEGETATIVE COVER
(CONTINENTAL U.S.)

- FOREST
- WOODLAND, BRUSHLAND, PRAIRIE

FIGURE 98

tions already familiar in the island kingdom. Plymouth was the town from which the Pilgrims left the Old World. Jamestown took its name from the ruling monarch of the time, James I.

As time passed, as the colonies grew and multiplied, Old-World labels and traditions continued to flourish. Virginia, one of the earliest provinces received its designation from "the Virgin Queen," Elizabeth I. Georgia, founded later under Oglethorpe, took its name from George II, King at that time. Charleston, in South Carolina, and Williamsburg in the Virginia colony, also reflected the British respect for royalty. As New England grew and flourished, a roster of the counties into which its eventual states were divided duplicates the listing of home shires from which the colonists came.[1]

Having once established outposts on the shores of the new world, immigrants followed, first in a trickle, then in a steady stream. Colonists they were, since nearly all looked west with determination, forsaking all but memories of home, firmly resolved to establish and expand Britain's colonial empire.

The colonial period excites us because of the boldness of spirit it expressed. For its

[1]Mencken, H. L., *The American Language*, abr. 4th ed., Ed. by McDavid, Ravin I., Jr., New York, Knopf, 1963.

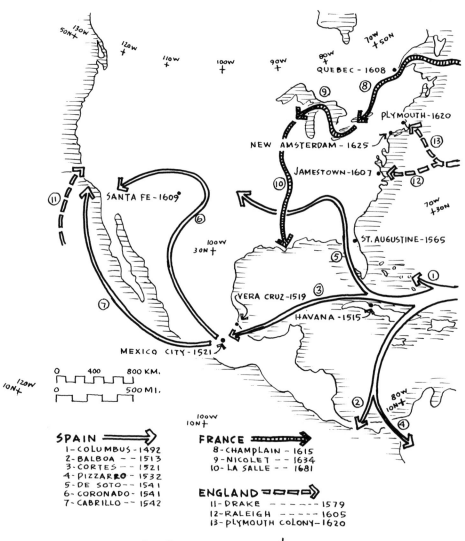

EXPLORATION & SETTLEMENT
NEW WORLD - 1492 TO 1681 A.D.

**FIGURE 99**

time, the daring shown must be equated to landing men on the moon today. The movement had to have brave leaders, flexible enough to adapt to situations completely foreign to the established European world.

Yet, custom and tradition were firmly implanted in the minds of these voyagers from another world. We tend to visualize pioneering in terms of the log cabin and the palisaded stockade. But, in fact, the introduction of the rough-hewn cabin as pioneer home appeared late, and in the lands beyond the Appalachians.[2] Even in their

[2]*Columbia Encyclopedia*, 3rd ed., New York, Columbia University Press, 1963.

beginnings, pioneer homes utilized hewn timbers and sawn boards. And, as soon as possible, native stone, and home-fired brick became the norm, because memory of "home" kept old methods alive.

St. Augustine, founded in 1565 in Florida, by the time the British drove the Spaniards out in 1763, was, in appearance, a Spanish town, with walled gardens laid out in the European manner of long-standing tradition, still much in evidence in the Spanish-speaking world, whether "Old" or "New" (see Fig. 100). The medieval need for defensive works had returned to the scene, as the pioneers felt need for protection against the unknown terrors of this new, vast continent.

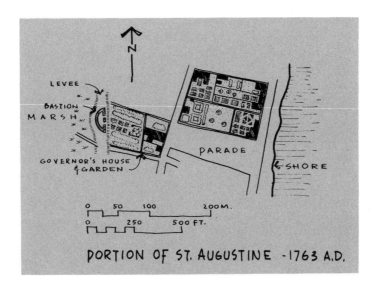

FIGURE 100

The need for protection against unknown elements took different forms when that need pertained to defenses against climate. While St. Augustine was blessed with a semitropical climate, the colonies in New England had a different kind of enemy with which to contend. New Hampshire and Massachusetts were early occupied by sturdy English yeomen, sons of the land, in contrast to the proud grandees of the Spanish settlements further south. The land the Englanders settled was poor and rocky in contrast to the fertile fields of England. Too, the climate, being continental and far to the west of the beneficent Gulf Stream, proved harsh and unpredictable. Consequently, in rural areas, farms tended to be small, with buildings built close to the village roads and with frugal practicality. Most significantly, house and service buildings were typically built close together, and interconnected, with the primary purpose of protection from the harsh winter winds and snows (see Fig. 101).

Note in Figure 101 the extremely practical arrangement of structures, and that the farm unit contained within its component parts, all that was needed for survival. As in much earlier times, every element provided for some necessity, with little or no energy spent on ornament, in contrast to developments in the much more benign South.

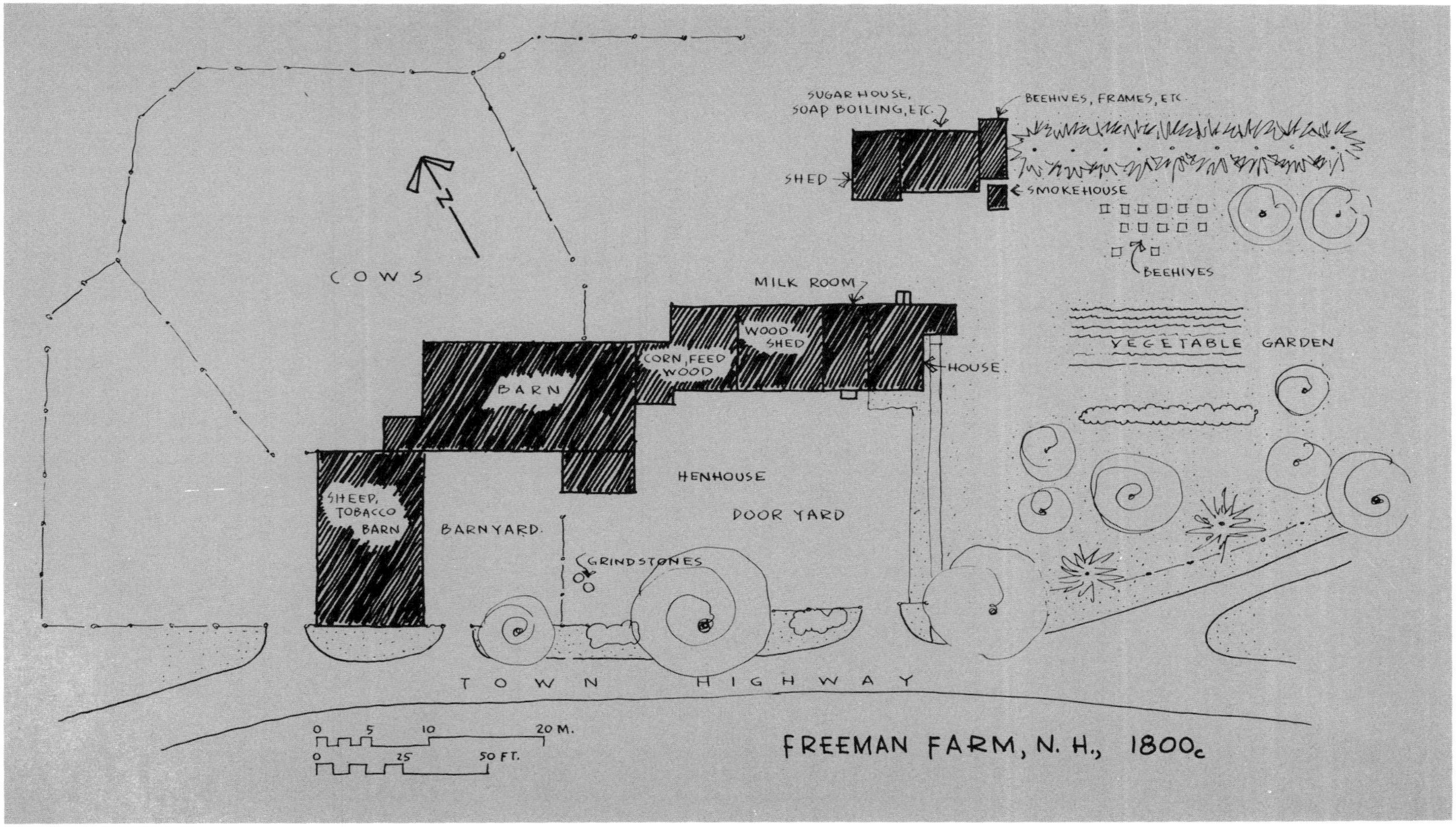
COWS
SUGAR HOUSE, SOAP BOILING, ETC.
BEEHIVES, FRAMES, ETC.
SHED
SMOKEHOUSE
BEEHIVES
MILK ROOM
WOOD SHED
CORN, FEED WOOD
BARN
HOUSE
VEGETABLE GARDEN
SHEEP, TOBACCO BARN
BARNYARD
HENHOUSE
DOOR YARD
GRINDSTONES
TOWN HIGHWAY
0 5 10 20 M.
0 25 50 FT.
FREEMAN FARM, N. H., 1800c

FIGURE 101

In relatively urbanized locations, as well, such as the seacoast town of Salem, Massachusetts (first settled in 1626), the European traditions of long vistas, axial approaches, symmetrically placed buildings and gardens gave way to the intense need for economy of energy, necessary for survival in the malevolent New England climate (see Fig. 102). Although "urban" dwellers apparently had greater economic resources than their country cousins, as evidenced by the addition of that purely decorative element, the flower garden, still, the major portions of town lots contained such utilitarian features as stables, fruit and vegetable gardens, and the ever-present beehives. A peculiar feature of the New England garden illustrated was the "forthright," a path leading lengthwise through the garden on the house axis. The likelihood that this was a much-reduced European major axis is strong, but the fact that it normally was simply terminated indicates that it was merely a vague memory on the part of the new Englanders of manor houses they had once known and admired. That the yards were fenced reflected the practice of communal cattle-herding. Every morning, the town herd-boy would follow a prescribed route, calling out the townsman's cow to join the lowing herd en route to common pasturage. In the evening, the reverse of the route would be followed, each cow instinctively returning to its accustomed stall.

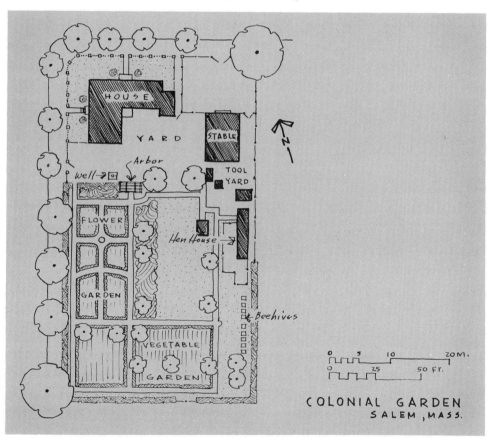

FIGURE 102

Time inevitably passes, as it did in the British colonies of the new world. Inevitably, too, as pioneers became settlers, as settlers became landowners, as landholders gained wealth, as rude villages became towns and eventually cities; greater control over environment, too became fact.

Blessed with a more moderate climate, the plantations and towns of the mid-South by the end of the seventeenth century had achieved status as centers of culture and learning. The frontier pushed westward to the Appalachian mountain valleys. Communities on the eastern seaboard lost their raw look, and became (Boston, Philadelphia, Charleston) smaller copies of European antecedents.

Founded as the "Middle Plantation," between the York and James River in 1632, in 1699 the community's name was changed to Williamsburg (after William III, King of England 1688–1702), and the city was named capital of the Virginia colony. As expression of the capital's lofty position, the College of William and Mary received its charter in 1693. Thus, we see visual evidence (Fig. 103) of old world culture transplanted, taking root, and flourishing in a new, but no longer strange, environment.

Eighteenth-century colonial Williamsburg exemplifies clearly "old forms in new places." Consider the town plan itself, with its major and minor axes. Although obviously an "old form," it implies new ideas evolving from the "new place" (the Colonies). Whereas at Versailles, the major axis focused on the French monarch, here in England's Virginia colony, the Governor's Palace heads the minor axis, while the major axis connects the College of William and Mary with the House of Burgesses. Thus early, the Virginia colonists began to show strong evidence of that independent spirit that led inevitably to revolt and a new nation.

The Governor's Palace itself, representing as it did royal authority, naturally followed eclectic patterns, drawn from those already thoroughly familiar in England and on the continent. The formal gardens, the north axis pointing to a vista over the countryside, the maze, the canal, and the bowling green, we have seen repeated many times elsewhere, as well as the palace green, an anglicized version of André Le Nôtre's *tapis vert.*

Now, as we approach the end of the eighteenth century, having watched the establishment of a beachhead on the eastern shores of the Western World, its consolidation, and the general "civilizing" of the seaboard, the three hundred years since Columbus' accidental discovery reveals a young republic, whose leading citizens already think in terms of expansion westward across the first major barrier, the Appalachians. American-born explorers[3] recounted to fascinated ears, their experiences in the broad reaches of the country's interior.

But the eastern slopes of the Appalachian Highlands, the Piedmont, and the Atlantic Plains (see Fig. 96) existed as a confederation of states, having ratified their constitutional government during the years 1787–1789. George Washington, Commander-in-Chief of the continental armies (1775–1783), having served two terms as the nation's first President (1789–1797) could now retire to his ancestral estate on the Potomac River, to devote himself finally and fully to the pursuits of a wealthy, cultured

---

[3]Daniel Boone had explored the Kentucky region between 1769 and 1771, and reported his delight at its prospects for development.

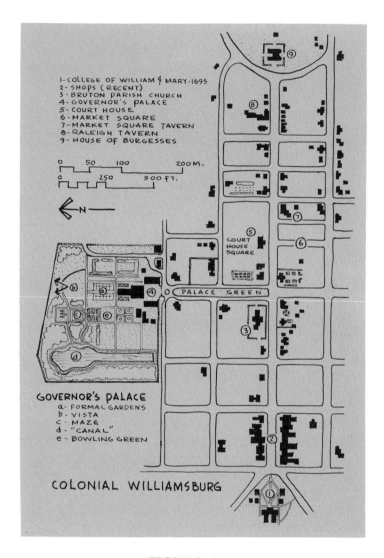

1- COLLEGE OF WILLIAM & MARY - 1693
2- SHOPS (RECENT)
3- BRUTON PARISH CHURCH
4- GOVERNOR'S PALACE
5- COURT HOUSE
6- MARKET SQUARE
7- MARKET SQUARE TAVERN
8- RALEIGH TAVERN
9- HOUSE OF BURGESSES

GOVERNOR'S PALACE
a- FORMAL GARDENS
b- VISTA
c- MAZE
d- "CANAL"
e- BOWLING GREEN

COLONIAL WILLIAMSBURG

FIGURE 103

gentleman of his time, which proved of astonishing breadth. Adept at mathematics, Washington had been a surveyor, during which time he first learned of the lands west of the mountains. As early as 1752, Washington inherited from his older half-brother, Lawrence, the post of district adjutant. As a Major, then, his duties included training militia, thus starting him on a second, and possibly most important, career as a soldier. From 1758 to the beginning of the revolution, Washington settled down to the life of a Virginia gentleman. As a member of the House of Burgesses in Williamsburg, Washington became a leader in the Virginia opposition to British colonial policy, serving in 1774–1775 as a delegate to the Continental Congress. He then took command (July 3, 1775) of the Continental forces fighting the British. Renowned as a military and political leader and also skilled as a supervisor of farmlands of some 1,319 hectares (3,260 acres), he was, by the end of the conflict in 1783, the most important man in the country.

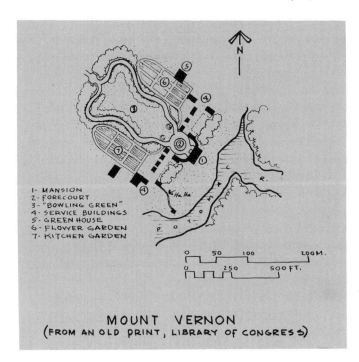

1- MANSION
2- FORECOURT
3- "BOWLING GREEN"
4- SERVICE BUILDINGS
5- GREEN HOUSE
6- FLOWER GARDEN
7- KITCHEN GARDEN

MOUNT VERNON
(FROM AN OLD PRINT, LIBRARY OF CONGRESS)

FIGURE 104

Preoccupied as he was, Washington's constant thought was devoted to his estate, Mt. Vernon, inherited in 1754 from Lawrence. Washington's skill as farmer, horticulturist, and surveyor led him, after the revolution, to complete the living portion of the estate in the form we know it today (see Fig. 104). "Mount Vernon is one of the best remaining examples of the plantations around which centered the highly developed social and economic life of the South in the eighteenth century."[4]

The mansion, its approaches, outbuildings, and gardens exhibit Washington's understanding of English estate-planning of the latter half of the eighteenth century, an understanding learned from his extensive acquaintanceships and wide correspondence. Accepting the dictates of site, Washington's positioning of the manor house on a high point, with extensive views up and down the Potomac, led him to say "No estate in America is more pleasantly situated than this."[5]

Axial treatment seemed inevitable to Washington. The approach from the public highway hundreds of meters away opened onto a rising vista of the mansion some 150 meters before approaching carriages arrived in the grassy forecourt. Yet, that approach followed "Capability" Brown's dictates, by being indirect, and Sir William Kent's, as he had commanded, "Nature abhors a straight line."

Yet, the mansion was flanked by symmetrical building groupings, while the flower and kitchen gardens equally flanked the purely English bowling green.

[4]*Handbook of Mt. Vernon*, Mt. Vernon Ladies Association of the Union, Washington, D.C., 1940, p. 8.

[5]*Ibid.*, p. 33. From the letters, diaries and will of General Washington.

Mount Vernon represents "old forms in new places," as an amalgam of Renaissance European forms with those of the English Landscape school. On the other hand, it represents the future, in that Washington seems to have understood the inherent values of site.

Squire Washington set the stage for the period of romanticism which followed when he wrote: "I can truly say I had rather be at Mt. Vernon with a friend or two about me, than to be attended at the seat of government by the officers of state and the representatives of every power in Europe."[6]

[6]*Ibid.*, p. 25.

# 16    The Beautiful and the Picturesque
## (United States, 1800–1850)

In 1851 J. B. L. Foucault[1] suspended a 61-meter (200-foot) long pendulum in the Pantheon in Paris, which, as it traced the path of its swing in sand on the floor, demonstrated the rotation of the earth. This device scientifically demonstrated a principle of physics to a wondering public. It also demonstrates a philosophical principle in history—that ideas of what is truly good, truly beautiful, veer from architectonic, man-dominated form to nature's forms adapted to man's use.

In the early 1800s, attitudes toward nature and views of the outdoor world tended to swing, albeit not with the regularity of a pendulum, toward idealized concepts of society, in which "all nature is a garden."

While the sixteenth-through-eighteenth centuries in the continental Northern Hemisphere illustrated the swing toward formalized control of grounds, as energy was available for the achievement of esthetic result, the first half of the nineteenth century saw a strong movement toward romanticized nature.

Naturalists of the young Republic had long reported on the rich variety in flora and fauna that abounded in the New World. William Bartram's[2] *Travels*, published first in 1791 was to English authors their major source of descriptions of the American wilderness and its inhabitants. As the young nation expanded westward, Audubon's *The Birds of America,* also began to describe accurately the wildlife abounding in the wilderness, then so predominant.

While such scientific endeavors provided factual data, an American literary tradition, begun during these decades (1800–1850), reinforced, not only in Europe, but among those dwelling along the "civilized" East Coast, a romantic view of nature. As early as 1823, James Fenimore Cooper (1789–1851) had written the first of the famous *Leather Stocking Tales,* titled *The Pioneers.* His *The Last of the Mohicans* (1826) presented a romanticized version of the noble Red Man, echoing sentiments earlier expressed by Shaftsbury and Rousseau. (Chapter 14).

Washington Irving (1783–1859), recognized abroad as one of the first American novelists, had in 1802–1803 published a series of humorous periodical essays on New York society. It was he who brought to the world's attention the Dutch background of the

[1]Jean Bernard Léon Foucault (1819–1868), French Physicist, is known for his researches on the speed of light, electromagnetism, and improvements in astronomic observations, as well as the Foucault Pendulum.

[2]William Bartram, (1739–1823). His father, John Bartram in 1728 planted near Philadelphia the first botanical garden in the United States. By exchanging specimens of western hemisphere plants with European botanists, Bartram introduced American plants to Europe and established some European species in the new world. William vividly described in *Travels* the plants and wildlife of the new nation.

153

Catskills and Hudson River valley in *Rip Van Winkle,* and *The Legend of Sleepy Hollow* (1820). By 1835, Irving had already produced *Tales of the Alhambra,* and romanticized the great western plains in *A Tour of the Prairies.*

The original colonies provided the long-established, now American, tradition of thorough control in urbanized centers, while beyond the mountains the great central core of the young republic already had begun supplying presidents. Andrew Jackson, first of the "wild westerners" had been elected in 1828 from Nashville, in Tennessee (Statehood 1796) on the strength of his successful battle against the British in the Mississippi delta below New Orleans. William Henry Harrison (President 1841; died in office), another military leader who successfully had opened Ohio and Indiana to settlement and statehood had lived most of his life west of the mountains. James K. Polk (President 1845–1849), came from Columbia, in the fertile lands of central Tennessee.

The young nation, by 1850, consisting of 31 states plus additional territories added through the Louisiana Purchase (1803), and lands ceded by Mexico after the Mexican War (1848), now occupied fully half the continental territory. While two-thirds of the states could still be regarded by Virginia ("Mother of Presidents") as raw frontier, the Eastern states considered themselves as having reached equality with Europe in culture.

The pendulum of history, then, swung away from eighteenth-century formalism to the opposite extreme, what Andrew Jackson Downing termed "the beautiful" and "the picturesque" in estate and suburbia.

Downing was the product of his era, but, more important, a strong influence on "improving" suburban and country homes, not only in the esthetic sense, but with a view toward inspiring minds to lofty ideals. His *Treatise on the Theory and Practice of Landscape Gardening, Adapted to North America, With a View to the Improvement of Country Residences,* published in 1841, established him as the chief authority on rural art.

Born in Newburgh, New York, October 30, 1815, Downing early fell under the influence of the esthetic taste and spirit of his era. His playground was the nursery run by his father and older brother. From this horticultural background, he had access to a field of study encompassing the whole countryside of the Catskills and Hudson River Valley. Much left alone as a child, he early became sensitive and responsive to nature.

Social and cultural influences of his New York State region molded Downing into a landscape designer who may have been the first American to study the natural beauty of site (he called it *genius loci*) as prelude to its enhancement by arranging and composing foliage masses. In his young manhood, Downing became the friend of Baron de Liderer, Austrian Consul, a mineralogist, botanist, and man of affairs who had a country estate near Newburgh (on the Hudson River's west bank, 80 kilometers [50 miles] north of New York City). Baron de Liderer helped to develop Downing's natural scientific curiosity.

At about the same time, Downing knew a young English landscape painter, Raphael Hoyle, from whom he learned "landscape composition." As scion of a successful nurseryman, Downing had entree to the many fine country estates of the region, some dating back to Colonial days. Thus, he came under the influence of the culture of his time and region.

Contemporary thought of this era (1800–1850) was basically English thought, which implies it was strongly influenced by the philosophies of Kent, Brown, and Sir Humphrey Repton.[3] Downing consequently became almost inevitably a follower of the English Lanscape School (see Chapter 14), but added his own modifications to the principles of Brown.

Whereas "Capability" Brown believed with Rousseau that raw nature, to be compatible with mankind, needed artful control, Downing recognized that his designs must fit the site as well as the American climate and culture. With Repton, in contrast to Kent and Brown, who saw all nature as a garden, Downing considered the "architectural" garden as having its place in the American scene, but in his view, secondary to the informal and natural.

Thus before his tragic death in a Hudson River steamboat accident in 1852, Downing, through his *Treatise* and other publications, by virtue of the fame he achieved in laying out the grounds of many influential residents of the valley region, achieved a position of strong influence on life-style in this period.

He had established a state agricultural school; was instrumental in seeing founded the National Agricultural Bureau in Washington; prepared plans for the nation's Capitol grounds, the Smithsonian Institution, and the White House.

By 1849, Andrew Jackson Downing, impatient with what he saw to be a lack of relationship of houses to their grounds, had decided to devote his attention to architecture. Having visited in England, he brought back, and established partnership with, a young English architect Calvert Vaux (see also Chapter 17).

Downing's theories of landscape design were based on the simplistic attitudes of his time. In *Cottage Residences*, he said:

> . . . I am still more anxious to inspire in the minds of my readers and countrymen livelier perceptions of the *beautiful*, in everything that relates to our houses and grounds. I wish to awaken a quicker sense of grace, the elegance, of the picturesqueness of fine forms that are capable of being produced in these, by Rural Architecture, and Landscape Gardening—a sense which will not only refine and elevate the mind, but open it to new and infinite resources of delight. There are perhaps a few upon whose souls nearly all emanations of beauty fall impressionless; but there are also many who see the Beautiful, in nature and art, only feebly and dimly, either from the want of proper media through which to view her, or a little direction as to where she is to be found.[4]

[3]Sir Humphrey Repton (1752–1818) succeeded Lancelot Brown in England as champion of the "natural" philosophy. Repton's *Red Books* used before-and-after sketches to illustrate how he proposed to "improve" the landscape pictures of the estates of his clients—a system of graphic description previously used by Lancelot Brown.

[4]Downing, A.J., *Cottage Residences, A Series of Designs for Rural Cottages and Cottage Villas, and Their Gardens and Grounds Adapted to North America*, New York, John Wiley, 1853, p. vi. With the permission of the American Life Foundation, Watkins Glen, N.Y.

One receives the impression that Downing's philosophies sought to counteract European travelers' reports on the roughness and crudity of life in the young republic. Charles Dickens, following his tour of the states in 1842, had produced *American Notes*, sharply criticizing America for its lack of cultural refinement. Alexis de Tocqueville, from the court at Versailles, had published *Democracy in America* in 1835, following extensive tours of this country. He, too, recognized, as a European, the extensive differences between this brash, young nation, and the highly cultured milieu he knew in France.

Brash and uncultured much of the continent appeared to European travelers, arriving from countries rich in long traditions of the gardener's art. At least in the Hudson River valley, Downing seems to have been possessed with the goal of counteracting this, to him erroneous impression.

Yet, there can be no question that Downing's executed works were the product of the preceding age. Bridgeman, Kent, and Brown had performed the initial experiments, and established the pattern of nature as art. Downing had visited England, and therefore must have experienced English homes and grounds. He had learned to appreciate art through Raphael Hoyle, an English landscape painter. As a serious student, he must have studied the reference works of the time, which may have included Sir Humphrey Repton's *Red Books*. Thus, he could, with confidence, illustrate, in the *Treatise on Landscape Gardening*, his views on what constituted "good" design (see Fig. 105).

Figure 105 partially describes one of Downing's basic principles, that a place may express the beautiful or the picturesque. What the sketches do not show, however, is Downing's insistence on recognition of "the genius loci;" that is, an understanding of basic visual site qualities. This principle constitutes Downing's major contribution to our understanding of the present state of the art.

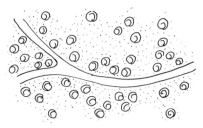

TREES GROUPED TO PRODUCE THE **BEAUTIFUL**

**FIGURE 105**

TREES GROUPED TO PRODUCE THE **PICTURESQUE**

(NO SCALE)

Each site (he probably called it, as others before him had done, "the situation") was unique, containing its own visual qualities. In his planning, therefore, Downing attempted to work with the basic scenic values inherent in the site, its land form, its specific character, and its vegetative cover. From this point, then, his designs proceeded.

The "beautiful," to Downing meant soft, flowing curves of land form, gentle, rounded tree forms, and moderated, slow-flowing or still waters. In contrast, the "picturesque" implied rugged, rough, angular land form, startling contrast in tree form (even including the dead trees so beloved by Kent), and fast-flowing, wild waters. He also recognized that any residential place which was to provide a sense of esthetic pride to the owner must function adequately in terms of the prevalent life style.

It is significant to note that one of Downing's major efforts was to provide for suburban property owners their own version of paradise (see Fig. 106). Represented here we see the end product of man's search, from his remote past to the present, for his own bit of land, organized to suit his needs and desires, the American dream-come-true in the long quest for "life, liberty and the pursuit of happiness."

A product of the industrial revolution, in which, theoretically, all men, by their labors, can buy a small piece of earthly paradise, the "suburban cottage" was put within the reach of every man. Downing estimated the cost of the residence at $1,800, and described in detail how cheaply other things, as shrubs, small trees, and perennials could be purchased.

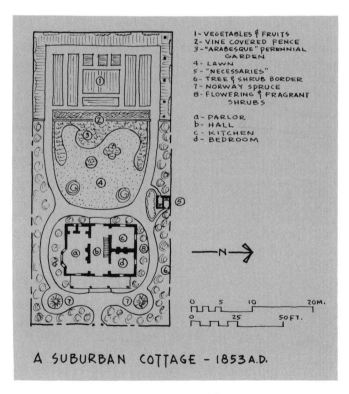

FIGURE 106

The plan forms stem from the past. Hogarth's dictum "the curve is the line of beauty" was expressed in the lines of the "arabesque" perennial garden. (Could it be that Downing had read Washington Irving's *Tales of the Alhambra,* or even discussed it with him?) The third of the plot devoted to fruits and vegetables ("In the suburbs of a town or village, the more common kinds of vegetables may generally be purchased as cheaply as they can be raised by the inmates of such a cottage. The more delicate kinds of fruit, and a few of the earlier or finer kinds of vegetables, may however, be produced, of fine flavor, and with more satisfaction to the proprietor, on the spot"),[5] hidden from view by the vine-covered fence, as it functioned to supplement diet, is reminiscent of the functional arrangement of the estate of an Egyptian noble of 2500 B.C.

> Quite an area, in the rear of the house, is devoted to a lawn, which must be kept close and green by frequent mowings, so that it will be as soft to the tread as a carpet, and that its deep verdure will set off the gay colors of the flowering plants in the surrounding beds and parterre. This little lawn is terminated by an irregular or "arabesque" border, varying in width from four to fourteen feet. The irregular form of this border is preferable to a regular one on account of its more agreeable outline, and more especially for the reason that, to a person looking across the lawn from any part of the walk near the house, this variety of form in the boundary increases the apparent size of the area of turf which it encloses.[6]

The lawn area is characteristic of the cultural background of America, deriving principally, as it did, from England.

However, Downing's own description of the residence indicated the already emerging "melting pot" of cultural backgrounds which the nation became. He used the term "piazza" for the porch on the front of the cottage, a term still heard to describe the same in the New England and Southern states. The derivation of the term is Italian.

The long-standing influence of talented amateurs like Downing is self-evident, as one compares the design illustrated in Figure 106 with the indigenous landscape architecture of today's suburban homes, more than 100 years after the publication of *Cottage Residences.* Observe how frequently there are curved walks, "arabesque" flower beds, and exotic evergreens planted as front-yard features in middle America.

Downing's concern for providing the average-income suburban dweller with his own economical version of the earthly paradise probably came after he had achieved success in designing for his earlier clientele, the estate owners along the Hudson.

[5]*Ibid.,* p. 34

[6]*Ibid.* p. 38.

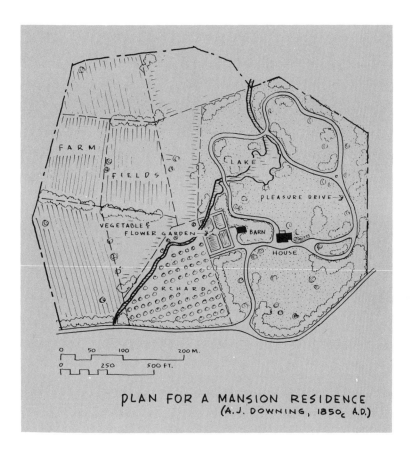

PLAN FOR A MANSION RESIDENCE
(A.J. DOWNING, 1850c A.D.)

## FIGURE 107

Figure 107 illustrates the plan for one of these midcentury (1850–) mansion estates. As was typical in England, a large portion of the grounds was devoted to current agricultural practices. But another portion of the acreage reminds one of Stowe, in Buckinghamshire, as it appeared after "Capability" Brown had completed his revisions of the gardens. Here (Fig. 107) one sees the "belt," trees massed along the borders to preserve the identity and privacy of the estate. Too, one visualizes the house on high ground, with great sweeps of meadow-like lawn, in one direction down to the lake, in the other across the "front lawn."

The major difference observed between Brown's Stowe, and Downing's New York estate, is that, in place of the pleasure walks, the American incorporates pleasure drives, thus prophesying the twentieth-century American recreation, driving for pleasure. Follow the driving lanes, and note how Downing created a series of open and closed vistas, a progression of landscape scenes. Such pictorial progression, initiated by Bridgeman, modified by Kent, and simplified by Brown, appears here as translated into the American idiom by Downing, and through him to Calvert Vaux, and Frederick Law Olmsted, Senior.

# 17      A Man Ahead of His Time
## (United States, 1850–1900)

Frederick Law Olmsted, regarded as the father of American Landscape Architecture, is described, "as a romantic, a trained engineer, an experienced farmer, a cosmopolitan man, a sharp observer and social critic, an accomplished writer, a proven manager, and a man of understanding and compassion."[1]

Born in 1822 in a rural America whose largest city, New York, had a population of only 123,000, Olmsted's life spanned the three-quarters of the century that saw the disappearance of the frontier and the shift from rural to urban living.

Olmsted, as he matured, pursued, with only a minimum of formal schooling, an astonishing series of careers. At the age of sixteen, Olmsted was "in turn a surveyor, part-time Yale student, bookkeeper, and sailor. In 1847, he established a widely acclaimed model farm on Staten Island. . . ."[2] He was, at times, a journalist, publisher, student of social attitudes, including a definitive work on social and economic conditions of the ante-bellum South (*The Cotton Kingdom*, 1861). For 2 years, during the Civil War, Olmsted served as secretary of the United States Sanitary Commission, predecessor of the American Red Cross.

However, what proved to be the most important career of his life, and the one which had vital impact on American life, began almost by accident.

Olmsted's practice of a new profession he called "Landscape Architecture" began during the era that saw occur most of the historic events that revolutionized his world. This was the great era of the railroad. From their timid beginnings in 1826, railroads had grown to span the continent by 1869. By the time of the World Columbian Exposition in 1893 at Chicago, rail lines constituted the major communication linkages throughout the nation.

As early as 1811, New York's commissioners of Streets and Roads provided in their plan for several open spaces in the gridiron of streets. These comprised, in total, some 182 hectares (450 acres) because, as their report stated, "those arms of the sea which embrace Manhattan Island render its situation, in regard to health and pleasure . . . peculiarly felicitous."[3]

[1]Fabos, Julius Gy; Milde, Gordon T.; and Weinmayr, V. Michael, *Frederick Law Olmsted, Sr., Founder of Landscape Architecture in America*, Amherst, Mass., University of Massachusetts Press, 1968. p. 10.

[2]*Ibid.*, p. 6.

[3]Olmsted, F. L., Sr., *Forty Years of Landscape Architecture, Vol II*, Ed. by F. L. Olmsted Jr. and Theodora Kimball, New York, Putnam, 1928, p. 20.

But, by 1844, William Cullen Bryant (1794–1878, poet and newspaper editor) advocated, in *The New York Evening Post,* a large public park. Four years later, Andrew Jackson Downing, in a letter to *The Horticulturist* made the same plea, using the parks of London as model and reproaching New Yorkers. By 1851, public clamor created the necessity of making provision for a major park space. In July 1853, the Board of Aldermen finally passed a legislative act authorizing the city to acquire the land that is now Central Park.

The Board of Park Commissioners, set up to govern what would become the most important park in the United States, by 1857 actively sought a superintendent. Olmsted, through a chance conversation at tea, was persuaded to seek the position and was appointed to that post in September 1857.

At the same meeting, during which Olmsted was appointed Superintendent, the board announced a competition for preparation of specifications and plans for laying out the park.

Calvert Vaux (formerly Downing's partner) asked Olmsted to collaborate with him in the preparation of a plan for Central Park. Olmsted and Vaux finished their plan, titled "Greensward," and submitted it on April 1, 1858, to be judged against 34 other sets of plans. On April 28, 1858, the Board voted "Greensward" the first prize in the competition.

Thus began Olmsted's long and fruitful career in landscape architecture, spanning the last half of ninteenth century America, a career which ended at the dawn of the twentieth century with his death in 1903.

Along with their "Greensward" entry in the Central Park design competition, Olmsted and Vaux submitted a comprehensive report, explaining in full their reasoning for every design feature of the plan.[4] They included in the report sound predictions as to the rapid growth of New York City's population as justification for creating such a huge (for its time) chunk of central parkland on Manhattan Island. In 1858, the raw acreage lay 2½ miles north of the population center. In other words, Olmsted and Vaux applied to their designs planning principles considered as sound today as they were revolutionary then.

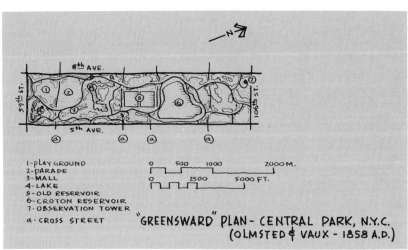

FIGURE 108

[4]*Ibid.,* pp. 211 ff.

The "Greensward" plan provided for:

1. Transverse roadways, at regular intervals, "sunk so far below the general surface that the park drives may, at every necessary point of intersection, be carried entirely over it, without any obvious elevation or divergence from their most attractive routes."[5]
2. Boundary planting ("Capability" Brown's belts) as a visual and sound buffer.
3. Vistas and views of "natural" scenery, as relief from the rigid grid pattern of the built-up city.
4. A grand avenue, or mall, where people could stroll, meet, and greet one another.
5. Long, winding carriage drives, now, as then, a source of delight and pleasure.
6. Bridle trails of sufficient variety and length to provide healthful exercise as well as pleasurable experience.
7. Pedestrian walkways winding up and down, in and around, the various terrain compartments, for the pleasure of casual strollers.
8. A parade ground, whose major purpose provided, for that period, room for marching maneuvers of foot troops, but "Such a broad open plane of well-kept grass would be a refreshing and agreeable feature in the general design."[6]
9. Playgrounds for active play.
10. Lakes for boating, attractive vistas, and, in winter, ice skating.
11. Flower gardens and an arboretum for those who wished to acquaint themselves with trees, shrubs, and flowers suitable to the environment.

In sum, Central Park, conceived in the fertile minds of F. L. Olmsted, Sr. and Calvert Vaux in 1858, and today still considered one of the most valid open-space developments, met the requirements of a great work of art. As reported in the preliminary paragraphs of the report accompanying the "Greensward" plan, "The Park throughout is a single work of art, namely, that it shall be framed upon a single, noble motive, to which the design of all its parts, in some more or less subtle way, shall be confluent and helpful."[7] This "work of art" responded then, and ever since, to a need of urban man for someplace in complete contrast to his otherwise architectonic environment.

[5]*Ibid.,* p. 218. These transverse park drives predate, by almost 100 years, today's limited access highways. Note, too, that grade separation was then handled unobtrusively in contrast to today's freeway monumentality.

[6]*Ibid.,* p. 223.

[7]*Ibid.,* p. 248.

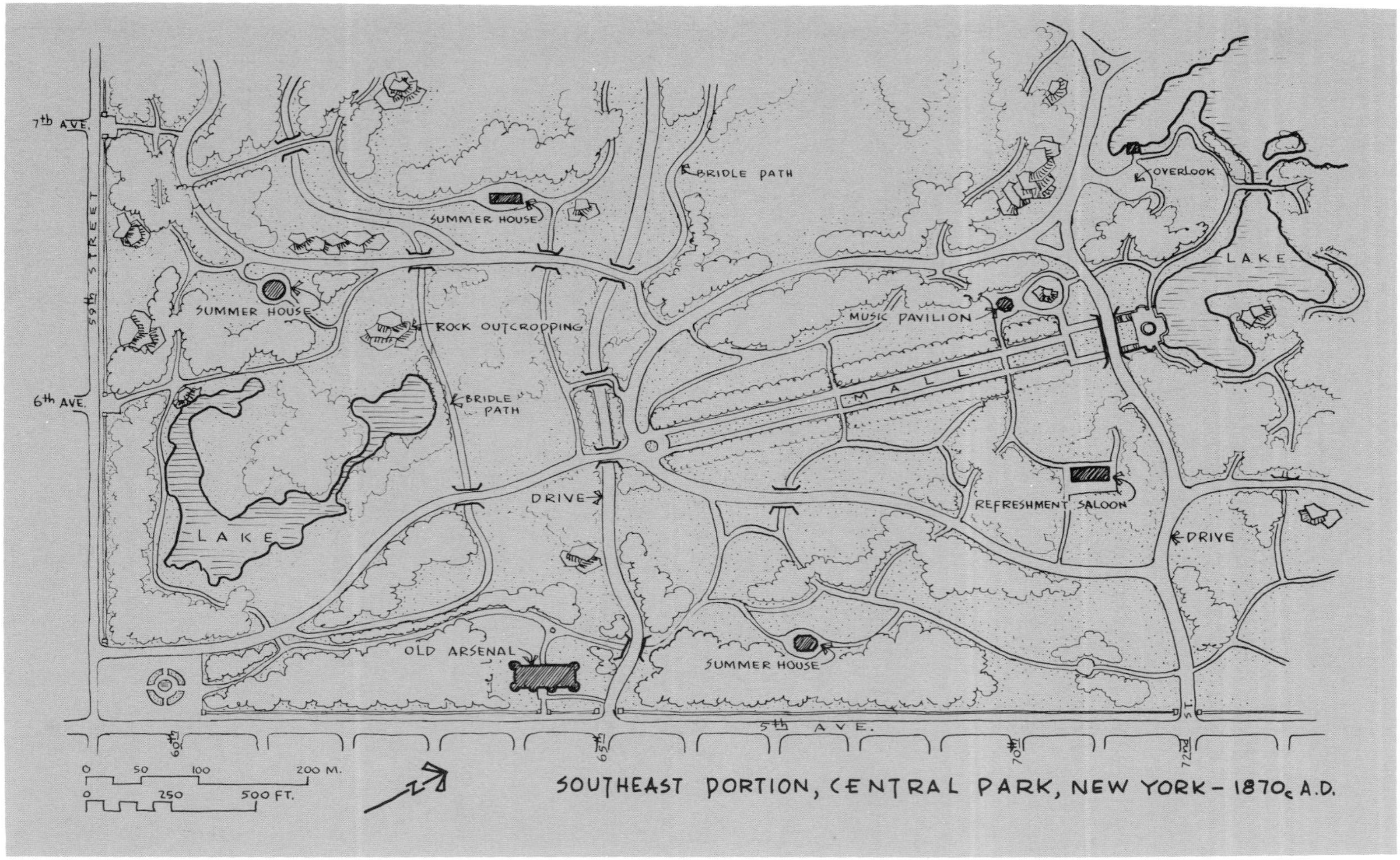
7th AVE.
6th AVE.
59th STREET
BRIDLE PATH
SUMMER HOUSE
SUMMER HOUSE
ROCK OUTCROPPING
BRIDLE PATH
LAKE
DRIVE
OLD ARSENAL
SUMMER HOUSE
MUSIC PAVILION
MALL
REFRESHMENT SALOON
OVERLOOK
LAKE
DRIVE
5th AVE.
60th
65th
70th
72nd
ST.
0 50 100 200 M.
0 250 500 FT.
SOUTHEAST PORTION, CENTRAL PARK, NEW YORK - 1870c A.D.

FIGURE 109

"Greensward" almost immediately established the reputation of the firm of Olmsted and Vaux, Landscape Architects. In succeeding years the partners prepared park plans for cities throughout the nation and Canada. Other well-known parks planned by the firm included: Prospect Park in Brooklyn, 1865–1888; Mount Royal Park in Montreal, 1873–1881, South Park in Albany, 1868, Belle Isle in Detroit, 1882–1883, and South Park in Chicago in 1871.

In addition to the commissions garnered by Olmsted and Vaux in park work, the impact of Central Park's plan on the nation sparked a national park movement which still comprises a substantial contribution to the United States economy. Olmsted himself, while in the west, became involved in a movement to establish Yosemite Park in 1890 thus touching off action leading to establishing the national park system as a means of preserving one of our precious natural resources, land (See also Chapter 18).

As Olmsted and Vaux plunged into a multifaceted practice, other kinds of commissions came their way. A. J. Downing had, long ago, recognized the strong movement of populations to the suburbs, made feasible by increased public transportation—especially the railroad.

In 1869, 13 kilometers (8 miles) west of Chicago, on the Chicago, Burlington and Quincy Railroad, Olmsted and Vaux created one of the first bedroom-communities, based on the concept of providing optimum living conditions within reach of a thriving commercial center. On acreage bordering the Des Plaines River, the landscape architects designed a community for 10,000 people, expressing the ideals of the period—attempting to combine country life and city culture.

Riverside (see Figs. 110 and 111) represents a culmination of romantic idealism, begun in eighteenth-century England and translated into North American idiom with nineteenth-century technological achievements superimposed. It provided the urban worker in a democractic, laissez-faire society with a place in the country, remote enough (in 1869, but today gobbled up in suburban sprawl) that the worker could raise his family in semirural surroundings. Yet its location would permit, should he choose, the suburbanite to have a pleasant canter on horseback into the city in the morning, riding back again to his cozy nest in the peace of early evening. Or, he could walk with his neighbors to the railroad passenger station to commute in comfort to Chicago's Loop.

Having achieved early recognition, and having established a sound reputation as astute, careful and vastly aware planners, this foremost of landscape architectural firms (Olmsted and Vaux, until Vaux's death in 1895, thereafter Olmsted, Olmsted and Eliot[8]) continued to offer a wide variety of services to public agencies and private clients.

Stanford University, planned in 1886 for Leland Stanford, Sr., in Palo Alto, California, remains today an outstanding example of campus design and planning, recognizing the needs of campus circulation and services. It also reflects the cultural background of the region, originally settled by Spanish missionaries. The Boston Architects with whom Olmsted collaborated, recreated, on a major campus scale, the essence of Spanish

[8]The firm, under the name Olmsted Associates, Inc. at present still exists in Brookline, Massachusetts.

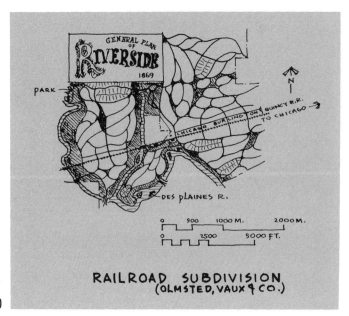

FIGURE 110

mission architecture, with cloistered quadrangles, and a central chapel. Olmsted's master plan recognized the relationship of the campus to the community, and yet gave it the dignified, monumental approach appropriate to a major university.

The monumental seems to have been a significant attribute of the terminal years of the nineteenth century. One of the most influential plans produced by Olmsted grew out of his collaboration with the architect Daniel Burnham in planning the World's Columbian Exposition held in Chicago in 1893.

International trade fairs grew out of medieval European cloth fairs, at which merchants from many countries compared their merchandise. Exhibitions of fine and applied arts date to eighteenth century France and England.

International scientific expositions began with the Crystal Palace exhibition in London in 1851, when Sir Joseph Paxton (1803–1865), English architect and designer of greenhouses, built the Crystal Palace, a great shell of iron and glass, to house the latest in science and industrial machinery. Another exposition which attracted world-wide attention took place in Paris in 1889, for which Alexandre Gustave Eiffel (1832–1923), French engineer, erected the Eiffel Tower in the Champs de Mars.

The young international power, the United States, eager to honor itself for the four-hundredth anniversary of Columbus' discovery of the "new" continent, sponsored an exposition in the bustling commercial center of Chicago—an exposition that proved to have tremendous impact on the nation itself, if not the world. Daniel Burnham, Chicago architect, and Frederick Law Olmsted collaborated in producing a major landmark in American urban design, the World's Columbian Exposition, on the former sand flats of Jackson Park on the shore of Lake Michigan.

Olmsted, responsible for site selection, carefully examined five possible locations for the exhibition. He would have preferred another site but the railroads refused to lay to it

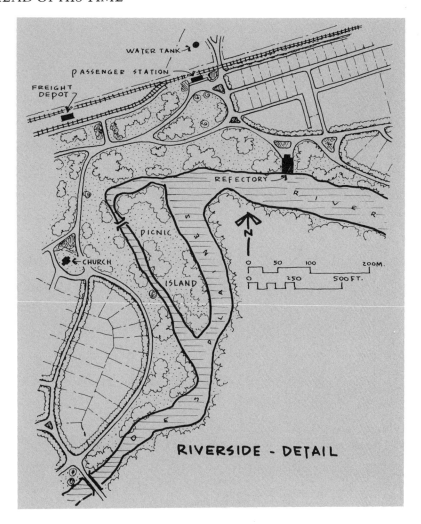

FIGURE 111

the necessary tracks, so Olmsted tackled the creation of a world exposition between the Illinois Central tracks and the lake.

The site plan (see Fig. 112) included a great Court of Honor, with a massive multijet fountain at the west end of its vast ceremonial basin, with Columbia herself rising in heroic proportions at the east end, backed by a Greek peristyle providing passage through to the pier jutting into Lake Michigan.

"Architecturally, the Exposition was a great popular success. The decision of the Exposition committee to design all major buildings in a uniform neoclassical Beaux-Arts style resulted in an imposing collection of huge plaster facades displayed to their best advantage by the public spaces Olmsted had insisted it was necessary to provide. Wondering visitors came to admire and returned home to imitate, convinced that their cities could capture some of the Exposition's grandeur."[9]

[9]Fabos, et al. op. cit., p. 91

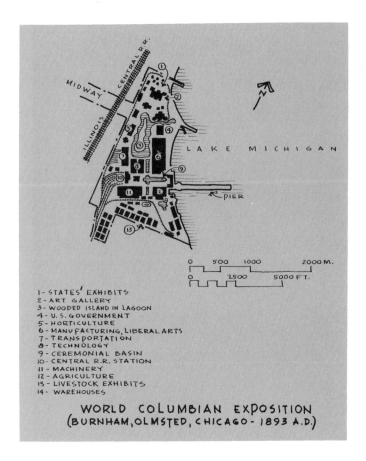

FIGURE 112

FIGURE 113

CEREMONIAL BASIN
COLUMBIAN EXPOSITION - 1893

The significance of Burnham and Olmsted's plan lay in the creation of a unified, harmonious whole out of a myriad of dissimilar forms, scales, and functions.

Yet, here, in a great display of the power of a muscle-flexing commercial-industrial empire, another significant impulse appears strongly expressed. The wooded island in its picturesque "naturalized" lagoon, Olmsted insisted, had its place, despite its apparent violation of classic theme. Romanticized nature, he perhaps felt, recognized a national nostalgia for the frontier wilderness of recent demise.

# 18                    The Arcadian Myth
### (Estates and Parks, 1890–1920)

Arcadia (Greek Arkadia) really existed. Originally a mountainous district of Greece, celebrated as the abode of a simple, contented pastoral people, Arcadia developed in the minds of late-nineteenth-century architects and landscape architects, a myth to be realized in an industrialized society.[1]

But not until an urban society stylized nature in its parks and estates did landscape architects achieve in this country the stature they commanded in Europe.

In the colonial period, formal gardens served as architectural devices extending floor plans into an intermediate zone where geometric patterns symbolized the "humanization" of nature. Symmetrical mazes of shrubbery and decorative walkways offered Tidewater aristocracy and New England gentry a defense against barbarism [see Chapter 15]. Within the boxwood hedges and mulberry plantings they could gracefully retire from a bitter struggle against the wild countryside. But the landscaped garden of the twentieth century was no island of civilization in a wilderness world. Rather, it stood in contrast to the mechanized world as an island of nature, 'a relief from the too insistently man-made surroundings of civilized life,' as Frederick Law Olmsted, Jr., wrote in 1923.[2]

This era of eclecticism, in which designers chose from the past those styles which seemed best suited to the given circumstances, also saw the peaking of individualism, as the industrial revolution rose to its zenith. Huge personal fortunes provided entrepreneurs the opportunity to become the patrons of architects and landscape architects.

By the last decade of the nineteenth century "George Washington Vanderbilt, age 33, could stand on the porch of his French chateau, near Asheville, North Carolina, and gaze

---

[1]Schmitt, Peter J., *Back To Nature; The Arcadian Myth in Urban America*, New York, Oxford University Press, 1969.

[2]*Ibid.*, pp. 56, 57.

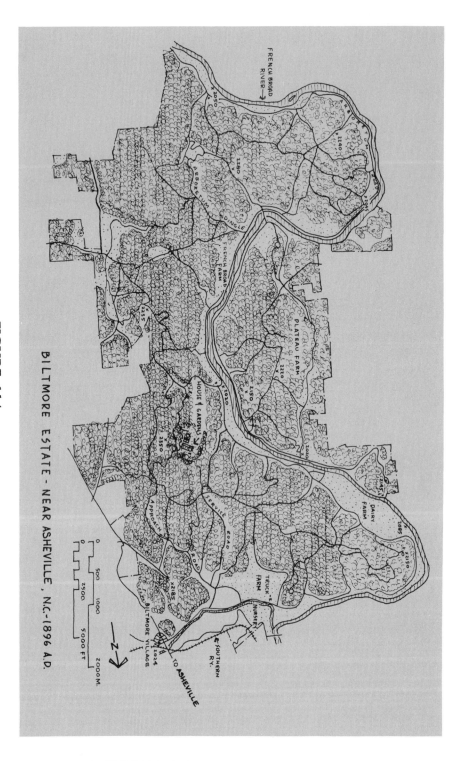

FIGURE 114

BILTMORE ESTATE - NEAR ASHEVILLE, N.C.-1896 A.D.

toward the Blue Ridge Mountains just on the horizon. All the land in between as far as the eye could see in any direction belonged to him."[3] The expansive estate Biltmore expressed, probably beyond his awareness, Vanderbilt's position as monarch of a financial empire in even greater scale than Louis XIV's Versailles had displayed his situation as a royal monarch.

Vanderbilt could command the attention of the leaders of the profession. Richard Morris Hunt, one of the founders of the American Institute of Architects, designed the great chateau while Olmsted, charter member of the American Society of Landscape Architects, designed the gardens and applied his skill in estate and park design to the 30 square kilometers (8 square miles) of the gargantuan estate.

We do not here imply, in any sense, that Hunt and Olmsted accepted their challenge in any way as fawning sycophants, as "kept ladies," as it were, or that they acted the role of Benvenuto Cellini, who had been "house artist" to cardinals in Italy, and royal masters in France.

Hunt very sincerely felt, in keeping with his time, that the mansion, in its majestic forest setting, had to appear a royal house. In the Beaux-Arts tradition, which demanded highly disciplined selection of the proper style, a regal French castle best expressed his client's concept for his country estate, set as a jewel in this uniquely American baronial park.

Olmsted, too, a product of his time, accepted the challenge of organizing the vast landholdings of Vanderbilt as an expression of the open display of wealth customary of a period in American history when the United States stood on the threshold of becoming a world power (see Appendix B).

In his typically far-sighted way (cf. Central Park), Olmsted viewed the resolution of his task as "an opportunity for private conservation often unavailable in public commissions."[4] The estate today exists as a semipublic preserve on both banks of the French Broad River, maintained as a unique example of that grandiose period when there were (financial) giants in the land. That it is a highly romanticized version of a pioneer farm in the wilderness merely reflects its fitness for its time. Andrew Jackson Downing had early (during the 1840s) written of the "life of a cultivated mind in the country." John Burroughs, Ernest Thompson Seton, Donald Mitchell, Editor of *Harper's* magazine, and Liberty Hyde Bailey, author of that most comprehensive and precise *Cyclopedia of Horticulture*, all contributed to the Arcadian mystique. They and men like them felt that they must guard the remnants of natural environment for an urban majority not quite capable of applying Arcadian principles in day-to-day situations.[5]

Apparently, in the vigorously expanding economy of a nation beginning to flex its muscle as a world power, the inevitable happened: the "iron horse" (the locomotive) had spanned the continent, steam-powered machinery was already giving way to electricity,

---

[3]Fabos, Julius Gy; Milde, Gordon T; and Weinmayr, V. Michael, *Frederick Law Olmsted, Sr., Founder of Landscape Architecture in America*, Amherst, Mass., University of Massachusetts Press, 1968, p. 86.

[4]*Ibid.*, p. 86.

[5]Schmitt *op. cit.*, p. xx.

and urbanization was rapidly overtaking the wilderness. A frontier had expired. As in England before, those who had tamed the wilderness began to look with fondness on nature, in the same romantic way an old war veteran, forgetting the mud and blood, reminisces with fondness over past battles.

Charles Eliot's description of the Cushing-Belmont place, an established (1800) country seat near Boston, illustrates the "back to nature" feeling of the last decades of the nineteenth century.[6] Eliot's description was highly literate, almost poetic, as he described the country seat as in "gently rolling countryside, where the lawn descends from the road northward to the pond, thence rises gradually toward the woods to the north." He continues lyrically to describe the "approach avenue, gently curved through arching trees," terminating in a wide gravel space for carriages, joining with the service road leading to the stables.

The Cushing-Belmont place reminds one immediately of Downing's Plan for a Mansion Residence (Fig. 107) of half a century earlier. Downing had adapted a Hudson River Valley working farm to the romantic ideals of his time. The Cushing-Belmont place had existed as a New England country seat since 1800. We may, with reason, suspect that in its original state, the farm had had the functional practicality of the Freeman Farm (Fig. 101). As time passed the estate changed hands (J.P. Cushing had been

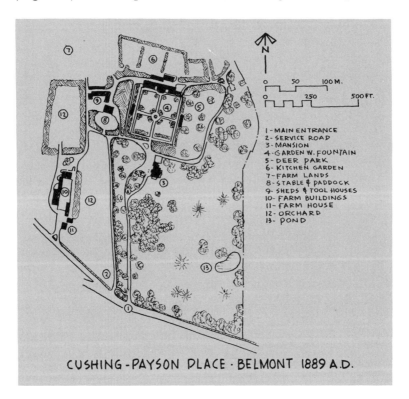

CUSHING-PAYSON PLACE · BELMONT 1889 A.D.

1 - MAIN ENTRANCE
2 - SERVICE ROAD
3 - MANSION
4 - GARDEN W. FOUNTAIN
5 - DEER PARK
6 - KITCHEN GARDEN
7 - FARM LANDS
8 - STABLE & PADDOCK
9 - SHEDS & TOOL HOUSES
10 - FARM BUILDINGS
11 - FARM HOUSE
12 - ORCHARD
13 - POND

FIGURE 115

[6]Eliot, Charles, *Charles Eliot, Landscape Architect*, 2 vols, Boston, Houghton Mifflin, 1902, pp. 246–250.

owner in 1853, remodeling the estate into "the most famous seat near Boston"[7]). As we see the estate in 1889, Eliot could be saddened to write that S.R. Payson, the latest owner, had sold the place to subdividers under rapidly growing urban pressures.

By the time of its submission to metropolitan expansion, this Belmont estate showed clear evidence of the gradual shift from practicality to the display of personal wealth. The great expanse of clipped lawn, the artful spacing of specimen trees, many of them exotic, the elaborate formal garden, and the "deer park" all give evidence of eclectic selection from the available smorgasbord of the past.

The Mather estate "Gwinn," designed by the architect Manning and the landscape architect Platt, in 1908 on the shore of Lake Erie near Cleveland, Ohio (see Fig. 116) illustrates clearly the spirit of its period. Even more subject to urban pressures, on the eastern fringe of then-exploding Cleveland, the industrial giant of Ohio's Lake Erie border, Gwinn was necessarily confined to a much smaller land area. Perhaps that is why Platt and Manning chose to express the coal baron's influential position by selecting an Italian villa as the appropriate style. As you have seen, Renaissance villas occupied relatively small tracts of land (cf. Fig. 116 with Fig. 73). Too, the house, situated as it was at the top of the Lake Erie Bluffs, could have reminded the designers of the grand villas lining the shores of Lakes Como and Maggiore at the top of the Italian boot.

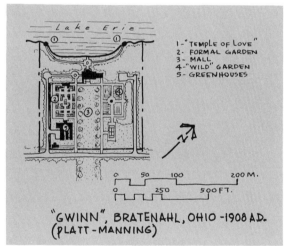

FIGURE 116

"GWINN", BRATENAHL, OHIO -1908 A.D. (PLATT-MANNING)

"Gwinn" thus echoes the classic past, combining Italian Renaissance geometry with the English "mall," whose own derivation stemmed from Le Nôtre's *tapis vert* at Versailles.

On the other hand, at Glen Cove, New York, on the north shore of Long Island, just 34 kilometers (22 miles) east-northeast of New York City, the Olmsted Brothers could, as late as 1922, design Ormston, the estate of J. E. Aldred, as a *ferme ornée*.[8] Ormston is

[7]*Ibid.,* p. 246.

[8]Marie Antoinette's playground at Versailles (Fig. 94) was the original *ferme ornée* or ornamented farm.

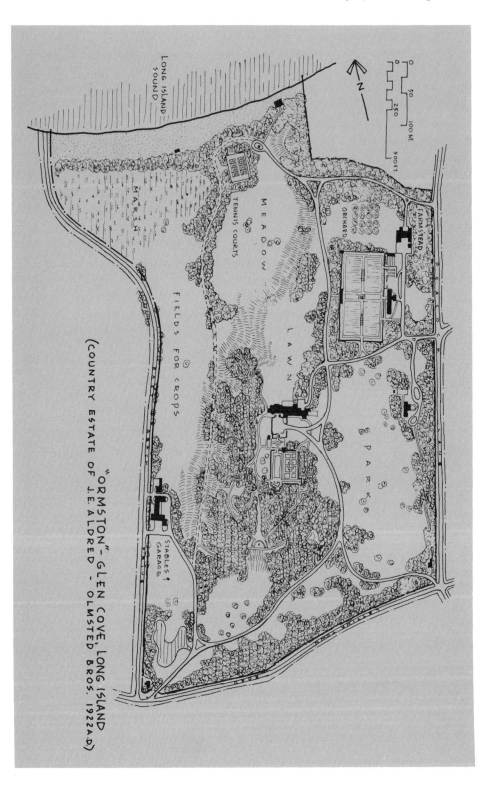

FIGURE 117

"ORMSTON"- GLEN COVE, LONG ISLAND
(COUNTRY ESTATE OF J.E. ALDRED - OLMSTED BROS. 1922 A.D.)

frankly eclectic, the formal gardens and mansion having been selected from French sources. Yet it reflects the firm agricultural tradition of the United States. As late as 1964, one could see sheep grazing on Long Island's north shore as close as 24 kilometers (15 miles) to Times Square. Thus, Aldred's country retreat, while expressing French monarchal splendor, overlaid by the American (English) love of outdoor sport (note the tennis courts and the extensive beach), touchingly includes a farmstead, orchard, and farm fields. Careful study of the plan reveals that the agricultural part of the estate must have been only a token, since it occupies such a relatively small proportion of the entire landholdings. With the exception of the farm fields, the bulk of the land is devoted to an almost regal park, a private expression of the early twentieth century felt need for adequate public parklands in and near cities.

As early as 1890, Charles Eliot wrote that the United States was well on the way to becoming urban. He was alarmed enough at the prospect to relate that "many of the rural counties of fertile Iowa have lost population in the last ten years."[9] Going further, Eliot expressed again the social conscience inherent in Olmsted's "Greensward" plan for Central Park (Chapter 17). In 1902, he wrote: "there is an important element in human nature which the town square cannot satisfy. This is that conscious or unconscious sensibility to the beauty of the natural world which in many men becomes a passion, and in almost all men plays a part."[10]

As early as 1888, Eliot had begun to study the problem of securing for American towns and cities adequate public parks. His analysis of parks available to the public in the major cities of the continent clearly indicated their inadequacy to provide the real needs he saw in the "newness of our civilization."

About metropolitan Boston, which he knew best, Eliot observed: "a crowded population thirsts, occasionally at least, for the sight of something very different from the public garden, square, or ball-field. The railroads and the new electric street railways which radiate from the Hub carry many thousands every pleasant Sunday through the suburbs to the real country, and hundreds out of these thousands make the journey for the sake of the refreshment which an occasional hour to two spent in the country brings to them."[11]

Eliot could not rest with merely writing about the problem. He proceeded to do something about it, calling, on May 24, 1890, a meeting of interested persons to form a committee for the preservation of scenery and historic sites in Massachusetts. This committee convinced the Massachusetts Legislature, aware that Niagara Falls and the Adirondacks in New York State were already state reservations, to enact legislation appointing, in 1891, a board of trustees to manage public lands.

By 1901 the state park and reservations movement had visible establishment.

---

[9]Eliot, *op. cit.*, p. 337.

[10]*Ibid.*, p. 341.

[11]*Ibid.*, p. 317.

Middlesex Fells and the Blue Hills became early examples of state and federal action to preserve natural scenery, following Henry David Thoreau's earlier precept "in wildness is the preservation of the world."[12]

So began, in the last decades of the nineteenth century, the state and federal park systems which, by 1960, constituted the basis for the $5 billion outdoor recreation industry.[13]

By 1910, the United States had created five national parks, all in the west,[14] and a growing number of states had allocations of major landholdings in parks and preserves. By 1928, every one of the 48 states had either state parks, forests, or game preserves.[15]

State parkland reservations became a necessary adjunct to the national park system, as they provided large tracts of scenic "wilderness" accessible to the public (as many of the federal reservations were not in the period 1899–1920) within reasonable proximity and at reasonable expense to the visitor. Yet even with the rapid growth of national and state park systems, the needs of crowded metropolitan areas required intensive planning on a regional scale to alleviate what, as early as the 1870s were becoming festering nuisances.

To cite just one example, by the 1870s, Boston had grown far beyond its original peninsula. "Landfill operations had created the South End and Back Bay districts on both sides of the original neck that joined the city to the mainland; as its population grew the city had also expanded its political limits to include the mainland, suburban townships of Roxbury [1867] and Dorchester [1868]. Draining these areas and forming the boundary between Boston and Brookline lay the Fens—a foul tidal swamp and creek left over from the days when all of Back Bay was a shallow body of salt water."[16]

Flood control and the eventual elimination of the stench of sewage dumped indiscriminately into the surface streams demanded immediate, pragmatic solution. By 1875, Boston created an independent park commission to deal with metropolitan problems of this nature.

The firm of Olmsted, Olmsted, and Eliot, Landscape Architects[17] provided functional, yet esthetic solutions to this major problem of Boston's exploding urban population. The purpose of the plan presented to the park commission (Fig. 118) was threefold: "to make an engineering solution the occasion for creating a needed municpal open space; to link newly annexed communities to the historic municipal center; and to provide, as in Central Park, a variety of forms of recreation—pleasure driving, picknicking, and education at the Arboretum."[18] Technical innovations of the plan included a major

---

[12]Title of a Sierra Club book, published 1962.

[13]Barlow, Raleigh, and Steinmueller, Milton H., "Trends in Outdoor Recreation," *A Place to Live,* Yearbook of Agriculture, Washington, D.C., U.S. Department of Agriculture, 1963, p. 299.

[14]Yellowstone, Yosemite, General Grant (California), Sequoia, Mt. Rainier, Grand Canyon (National Monument).

[15]Nelson, Beatrice Ward, *State Recreation, Parks, Forests and Game Preserves,* Washington, D.C., National Conference on State Parks, Inc., 1928.

[16]Fabos, et al., *op cit.,* p. 57.

[17]F. L. Olmsted, Sr., F. L. Olmsted, Jr., and Charles Eliot.

[18]Fabos et al., *op, cit.,* p. 59.

trunk sewer, tide gates in the Charles River, and the use of the Fens parklands as a temporary storage basin for runoff. In addition, the plan created a linear park system linking older with newer sections of the city. Much of the plan remains today as a monument to the planning genius of F.L. Olmsted Jr., and his coworker, Charles Eliot.

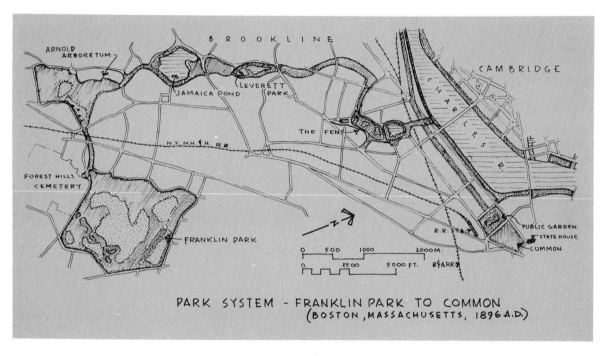

PARK SYSTEM - FRANKLIN PARK TO COMMON
(BOSTON, MASSACHUSETTS, 1896 A.D.)

FIGURE 118

Yet the pendulum of time was once again to swing, away from the romantic vision of the Olmsteds, father and son, and the Cambridge-bred Charles Eliot. Geometry in the fabric of urban tapestry, echoed in the diagonal street-pattern proposed for Cambridge (see Fig. 118), was once again to dominate, as remembrance of the Columbian Exposition fostered the "City Beautiful."

# 19             Make No Little Plans
## (The City Beautiful Movement, 1893–1920)

Daniel H. Burnham, in 1907 formulated a credo that has become the motto of city planners: "Make no little plans; they have no magic to stir men's blood and probably themselves will not be realized. Make big plans: aim high in hope and work, remembering that a noble, logical diagram once recorded will never die, but long after we are gone will be a living thing, asserting itself with ever-growing insistency. Remember that our sons and grandsons are going to do things that would stagger us. Let your watchword be order and your beacon beauty."[1]

The seeds of the City Beautiful movement had been planted in France centuries before by André Le Nôtre and his most important patron, Louis XIV, at Versailles. This implantation in the minds of men had borne fruit in the original plan of Washington, where our first president had commissioned Pierre L'Enfant[2] to prepare plans for the nation's capital.

The plan was not executed at the time, because L'Enfant fell into disfavor with Thomas Jefferson, apostle of agrarian democracy. However, in 1889 the designs were resurrected from the archives and in 1901 were executed by the Capitol Planning Commission, of which Daniel Burnham was a chief member.

In sharp contrast to the romantic scheme proposed by Andrew Jackson Downing in 1851, the plan for Washington, D.C., in the first year of the twentieth century reflected the classic order dictated by the Ecole des Beaux Arts in Paris, arbiter of the period for everything in esthetics considered useful and beautiful.

The strong Beaux Arts influence of the latter decades of the nineteenth century had achieved its greatest impact on the American mind in 1893, when the World Columbian Exposition (see Fig. 112) opened. "Wondering visitors came to admire and returned home to imitate."[3] Immediately dubbed White City because of its consistent snowy-white pseudoclassic architecture, the 1893 fair represented everything that the United States urban environment was not. It so impressed visitors with its scale and ordered, classic beauty that, after the fair, every large city with any pretension of self-worth planned to become a City Beautiful.

---

[1]Moore, Charles, *Daniel H. Burnham, Architect, Planner of Cities*, Vol II, Boston, Houghton Mifflin 1921, p. 147.

[2]L'Enfant, Pierre (1754–1825) American soldier, engineer and architect. Born in France, enlisted in the continental army of the United States and rose to rank of Major.

[3]Fabos, Julius Gy, Milde, Gordon T.; and Weinmayr, V. Michael, *Frederick Law Olmsted, Sr., Founder of Landscape Architecture in America*, University of Massachusetts Press, 1968. p. 91.

As the movement gained impetus toward solving the problems of cities, Daniel Burnham's reputation grew with it. Commissioned by the city of San Francisco in 1905 to plan that peninsular metropolis, he conceived his task as an opportunity to replan the city after the great earthquake and fire of 1906. Unfortunately for Burnham only the Civic Center portion was built, as the basic grid pattern of the city had too much landholding tradition behind it to permit the city fathers to slice diagonal grand boulevards through San Francisco's fabric. Only Baron Haussmann, in Paris, in the 1850s, had accomplished that grand scheme for Napoleon III.

On the other hand, the grand idea still had power to stir the minds of men. The Commercial Club of Chicago commissioned Burnham to replan the city along the lines dictated by the time, and so finely exemplified a few years previously in the Columbian Exposition. The basic need of Chicago was for resolution of traffic problems arising from the city's division into independent gridiron sections. The importance of Burnham's plan was not in the wide esplanade paralleling the lakefront, with its grand vistas and cultural center, but that it regularized in a comprehensive way this greatest of America's commercial metropolitan complexes.

The great volume of documentation comprising the plan included proposals for ring roads (cf. the inner and outer belts seen today), a series of major parks, connected by green belts, orderly systems of transportation, and decisions about population densities and growth potentials.[4]

These, however, were practical matters, devoted to efficiency. What captured the imagination, not only of Chicago, but of most other early-20th-century cities, was the grand lakefront plan, with its classic yacht harbor, its imposing series of grandiose buildings, esplanades, fountains and plazas. (see Fig. 119). From the impressive marine entrance to the city, a grand boulevard (Congress Street) led inland to a Civic Center, dominated by a massive monument to civic pride, its dome even more dominant on the skyline than that of St. Paul's in London or St. Peter's in Rome.

The national impact of such visually impressive plans as that for Chicago exploded almost instantaneously in most state capitals, as they rebuilt using "civic center" schemes. As just one example, the Planning Commission of Columbus, Ohio, in 1908 planned a major restructuring of its own civic center. The simple, massive neoclassic State House was to be set, as a jewel on velvet, in a major series of formally balanced public and commercial structures worthy of a new Rome. East of the capitol building was to be erected a new city hall. To the west, flanking a grand mall, were to be other public services. Across the Scioto River, spanned by two pedestrian bridges (see Fig. 120), the axis terminated in a domed armory, flanked by public baths and a technical school.

Although never executed, the 1908 civic center plan for Columbus expressed its period in several ways. Note, for example, in the cross-section accompanying the plan, the presence of 22-story office buildings just west of High Street. Half a century before, in 1851, Elisha Graves Otis had demonstrated, at the Crystal Palace in London, a freight

---

[4]For a detailed account of the Chicago Plan see: *Plan of Chicago*, prepared under the direction of the Commercial Club during the years 1906, 1907, and 1908, by Daniel H. Burnham and Edward H. Bennett, Architects, Edited by Charles Moore, Chicago, The Commercial Club, 1909.

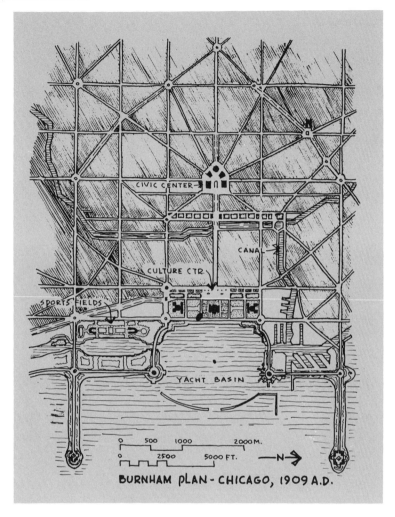

BURNHAM PLAN - CHICAGO, 1909 A.D.

FIGURE 119

elevator equipped with a safety device to prevent its falling should the cable break. By the 1870s, Sir William Armstrong's hydraulic principles had been applied to make elevators even more efficient. By the end of the nineteenth century, operation of elevators by electric motors had become the chief method used to make possible high-rise office buildings. Another expression of early-20th-century technology appears in the street railway tracks laid along the principal traffic ways, and providing public transportation to the principal activity centers.

One should also note, in the plan for the Statehouse ground, the commission's concession to nostalgia, the romantic tradition of the previous century. The then-existing majestic elms had been retained, in true Downing expression of the "beautiful." Only as late as 1964, the vestige of the now century-old pattern succumbed to progress, in the form of an underground parking garage, making complete revision of the plantings necessary.

Today, we look back on the City Beautiful movement with scorn and derision, from

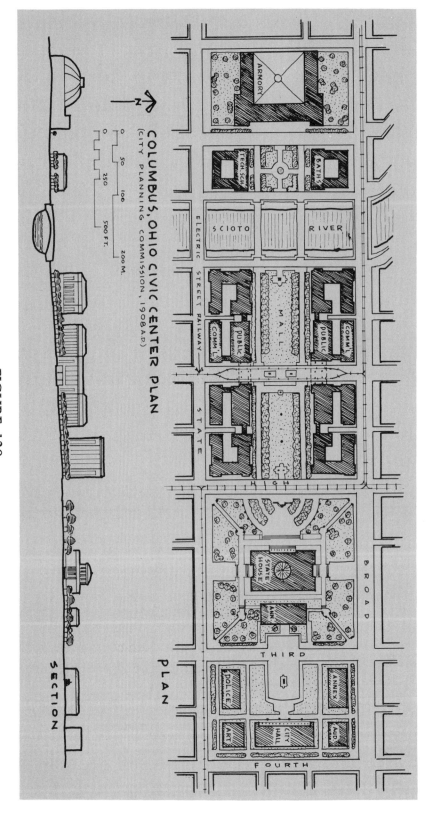

FIGURE 120

our lofty position of planning concepts devoted to safety, economy, efficiency, and life-support systems. Louis Sullivan, early advocate of what we now know as contemporary architecture, had said, upon viewing the Chicago plan, that the city beautiful movement would set back planning 50 years.

Perhaps Sullivan's prophecy stated truth, but in aspects of urbanized life other than city showplaces, the industrial revolution spawned movements toward improvement in housing, made widespread in impact by Ebenezer Howard, who popularized the Garden City concept.

# 20

# Garden Cities
## (1400–1940)

"A Citie is a perfect and absolute assembly or communion of many townes and streets in one" (Aristotle, *Politics*, as translated in 1598).

Just as man, from earliest times, having acquired sufficient knowledge and capacity to utilize energy, established in private his own earthly paradise, so in public he has concerned himself with lofty ideals as to community.

The ancient world had a rather static view of community, as illustrated by the gridiron patterns of cities planned by Hippodamus of Miletus, as he provided the uniform structure of Greek colonies.

Vitruvius, of the Augustan age of Rome added formal and structural considerations, recognizing sacred, public, and private precincts in his radially arranged schemes, indicating eight principal streets, carefully oriented to avoid direct alignment with the presupposed eight prevailing winds. His ideal, though recognizing at least one of the physical factors today commonly considered, consisted primarily of formalized patterns observing the cleavage between the higher and lower classes of citizens.

The Judeo-Christian tradition, powerful during the Middle Ages, added another dimension, the spiritual, to the ideals previously recorded. Thought centered around Jerusalem, as the heavenly city, rather than the reality observed by the crusaders during their sojourns in the Holy Land. The spiritual idealists appreciated only the sharp distinction between the holy city and the sinful town. These attitudes gave to the architectural image of the ideal community the strength of a universal moral symbol.[1]

The Renaissance, too, had its contributors to idealistic planning, as represented by Leon Battista Alberti's (1404–1472) publication of *De Re Aedificata*, in one volume of which he outlined his ideal, which allowed variations in plan to fit specific sites. The humanization that began with the period apparently for the first time considered society as egalitarian. It may be supposed, then, that Alberti was the precursor of modern functionalism.

Sir Thomas More in England (1478–1535) wrote *Utopia* (1516) as a fitting expression of his ideal community enjoying social, legal, and political perfection. Typically English, More's Utopia advocated integration of town and country, and limited community size to 6,000 families.

---

[1]Rosenau, Helen, *The Ideal City in its Architectural Evolution*, Bristol, England, Western Printing Services, 1959.

Toward the end of the period, there appeared large numbers of ideal civic forms whose basis was formal order in which geometric patterns dominated, reflecting the concern of the time with geometry, that noble science which so enriches and adorns the mind, expressing, in the philosophy of the time, not only the wonderful properties of nature, but also the most important truths of morality. Renewed interest in the Classics, especially the writings and drawings of Vitruvius, led to a desire for symmetry and order.

Vincenzo Scamozzi (1522–1616), in 1615 published *L'Idea della Architettura Universale.* In it, he expressed the classic Vitruvian form (see Fig. 121), modified to meet current (Renaissance) concepts of civil defense. Its moats and canal supplied water and, in addition to the city wall, provided protection. The residential precincts and the classic medallion shape clearly expressed the predilection of the time for geometric order (cf. Italian villas and French chateaux). Public squares, five in number, balance the mass of housing with their orderly presentation of spaces. A sixth, smaller plaza was introduced as a balancing foil for the canal penetrating the civic pattern.

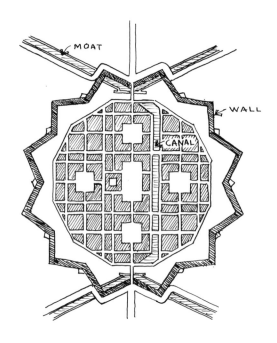

IDEAL CITY - 1615A.D.
(VINCENZO SCAMOZZI)
(NO SCALE)

FIGURE 121

The eighteenth century saw the beginning of the Industrial Revolution, with its consequent crowding of families into close quarters near their sources of livelihood. English Puritanism, the nascent social sciences, and the burgeoning romanticism spawned by the English Landscape School combined, by the nineteenth century, to produce a whole series of experiments in utopian socialism.

Robert Owen (1771–1858), a successful cotton manufacturer in Manchester, in 1800 moved to New Lanark, Scotland, where he and others purchased the mills of David Dale. There he reconstructed the community into a model industrial town with good housing and sanitation, nonprofit stores, schools, and, for the time, excellent working conditions. In spite of these novel ideas, the mills continued to earn profits.[2]

The New Lanark experiment became famous in England, and Owen attempted to spread his concepts to the New World. Though unsuccessful, Owen's New Harmony, in Indiana, created in 1825, furthered the concepts of cooperation, social justice, and improved environment of the United States.

Owen's influence had its impact. James Silk Buckingham (1786–1855) published, in 1849, *National Evils and Practical Remedies*. In it he described the city of Victoria, named for the then-reigning English monarch. Victoria represented an urban ideal for 10,000 inhabitants. To be built in open country, the plan was to be rectangular. That the inhabitants were to lead a virtuous life and practice temperance may be illustrated by Buckingham's roster of street names, laid out at right angles and on the diagonals of the square:

Avenue of Peace
Avenue of Fortitude
Avenue of Charity
Avenue of Hope
Avenue of Faith
Avenue of Justice
Avenue of Unity

As early as 1827, J. B. Papworth, an English architect, planned a new town on the South bank of the Ohio opposite Cincinnati, which he named Hygeia after the Greek goddess of health.[3] Although the town never came to fruition, it forecast Ebenezer Howard's *Garden Cities of Tomorrow*.[4]

Howard's ideals included low population density, park and garden development, and small townships so located in reference to a central metropolis that handsome, yet functional greenbelts, or countryside (see Fig. 122), would surround both central city and satellite communities. Howard, much more the pragmatist than many of his idealist predecessors, took into account the economic conditions of his time, but also was aware of the pressing need for reform in the urban pattern he knew.

He expressed his philosophy in contemporary terms, describing three magnets which did, or should, draw people. The town he described as a place closing out nature, which, while providing high money wages and places of amusement, also created confinement, foul air and murky skies. The country, second of the three magnets, had as values the

[2]Choay, Francoise, *The Modern City: Planning in the Nineteenth Century*, New York, George Braziller, 1969.

[3]*Ibid.*

[4]Howard, Ebenezer (1850–1928), *Garden Cities of Tomorrow*, London, Faber & Faber, 1945.

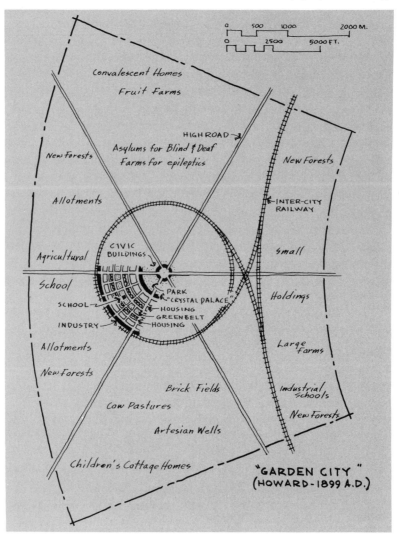

FIGURE 122

beauty of nature and its fresh air and abundant water. In contrast, however, the country possessed its own faults, including unemployment, lack of drainage, lack of amusement, and low wages.

To Howard the "garden city," the third magnet, possessed all the advantages of the country plus the social amenities of the town, which, if combined as Howard proposed, would serve mankind to the millennium.[5] Bright homes and gardens, adequate opportunity for the enterprising, freedom, and cooperation would prevail thus enlarging the individual "earthly paradise" concept to encompass all people, all classes of a complex, industrial society.

---

[5]"Millennium," in the sense here used, refers to the thousand years mentioned in Revelations **XX**, during which holiness is to be triumphant. Some believe that during this period Christ will reign on earth. Hence, the millennium is a period of great happiness and good government.

Garden City (Fig. 122) forecast twentieth-century urban-planning ideals, carefully balanced to the economy and technology of the end of the nineteenth century. Major intercity communication was to be by rail, with "high roads" as supplement.

The city itself was to comprise 809 hectares (2,000 acres), while the rural holdings of the corporation (a holding company which would purchase all lands and collect all ground rents, thus ensuring not only equality of opportunity, but economic profit to the corporation) comprised the remainder of the total land holdings of 2428 hectares (6,000 acres).

The town should be limited to a population of 32,000, comfortably and spaciously housed along the perimeters of a greenbelt. Inward from the cooperative housing lay the civic center, shops, amusement and cultural facilities, while the industrial zone lay on the perimeter of the town adjacent to a ring rail line.

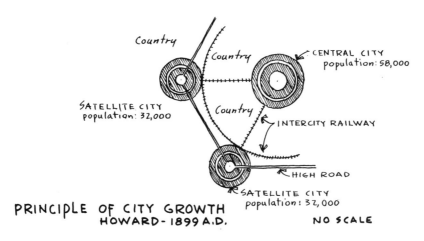

PRINCIPLE OF CITY GROWTH
HOWARD - 1899 A.D.

FIGURE 123

Outside of the satellite town would lie all the ancillary functions, such as garden plots, truck and dairy farms, forests, water supply, and the recognized health and welfare institutions necessary to a viable community.

Though Howard realized his diagrams could not be exactly reproduced, but depended on site selection, his concepts soon had their effect. Both Letchworth and Welwyn Garden City, in England, are existent examples of the application of the garden-city principle. Letchworth, designed by Raymond Unwin (1863-1940), 55 kilometers (34 miles) north of London, was the first of the garden cities, founded in 1903, followed by Welwyn Garden City, 38 kilometers (24 miles) north of London, established in 1920.

The garden-city movement gained impetus in the early years of this century, and, in the United States, came to fruition, in 1928, in Radburn, New Jersey.

Clarence Stein and Henry Wright, urban designers, to a great extent carried on the work begun by Ebenezer Howard and Sir Raymond Unwin. Stein and Wright,[6] while

---

[6]Stein, Clarence S., *Toward New Towns for America*, Liverpool, University Press, 1950.

accepting the economic and social philosophies of their predecessors, introduced a new dimension in designing Radburn, made necessary by Henry Ford's production-line technique, making the Model T available to everyone at costs $900 less than his closest competitor. Radburn, in its initial concept, was to provide a complete, automobile-oriented city, coming to grips for the first time with the necessity of separating vehicular and pedestrian traffic.

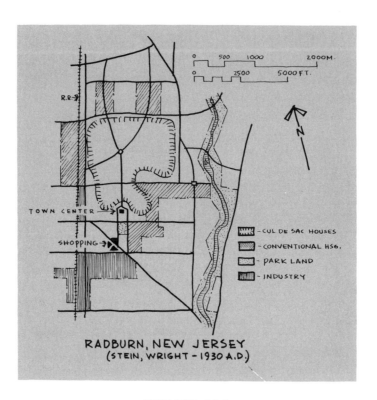

FIGURE 124

As finally executed and as it exists today, the garden cul-de-sac principle, for economic reasons, was not fully realized. Parts of the community became throwbacks to the single-family subdivision pattern then and now prevalent. However, a large enough percentage of garden-oriented planning prevailed to assure the success of the project as a means of providing much more amenity than the usual engineered solutions.

The community plan gave direct pedestrian access from the living areas of individual housing units (see Figs. 125 and 126) to a linked system of parklike pathways, recreational nodes, schools, and active physical activities, as well as the town center and shopping facilities.

Radburn's plan influenced other planning, other sites. Chatham Village (1937) in Pittsburgh, by Ingham and Boyd, architects (Stein and Wright were site planners and consultant architects) remains today a demonstration of the values inherent in the Radburn plan.

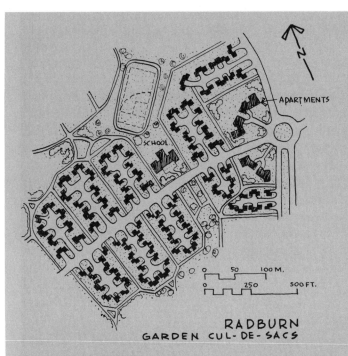

RADBURN
GARDEN CUL-DE-SACS

FIGURE 125

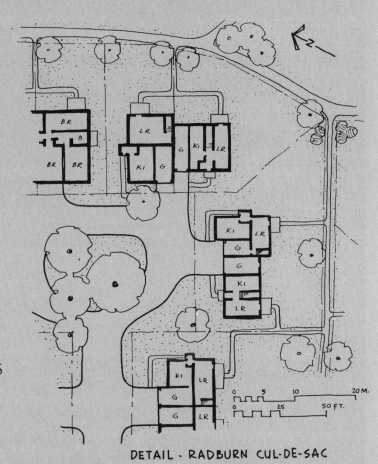

FIGURE 126

DETAIL - RADBURN CUL-DE-SAC

As the great depression of the 1930s emphasized the crying need for social planning on a national scale, other, federally financed communities based on Howard's dream, and the Stein-Wright example, came into existence across the nation. Greenbelt, Maryland (Hale Walker, town planner), made possible by the Emergency Relief Appropriation Act and the National Industrial Recovery Act of 1935, came into being that year, as a community of homes for low-income families. Greenbelt, and others which followed, demonstrated garden-city principles. They provided access to industrial employment and were therefore planned for both work and living.

In the end, only two other "greenbelt towns" were constructed under the New Deal. Greendale, Wisconsin, 11 kilometers (7 miles) from Milwaukee; and Greenhills, Ohio, north of Cincinnati became the additional demonstration units.

The approach of World War II, with its concomitant industrial prosperity, led to the decline of this special kind of social planning, but also presaged other ramifications in the land-planning process. Mankind seems to have found it easier to design the physical relationships of land to dwelling places than to understand psychological and sociological implications of those forms. Technology and widely improved international communications, perhaps inevitably, made possible a movement toward function in design, both in building, and in land uses.

# 21    Form Follows Function
## (United States, 1920–1950)

Horatio Greenough, born in Boston in 1805, early exhibited an interest in art, especially sculpture. After graduation from Harvard in 1825, he spent most of the next 25 years in Italy, during which time he produced a memorable series of articles on architecture. During his sojourn in Florence, he also produced some of the first important sculptural pieces by an American artist. He returned to Massachusetts in 1851 and died in Somerville in 1852.

Greenough's significance to this narrative rests in his theories of the relationship of form to function. "Beauty is the promise of function," wrote this sincere critic of the eclectic classicism in architecture of his time. By 1831, Greenough's theories on architecture had developed through his acceptance of the functional theories of the Venetian architect Carlo Lodoli and the French architect Claude Nicolas Ledoux (1736–1806) who had prepared designs for an ideal city called Chaux for the salt mines of the Franche-Comté. Though never built, Chaux represented not only a model community, but also expressed Ledoux' philosophy of functional relationships.

Greenough, influenced by these European concepts, in 1852 published *The Travels, Observations, and Experience of a Yankee Stonecutter*, in which he stated his belief in nature as the authority for functionalism. Elsewhere, he wrote: "The law of adaptation is the fundamental law of nature in all structure."[1]

Just as he recognized functionalism in nature, Greenough admired function in man-made objects. The sailing ship, for example, he saw as a clean, clear adaptation of form to function, of necessity functional in all its parts, stripped of unnecessary ornamentation, but perfectly adapted in proportion, form and scale to its relations with movement dictated by wind and water.

We can trace Greenough's theories of functionalism down to its greatest advocate, Frank Lloyd Wright, by realizing that Wright's mentor, Louis Sullivan, was first employed in the Philadelphia architectural firm of Frank Furness, who had learned of Horatio Greenough through his association with Ralph Waldo Emerson, who, in turn, had discussed architectural theory at length with Greenough. Thus is the flow of history

[1]Greenough, Horatio, *Form and Function; Remarks on Art*, Ed. by Harold A. Small, Berkeley, University of California Press, 1947, p. xix.

proven. Thus does the seed of a concept, while lying dormant for a while, eventually sprout, and from its roots within the soil of history, produce a mighty tree, whose branches influence environment favorable to the implementation of the idea.

That environment, an area of thought and belief, was carved out of a wilderness of eclectic concepts of what was beautiful and good. The romantics had influenced designers for generations, from the time of Shaftsbury in England, Rousseau in France, Downing and his compatriots in America. American artists in the nineteenth century, as might be expected, looked toward the ancestral nations, England in particular, for confirmation of their feelings about what was perfection.

As economic power burgeoned in the United States (cf. Chapter 18), the wealthy toured Europe, and, in many cases literally transported not only ideas, but objects of art, up to and including entire French, English, or Italian mansions, back to the United States to be re-erected as the nuclei of English Manorial Estates, French Chateaux, or Italian Villas. The great period of European-dominated estate building took place in the period after the Spanish-American War, up to World War I, and was only forced to its death by the Great Depression of the 1930s.

Voices already cried in the wilderness, however. H. H. Richardson, in the Victorian era, though utilizing classic forms, experimented with them, arranging them in new patterns. Frank Lloyd Wright had built his first "Prairie House" in the midwest in the dawn years of the twentieth century. By 1920, Gropius' Bauhaus produced "machines for living," in stark contrast to the elaborate Art Nouveau engendered in France.

The grand era of the steamship and the affluence of the time added another dimension to the picture. Commodore Perry, having gained recognition as captain of an early naval steamship and in the Mexican War, on March 31, 1854, had succeeded in signing with the Japanese Shogun, a treaty that opened to the world a nation previously isolated.

As the trickle of tourists to Japan became a flood in the first quarter of the twentieth century, an entirely contrasting culture caught the fancy of the Occidental world. These island Orientals, having adopted Buddha from India by way of China, modified Buddhism and its concomitant mystic philosophies (Confucianism, Shintoism, and Taoism) into a whole way of life, amazing to the westerner in its stark contrast to Anglo-Saxon Calvinism, dominant in the West.

The Judeo-Christian philosophy presupposed that the earth is man's, and that he should "dominate and subdue" it. The Oriental philosophies, on the other hand, recognized that man was only one of the myriads of creatures of the globe, and that all parts of nature, including man, were one. Thus, the Oriental mind established patterns and forms of expression based on a geometry which the Westerner came to call "occult." In contrast to Western geometry, based on the square, triangle and circle of Pythagoras, Oriental geometry's recognition of nature's forms accepted nature's balancing forces. "Yin and Yang" perhaps expresses occult balance best. It implies contrasts between storm and calm, female, male, and vertical and horizontal, smooth and rough, soft and hard.

The Orientals, especially the Japanese, further accepted the principle that progress in art is progress toward simplicity. To the Japanese, one simple object, carefully and

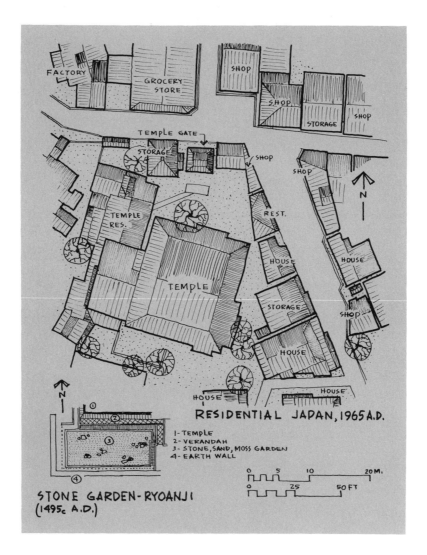

FIGURE 127

lovingly placed in proper relationship, both in scale and proportion, to its surroundings, engendered, in the eye and mind of the sensitive observer, whole clusters of mental images, the simplest arrangement becoming to the mind's eye whatever the observer's feelings wished it to become.

The Garden of the Buddhist monastery of Ryoan-ji (see Fig. 127) in Kyoto, Japan, "surely one of the ten outstanding gardens of all time, is an abstract composition of stones and moss in a bed of raked gravel simulating the sea; this walled garden space extends the limits of the monastery refectory and terrace. Designed as a garden for contemplation, its distinction lies in its simplicity. . . ."[2]

[2] Simonds, John O., *Landscape Architecture, The Shaping of Man's Natural Environment*, New York, F. W. Dodge Corp., 1961, p. 176.

Western designers accepted the esoteric Oriental geometry and translated it into western terms coupled with the end-products of Occidental technology. In this sense, a new approach to the design of outdoor space evolved.

Additionally, Americans, products of a geography full of wide open space, saw in Japan a foretaste of their own crowded future (see Fig. 127).

> One thing seems clear. The time when most of us can go home to a private house as detached from its neighbors as it is now is running out. It ran out quite a while ago in Japan. In America, boys still fly kites and gasoline-engine-powered model airplanes tethered to 15-meter (50-foot) wires. In Japan, where most of 100 million people live on an island the size of Oregon and one-tenth of that population lives in one city, boys have learned to fly a kind of cicada called *semi*. Long nylon ribbons are attached with a drop of plastic glue to the insects, which are tethered to a 3-meter (10-foot) thread. It seems every bit as much fun as flying kites or model airplanes and takes up far less space. The *semi* planes can be flown, two or three at a time, any time and almost any place.[3]

In crowded Japan, Americans were exposed to and made aware of a sense of scale absolutely contrasting to our own. Compare, for example, the portion of the land-use map of Saiwaicho, Kanagawa, Japan (Fig. 127), with the detail of a Radburn, New Jersey cul-de-sac (Fig. 119). Incidentally, Japanese visiting our country are frequently as astonished at the expansive U.S. scale of open space as the American tourist is at the feeling of compactness he gets in Japan.

Some designers, even at the beginning of this era of functionalism, seemed to have an awareness that the "frontier" was long gone. The advent of the automobile—and its concomitant permissive mobility—was probably the single important technological factor causing the shift in the United States from a predominantly rural to a predominantly urban population (compare 1920 population figures with 1950, Appendix B).

As early as 1924, Fletcher Steele, Fellow of the American Society of Landscape Architects, practitioner and lecturer in his chosen profession, in his book *Design in the Little Garden*[4] prophesied the age of functionalism.

Four years before Stein and Wright showed their Radburn scheme, Steele advocated the reversal, in housing, of the common practice of living-room-facing-the-street, kitchen-facing-the-rear of the property. Steele recognized the change in life style from

---

[3]Smith, Richard Alan, "Crowding In the City: The Japanese Solution," *Landscape*, vol. 19, no. 1 (July 1971), p. 33. Reprinted by permission of *Landscape*.

[4]Steele, Fletcher, *Design In The Little Garden*, Boston, The Atlantic Monthly Press, 1924.

one of homecraft self-dependence, to an interdependent, mass-production economy. No longer, he felt, did the household need large areas behind the house for the formerly necessary service functions, but the backyard should serve as outdoor living space, while the service functions, coming as they did from a whole network of urban services, would be more efficiently served from the street side. The term "garden" no longer meant what it had to Downing, a collection of flowering plants, shrubs, and vegetables; but Steele changed it to mean "outdoor living room."

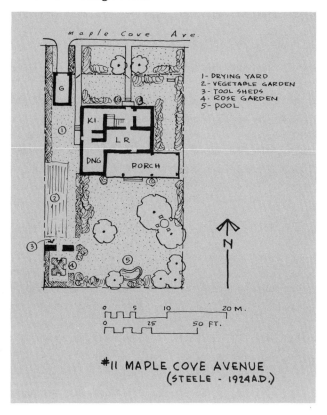

FIGURE 128

Figure 128 identifies the plan's functionalism, as well as its contemporary technology. The garage is placed well-forward, thus "modernizing" the plan. The first garages were carriage houses, usually placed well away from homes in former times, since the smelly stable was logically nearby. In the plan of 11 Maple Cove Avenue, all service functions are related to the service side of the dwelling, thus freeing the remainder for outdoor living. Note the arrangement of rooms. Both the living and dining rooms face on the outdoor living area, which, though frankly accepting romanticism in terms of lawns and plantings, nevertheless exhibits a sense of private living space, reinforced by the generous porch, which Steele admits probably should be screened for protection from insects. The plan also shows, by the absence of a fireplace, contemporary technology, since the house must have central heating.

Another phase of the shift toward functionalism occurred in Europe, as a revolt against Art Nouveau, which had achieved its greatest vogue there in the 1890s. Christopher Tunnard described the theory of functionalism as having three approaches:

*The functional approach*—Aesthetic values lie in the simple statement, in economy of the means of expressions, and in discarding "the old clothes of a past age," which are the Styles . . .

*The empathic approach*—Nature is not to be regarded as a refuge from life, but as an invigorator of it and a stimulus to body and mind. Nature is therefore not to be copied or sentimentalized, neither is she to be overriden.

*The artistic approach*—The profitless search for decorative beauty, a purely relative quality, is abandoned in the creation of the work of art. An appreciation of the interrelation of all true forms of art and of artists themselves results in a broadening of the power of expression and in the cooperation needed. . . .[5].

In exegesis of his thesis, Tunnard chooses St. Ann's Hill, Chertsey, an estate in the South of England. He traces the development and periodic modifications of the tract from its origin in a virgin tract of Windsor forest in the seventeenth century to its form in 1938. In the beginning, the rectilinear geometry of the eighteenth century dominated. Expansion of grounds occurred through the late Renaissance and the Landscape School era, but the formalized garden plots, relatively remote from the house, were never destroyed, as in many such estates, under "Capability" Brown's influence. The house itself passed through a relatively rapid period of expansion in the nineteenth century, but in the 1930s, the original Renaissance structure, plus its additions, was removed, and a new house built of reinforced concrete, obviously influenced by the works of Le Corbusier on the continent (see Fig. 129).

The curvilinear geometrics have Art Nouveau overtones, so that the house and its immediate environs appear transitional. Tradition exists in the presence of the walled forecourt. The Brownian philosophy of "all nature is a garden" is represented by the southern exposure of the living areas onto the spacious, sloping lawn, dotted here and there with clumps and groupings of retained mature trees. There is also functionalism represented in the careful relationship of the house and its ancillary elements (the swimming pool and terraces) to the sloping land form, as illustrated in the plan by the flights of steps leading deftly from one level to another.

---

[5] Tunnard, Christopher, *Gardens in the Modern Landscape,* London, The Architectural Press, 1938, pp. 106, 107.

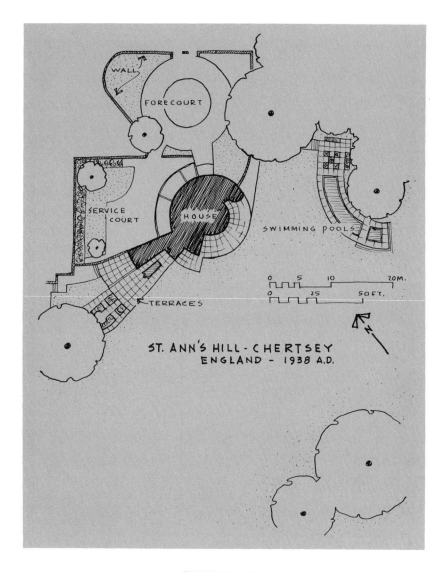

FIGURE 129

Advances in technology during the past half-century have tended to reduce the apparent size of the world, creating a much broader interchange of thought in the design professions. In the early 1900s, aviators had already demonstrated the feasibility of air travel to various parts of the world. World War I motivated aviation research and development. In the 1920s, Europe at first outstripped the United States in air transportation, but the United States later forged ahead. Barnstorming by daredevil flyers in surplus World War I aircraft made the public air-conscious.

By 1925, the first airmail service began, and by the 1930s the transport of passengers became profitable enough so that air travel extended to foreign countries, beginning with Pan American's "China Clipper" in 1934. World War II saw the development of jet propulsion, so that today, rapid air-travel commonly occurs on a global basis.

Other means of communication, too, shrank the world in a time sense. KDKA, Pittsburgh, became the first commercial broadcasting station in the United States in 1920. Since, radios have become standard household fixtures and traveling companions.

Subsequent research into Hertzian-wave transmission produced Facsimile (the transmission of graphic material by wire or radio), and radio telephony made possible virtually instantaneous voice communication to any place on the globe.

By 1928, electronic scanning had been patented. Television equipment was laboratory perfected between 1930 and 1940, so that, almost immediately after the end of World War II in 1945, commercial television became marketable.

The training of young people in the design professions, with the new and expanding possibilities for intercommunication, rapidly acquired an international flavor. What teachers and students thought best from all cultures began to fuse into an international style, whose regional modifications, based on local technical possibilities or limitations, produced the minor differences their planning showed.

Thomas Church, California landscape architect, acquired fame through publications in the popular press, and, by 1955, produced a book, *Gardens Are For People*.[6] In it, he explained the revolt in design against the imitative influences of the previous era, especially the kind of collector's mania evident in the Victorian age. Church's designs, especially in California residential works of the mid-century period exhibit the functionalism taught so effectively by the Bauhaus, but overlaid thereon appeared an Oriental (specifically Japanese) influence, in terms of plan forms, and occult balance (see Fig. 130).

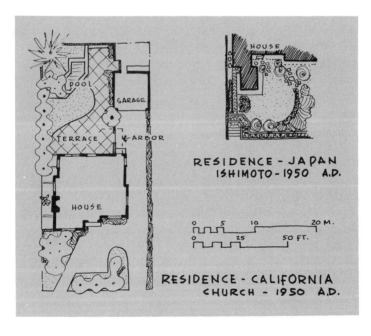

FIGURE 130

[6]Church, Thomas, *Gardens Are For People*, New York, Reinhold, 1955.

It seems natural, in retrospect, that these plan forms, soon popularly known as "California Style" should have originated on our West Coast, as that region has long had commercial relationships with the Orient. On any given day, in West Coast ports, one can find at least one vessel flying the Japanese flag.

Note how closely the plan form of the California residence (Fig. 130) resembles that of its Japanese counterpart. The only significant differences appear to be those of scale, technology, and life style. Church's client required an ample paved terrace for outdoor activity, the floor of which appears to be of mass-produced, modular units. The Japanese life style, on the other hand, required development on a much reduced scale, and the ground spaces appear to follow traditional Japanese concepts, that the garden was a place to be viewed from the house rather than (in the American idiom) an activity area.

Another significant aspect of internationalism appeared at the same time. The Japanese, immediately following the ending of hostilities in World War II, began to look to the Western World, particularly the United States, for inspiration toward "modernizing" their ancient cultural traditions.

Influenced through travel, communication, and education in the Western hemisphere, Japanese designers produced garden forms considered "Western," but adapted to the Japanese idiom (see Fig. 131).

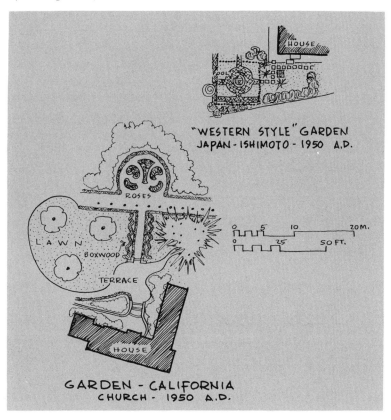

FIGURE 131

Scale and local technology constitute the basic differences in the compared examples of Figure 131. While, in Church's garden, the scale is "western," the Oriental influence shows in the modulation of circular geometry. In the "Western-style" Japanese garden, Occidental influence appears in the frankly symmetrical paths surrounding the garden pool. Even so, the contrast in scale maintains the traditional idiom of expansiveness on the Western continent as opposed to the insular Japanese scale.

With the rapid shift, under technology-oriented societies in which, since World War II, the focus of attention aims at urban problems, buildings and places for people took on an even more pronounced cosmopolitan flavor.

The work of Kenzo Tange, Japanese architect, clearly illustrates the turn toward international architectural style. In his book *Kenzo Tange 1946-1969, Architecture and Urban Design*, Tange expresses to perfection the character of the present phase in architecture: economy, emotionalism, symbolic shape, urbanization, and structurism.[7]

Tange, born in 1913 in Japan, received his architectural training at the University of Tokyo, finishing in 1942. He has since traveled widely, and given lectures in Europe and America. His firm constitutes a team enterprise (its precursor was the Bauhaus), with no attempt to produce specialists. The firm uses consultants of all kinds when the situation demands their knowledge.

The Tange philosophy may be summarized as follows: "The basic theme of urban design is structuring. Science and technology so permeate our lives that it is only on this basis that we can arrive at a new unity of the arts . . . we need a symbolic approach to architecture and urban space in order to secure humanity, human meaning and human value in architecture and urban space."[8]

Tange has achieved world reknown and received many awards during the years since World War II. He first won international recognition by winning a competition, in 1949, for the design of the Peace Center at Hiroshima, ground zero for the dropping of the first atomic bomb. Commissioned to prepare designs and supervise their execution, Tange's firm saw the Peace Center completed by 1956 (see Fig. 132).

The plan creates an open plaza, at the conjunction of two major streams flowing northward through the city. A memorial monument to the victims of the bombing provides the focal point of the plaza, designed to accommodate up to 50,000 people during memorial ceremonies. The momument itself, a saddle-like arch of hyperbolic paraboloids is "redolent of modern engineering, but also recalls the ancient Japanese tombs of rulers." [9]

The Peace Center plan blends "Western" technology and cultural forms with Japanese tradition. The centrally located museum is a rough concrete box set on reinforced concrete columns 6 meters in height (19.65 feet). The museum is reached by a free-standing stair beneath the box. The auditorium-hotel and community center buildings flanking the museum also express contemporary technology in their similarity of expression.

---

[7]Tange, Kenzo, *Kenzo Tange, 1946–1949, Architecture and Urban Design*, Ed. by Udo Kulterman, New York, Praeger, 1970, p. 8.

[8]*Ibid.*, p. 241.

[9]*Ibid.*, p. 16.

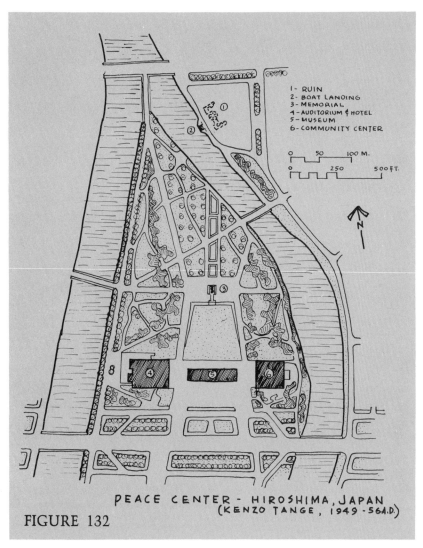

FIGURE 132

PEACE CENTER - HIROSHIMA, JAPAN
(KENZO TANGE, 1949-561.D.)

1- RUIN
2- BOAT LANDING
3- MEMORIAL
4- AUDITORIUM & HOTEL
5- MUSEUM
6- COMMUNITY CENTER

Adapted from Kultermann, Udo, *Kenzo Tange, Architecture and Urban Design 1946–1969*, Zürich, Verlag für Architektur Artemis, 1970, p. 20.

The Peace Center plan further melds "Eastern" and "Western" cultural tradition in its organization. Circulation systems, lawns, and plantings seem to reflect a number of cultural traditions. Straight paths and formal rows of trees represent Renaissance European formalism. Lawns and winding paths amalgamate Brownian romanticism with Japanese "natural" patterns, while the groupings of lower plant masses reflect the Japanese sensitivity to the creation of controlled environments.

Although representative of the dominance of the architect in urban design during its decades, the Peace Center illustrates awareness of the art of site planning, or the art or arranging an external physical environment in complete detail. The Peace Center, a place of community assembly, lay within the scope of a 15-year site plan for reconstructing an almost completely destroyed city.

# 22

# They Deal with
# Structures and the Land
## (United States, 1950–1965)

"Site planning is the art of arranging an external physical environment in complete detail. Site planners are all those who deal with structures and the land, whose plans can be carried out in one continuous foreseeable process, according to one original design, under the control of one agency, inclusive of all the details of engineering, landscaping, and architecture."[1] The art of site planning constitutes a process, rather than a specific skill applied by a specialized profession. Site planning, in the sense of arranging his external physical environment has existed, in at least rudimentary form, from the time of man's earliest self-consciousness.

The external forces of the natural environment (wind, sun, temperature, and rain or snow) dominated site-planning consideration during primitive times, while man learned to control his living spaces. As man gained competence in technology, site planning acquired social and symbolic aspects. After he learned civilized ways, organized external aspects of the physical surroundings became quite complex. In early civilizations, communities characteristically organized themselves in relation to symbolically chosen temple sites, located and oriented for spiritual reasons, and often in regard to the cardinal points of the compass (more precisely, related to the changing horizontal and vertical angles of the sun).

Throughout history, from that time to this, the site planning process has waxed and waned in importance, depending on whether it was dominated by arbitrary decision or based on the best understanding of cultural and physical conditions known at the time. The temples, palaces, and city of Peking, for example, founded as Cambulac, under the reign of Kublai Khan in about 1260 A.D., had its site and orientation carefully selected by soothsayers, on the basis of complex ritual. On the other hand, geography, defense, and strategic location dictated the origin and growth of the city of Paris. Originally an iron-age village built on what is now the Ile de la Cité for defense, Paris became, in Roman times, a strategic strong point at the juncture of a north-south military road through Gaul to the Germanic frontier, with the river Seine providing access to the English Channel.

As life has become ever more complex, planners have become ever more aware of the need for comprehensive site planning, so that programmed human activities could best fit a given set of physical circumstances. Today, site planning has a recognized status as a means of marrying program to site. The origin of the process may be traced at least back to 1495 when Leon Battista Alberti, in *De Architectura* (see also Appendix B) commented on the need, in selecting a house site, for considering wind direction, topography, potable water supply, firm ground, and availability of building materials.

---

[1]Reprinted from *Site Planning* by Kevin Lynch by permission of the M.I.T. Press, Cambridge, Massachusetts. Copyright © 1962 by the Massachusetts Institute of Technology.

All of these physical restraints have since been considered, in greater or less degree, with adaptations based on the owner's ego. You will recall, for example, Count Vitalione's decision in 1632 to rebuild a small, rocky island in Lago Maggiore into what he soon termed "Isola Bella" (Fig. 74). The site planning challenge here ignored, in fact defied, the natural exigencies of environment, so that the Count could express his own ego.

While it is true that the first half of the twentieth century saw many erroneous decisions made, based on the assumed values of those in the design professions from a small social class, by midcentury, planners had learned that values, habits, and objectives of the users, not the designer's own values, must dictate sound planning.

Typical user goals are:

1. Functional adequacy: Space adequate for the necessary or desired activities.
2. Optimum communication: Access to and from the site; adequate means of moving goods, people, and information within the site.
3. Freedom of choice: Where individuals are concerned, allowance of maximum choice human interaction.
4. Cost: Achievement of the development at least cost in labor, materials, and organizational effort. (Note: a cost that is still frequently ignored involves long-term maintenance costs, beyond initial construction costs.)
5. Health and comfort: Health, safety, comfort of users.
6. Adaptability: Flexibility of site arrangement to adapt to future modifications of function. (Example: a military base, upon abandonment, might become a school complex.)
7. Image quality: Visual form, conveying integration into a unified whole, and displaying to the world, in visual form, the site's function.

The above systematized checklist has to do with activities and facilities programmed to fit a site. We next consider the site itself, as it provides potentials for, and sets limits on, the program.

During less-technologically developed times, man's recognition of site potential and limitation was necessarily more advanced than today. Today's machinery, literally capable of moving mountains, gives men the technical capability of creating any sort of site surface deemed desirable. Men dredge up whole new living-recreational complexes along the coastlines of Florida, new Venices by the thousands of hectares, with spacious house lots lying conveniently between auto roadways and motorboat canals. Planners now have the technical skill to build whole new cities anchored in the seas just off the coastline, such as the new city planned by Kenzo Tange for Tokyo's harbor.

Fortunately (or unfortunately, depending on one's point of view), in most places such violent departures from acceptance of natural site potential and limitation are not yet considered necessary or economically feasible.

One thing is certain. Each site is unique, because of the complexity of the forms and patterns of which it is constituted.

Site planners today take for granted that thorough investigation of existing site-conditions proves a necessary preliminary step to adequate arrangement of physical elements for man's use on that site.

Such investigations include:

1. *Subsurface.* Geologic (rock) structure undergirds the whole of the earth's surface. For each site, the type of rock and its depth below the surface places limits on, or provides potential values to, whatever is to be constructed. In most places, for instance, it is uneconomical to erect a high-rise structure on soils where bedrock lies more than 100 feet below the surface. On the other hand, below-grade structures may be infeasible where bedrock appears too close to the surface.

Rock structure and its chemical composition dictate the type of soil appearing on the site, which in turn effects the level of the water table and the percolation of water more or less horizontally through such soil. Some soils readily support building foundations, roadways, and paths, while others prove unstable for such uses.

2. *Surface soil* (most often referred to as topsoil). Closely related to subsurface soils, topsoil dictates the kinds of trees, shrubs, and other plants growing on the site. Vegetative cover, its kind and density, in turn provide habitat for native animal life. Whether or not these last may be considered important to planners, of course depends on the goals and objectives about the land's use. On the other hand, in our present state of ecology-mindedness, the life cycles inherent on sites may often determine kinds and intensities of uses to which the site should be put, depending on the quality and uniqueness of the site's living communities.

3. *Surface characteristics unique to each site.* These include the plant and animal communities, and, just as importantly to proposed uses, the topography, or land form. Land form often determines plan organization. Designers must relate planned activities to topographic features as they indicate placement of buildings, as they provide or limit movement about the site, and as they dictate land uses.

Land-slope varies from flat to very steep. Extremely flat sites create problems in removal of surface water. Very steep slopes make movement up and down them difficult, and cause erosion problems. Experience has shown that where surface erosion can occur, it probably will. Over time, erosion tends to increase, unless sometimes-costly measures are taken to prevent it.

Topography also provides, on high ground, opportunities for commanding views, while valleys permit natural-land-form enclosures, creating areas protected from the elements.

The critical element, more frequently recognized today, is that man's excessive disturbance of the natural topography tends to create troublesome and, in extreme cases, hazardous effects on life and property—witness the mud slides prevalent on the California coast.

4. *Climate and microclimate.* Each site, exposed to wind, sun, rain, snow, and temperature fluctuations, has its own unique properties dependent on topography, and its relation to sun and wind. South-facing slopes obviously receive more energy from the

sun than north-facing ones. Hill crests provide barriers to winds, as they cause the force of gusts to deviate upward, creating pockets of calm on their downwind side.

Adequacy of rainfall may help determine the type and extent of vegetative cover needed to control the ground surface. Conformation of the land and its exposure to wind may determine location of snow drifts in those geographic areas subject to snowfall. Frost and fog pockets may occur in certain kinds of topographic situations.

Beyond these general considerations, within the site may exist microclimatic conditions substantially differing from one part of the site to another.

While we have discussed site conditions as nature provided them, most sites today are located where man has had impact. Man-created site factors include:

1.  Accessibility of the site to external facilities, such as schools, shopping, places to work, or sources of labor supply or raw materials, and the transportation network that serves the site.
2.  Relationship of site to human activities in its immediate vicinity. Obviously, certain human activities are incompatible with others, as a cement plant next-door to a housing area. We ask the question (or should) will our site be a good neighbor to adjacent land uses, or will the neighbors be compatible to our proposed land use?
3.  Service facilities, such as water, gas, electricity, and sanitary sewage installations must be available, or be provided within the economic limit of project feasibility. The more urban the site, the more these man-made conditions influence site possibilities.
4.  Legal restrictions, such as zoning, subdivision regulations, building codes, tend to provide or limit opportunities for site development, as well as established rights of way, easements, or deed restrictions.

In any case, site planners approach site analysis in two ways. Personal visits to the chosen site provide to the trained mind a mental image of the site and its potential. Then, with a detailed survey in hand (a plan of the site indicating topography, natural and man-made features, property boundaries, and access roads) the planner records thereon his visual and aural impressions, to assist him in remembering, as he proceeds with his plans, the many and varied conditions which tend to control how he uses the site.

Figure 133 shows a portion of a typical site survey. It records existing vegetation, topography (by dotted and dashed contour lines), existing streams, rock outcroppings, as well as such man-made features as roads and available underground utilities (sanitary sewer denoted S; storm drain, SD; water lines, W). At "a" the land is relatively flat (2-foot rise from left to right in 90 feet), while at "b" it is steep (2-foot rise or drop in 10 feet).

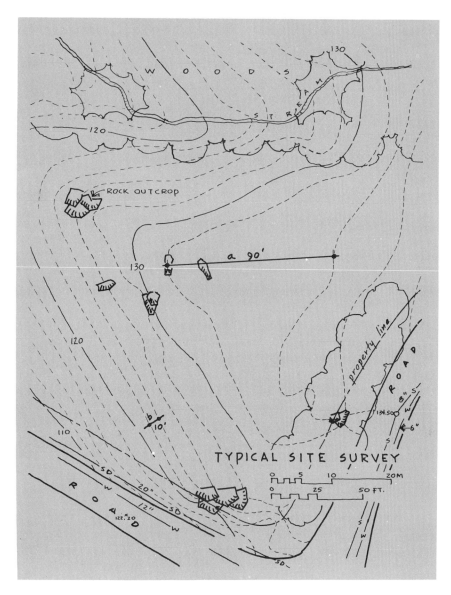

FIGURE 133

The land-use program called for low rent housing. Therefore, site analysis included studies relating the desired housing density to the existing land features. Apparently (see Fig. 134, planned development on the site shown in Fig. 133), planning demanded considerable open space for amenity and play space for children. Consequently, the site planner chose to wrap the housing units around the level area, thus preserving it, and also providing a roadway encircling the units. Obviously, economics and desired housing density dictated, in this case, eliminating existing trees and placing the existing stream underground in a storm drain.

Each site and the land uses programmed for it require unique approaches to site analysis and site planning, as illustrated in Fig. 135. In an urban area, the site at first might appear restrictive, considering the number and scale of functions planned for it (Fig. 135). However, the site planner (a landscape architect), with the architect's collaboration, used the site to full advantage, providing the Fireman's Fund Insurance Company with the desired image, as well as providing optimum amenity.

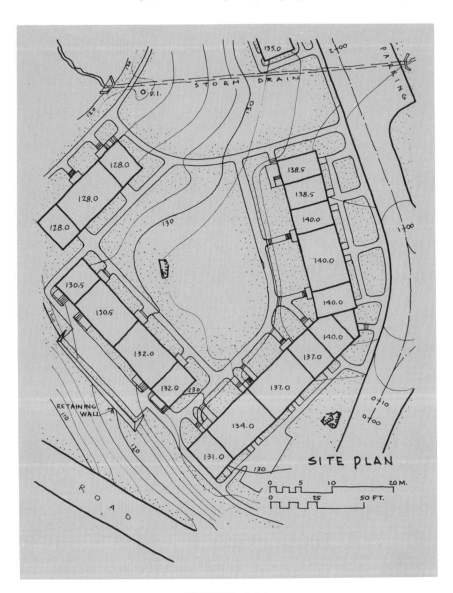

FIGURE 134

Considerable care was taken in the arrangement of the building, parking areas, and levels to save all existing trees. Some of the trees were left on mounds of earth where the ground was depressed, and others were contained in wells where the ground was raised. In all cases, special pruning, feeding, aeration, and watering were done during construction to help the trees make the necessary adjustments.

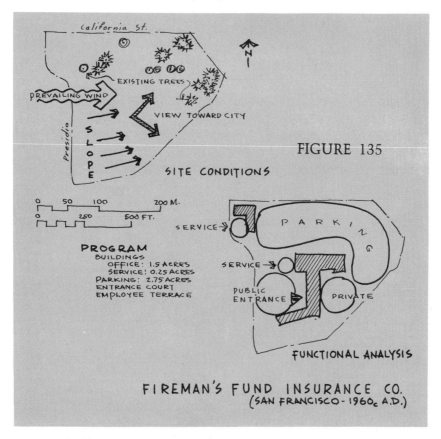

Courtesy Edward B. Page, Architect (Adaptation).

The most impressive of the trees saved are the beautiful specimens of Monterey cypress in the parking area on the California-Street side of the building. Here, too, three very large blue gums are retained. In some ways, the most distinctive specimens saved are the large red-flowering eucalyptus near the corner of California and Presidio, and the magnificent native toyon or Christmas berry in the parking area above Presidio. In addition to these, six live oaks and a very large redwood and Monterey pine are saved.[2]

[2]Eckbo, Garrett, *Urban Landscape Design*, New York, McGraw-Hill, 1964, p. 47.

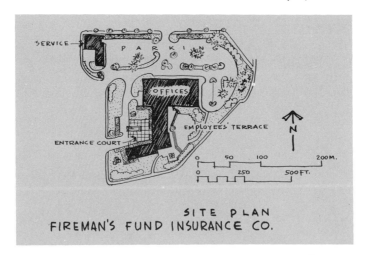

FIGURE 136

SITE PLAN
FIREMAN'S FUND INSURANCE CO.

Courtesy Edward B. Page, Architect (Adaptation)

Eckbo carefully tucked the employees' terrace into the building angle, away from the prevailing wind, and depressed it to insure privacy (Fig. 136).

Contrast the opportunities and restrictions embodied in an urban site with the broader, more complex, potentials and limitations in the site planning of a rural site (see Figs. 137–140).

Simonds and Simonds, landscape architects in Pittsburgh, received a commission to evaluate a piece of farm property in western Pennsylvania, to determine its feasibility as a high-school site. Once they had received the topographic survey of the site (Fig. 137) and had looked into the geological, political, and climatic conditions governing its use,[3] the next logical step in the site-planning process was to visit the site, with a copy of the topographic survey, for purposes of evaluating, in person, potentialities and limitations inherent in the existing site conditions.

The on-site examination revealed (in view of intended land use), among the items noted on Figure 138, that the key to best site-use was the purchase of a triangular piece of the adjacent farm to the south. Interestingly enough, the owner of this piece of ground proved to be extremely sympathetic to the idea of establishing a high school on the proposed site, and therefore was willing to negotiate, thus making optimum site-utilization possible. Site planning includes broad ramifications in the area of human relations, beyond the purely physical realities. This example points out the complexities of the site planning process. Since environmental design invariably involves people, their reactions to the designer's intent must be an integral part of the design process. In the case in point, the neighbor proved favorably inclined to the general intent. Experienced planners realize, of course, that this fortuitous circumstance is relatively rare. More frequently, neighboring landowners tend to resist change.

The personal site visit proved its importance further in the example as it showed several alternatives for locating school structures as well as natural features desirable to preserve, possible vehicular entry points, and problems (for example, moving of an electric utility line).

---

[3]Geological studies showed that coal resources underlaid part of the site and that there had been an oil well drilled elsewhere on the farm property. The county controlled one of the bounding roads, the township the other. An operating strip mine lay north of the site, while land to the south was being farmed.

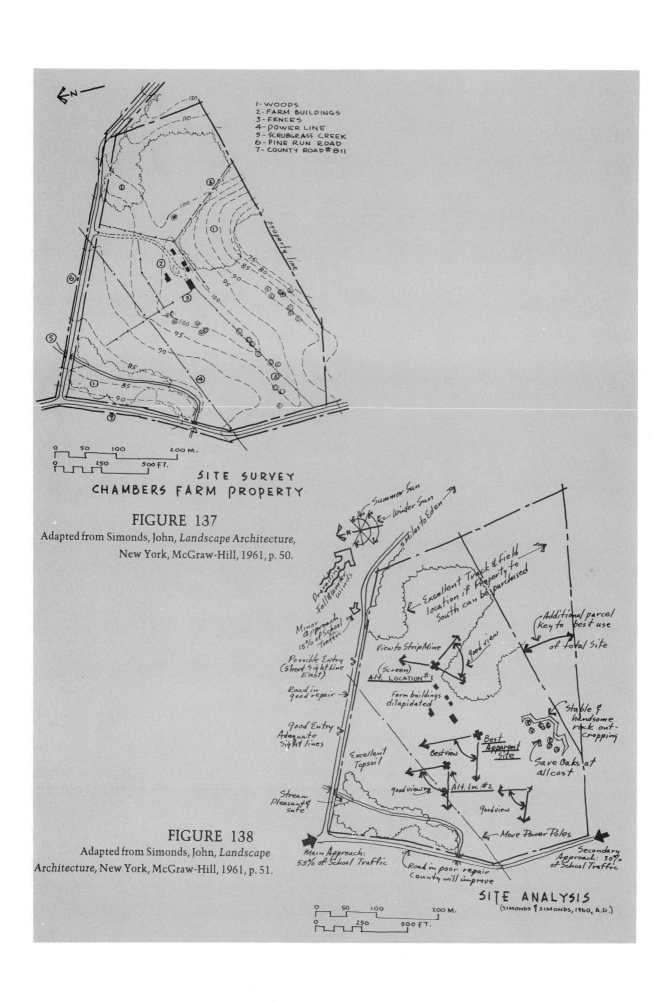

1 - WOODS
2 - FARM BUILDINGS
3 - FENCES
4 - POWER LINE
5 - SCRUBGRASS CREEK
6 - PINE RUN ROAD
7 - COUNTY ROAD #811

SITE SURVEY
CHAMBERS FARM PROPERTY

FIGURE 137
Adapted from Simonds, John, *Landscape Architecture*,
New York, McGraw-Hill, 1961, p. 50.

FIGURE 138
Adapted from Simonds, John, *Landscape
Architecture*, New York, McGraw-Hill, 1961, p. 51.

Summer Sun
Winter Sun
5 Miles to Eden

Prevailing Fall & Winter Winds

Excellent Track & field location if Property to South can be purchased

Additional parcel Key to best use of total site

Minor approach 15% of School Traffic

View to Strip Mine

Good view

Possible Entry (Short Sight Line East)

(Screen) Alt. LOCATION #1

Stable & handsome rock out-cropping

Road in good repair

Farm buildings dilapidated

Save Oaks at all cost

Good Entry Adequate Sight lines

Best Apparent Site

Excellent Topsoil

Best view

Good view

Alt. Loc. #2

Good view

Stream Pleasant & safe

Good view

Move Power Poles

Main Approach: 55% of School Traffic

Road in poor repair County will improve

Secondary Approach: 30% of School Traffic

SITE ANALYSIS
(SIMONDS & SIMONDS, 1960, A.D.)

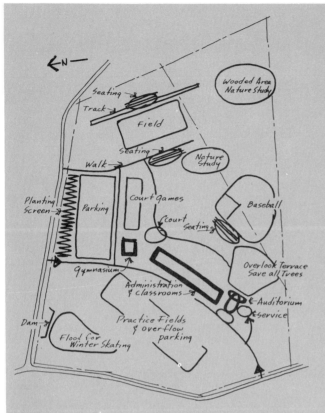

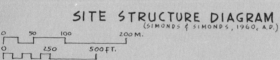

## SITE STRUCTURE DIAGRAM
(SIMONDS & SIMONDS, 1960ᶜ A.D.)

### FIGURE 139

Adapted from Simonds, John, *Landscape Architecture*,
New York, McGraw-Hill, 1961, p. 52.

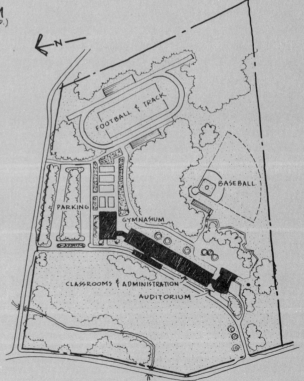

### FIGURE 140

Adapted from Simonds, John, *Landscape Architecture*,
New York, McGraw-Hill, 1961, p. 53.

## SITE PLAN
(SIMONDS & SIMONDS - 1960ᶜ A.D.)

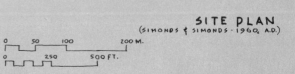

Site analysis goes far beyond property boundaries, as indicated by the notations about travel to and from the selected site by the potential users. The wise site-planner understands that a specific site must be evaluated in its total relationship to the world into which the site and its proposed uses are to fit.

Based on careful site analysis, the planners prepared a series of studies, each of which attempted to take full advantage of the potentials of the site, while recognizing its limitations. Figure 139 illustrates one such study. Such studies reveal functionally sound relationships of the required land uses and determine the land area required for each, including access points to the site, and the paths of circulation among the various elements, once the user gets to the site.

Site structure diagrams, after careful study by the design team, evolve into a final decision, selecting from among numerous alternatives, the one (in this case, Fig. 140), which seems best to meet all the design criteria.

Then, and only then, the site plan (Fig. 140) was prepared in measured detail for presentation to the client for his approval. Compare the site structure diagram with the site plan. In the structure diagram, the landscape architects felt the stream could well be utilized as an amenity and provide an additional source of winter activity. In the accepted site plan, however, apparently for reasons of economy, the proposed dam and skating pond have been left out.

Perhaps the school board (the client) will, in later years, find it wise to add the skating pond to the school site facilities. Planning involves mutual establishment of priorities for site development, by both planner and client. As mentioned earlier, and as here illustrated, site planning must consider not only the static development of immediate needs, but must be flexible enough to permit change as future needs become apparent.[4]

Site planning also proves a valuable tool to the design professions as a tool for organization of relatively complex functions on large sites in the context of our highly industrialized society.

General Motors Technical Center occupies 325 hectares (800 acres) on a flat plain north of the city of Detroit, Michigan. The design team frankly recognized the rectilinear geometry of the site (Fig. 141), organizing the programmed activities and structures as a series of interrelated rectangles, in plan, around a patently geometric lake. The rigidly geometric plant masses complement a series of complex cubic building forms, creating a three-dimensional image of highly sophisticated order.

It should be noted that this automotive research center is scaled to its purpose. The individual person, unless moving through the site in a car, feels out of place, overwhelmed by the immensity of the visual spaces; yet, moving from place to place in the complex in a car that feeling of vastness is no longer apparent.

In contrast, examine Figure 142, the plan for the campus of the National University of Mexico, located in the Pedregal, a site of volcanic origin south of Mexico City. Here is a site of approximately the same scope as General Motors Technical Center, yet the programmed activities are of a much higher order of complexity and are scaled to people,

---

[4]Figures 137–140 adapted from Simonds, John O., *Landscape Architecture, The Shaping of Man's Natural Enrivonment*, New York, F.W. Dodge Corp., 1961.

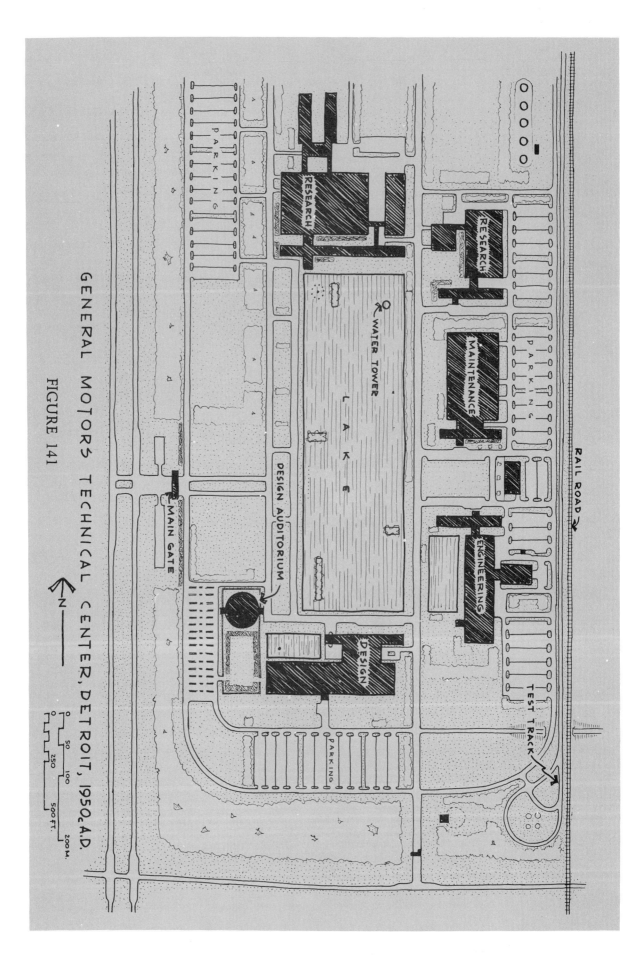

GENERAL MOTORS TECHNICAL CENTER, DETROIT, 1950₌A.D.

FIGURE 141

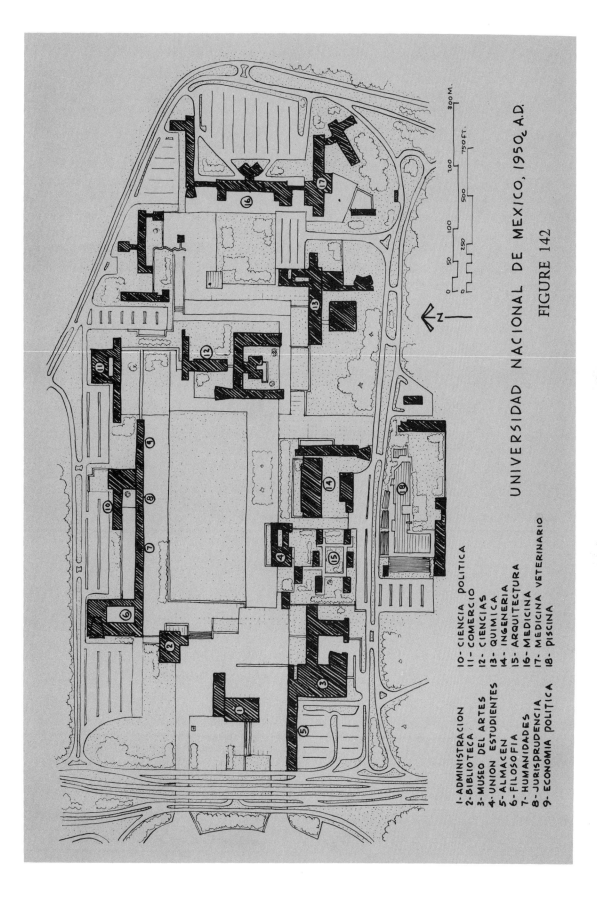

1- ADMINISTRACION
2- BIBLIOTECA
3- MUSEO DEL ARTES
4- UNION ESTUDIENTES
5- ALMACEN
6- FILOSOFIA
7- HUMANIDADES
8- JURISPRUDENCIA
9- ECONOMIA POLITICA

10- CIENCIA POLITICA
11- COMERCIO
12- CIENCIAS
13- QUIMICA
14- INGENERIA
15- ARQUITECTURA
16- MEDICINA
17- MEDICINA VETERINARIO
18- PISCINA

UNIVERSIDAD NACIONAL DE MEXICO, 1950c A.D.

FIGURE 142

rather than cars. All this is accomplished through an intelligent ordering of functional relationships, taking advantage of the geologic reality of grade changes necessitated by the relatively rugged terrain. The campus is ordered, by virtue of the visual order of building-mass relationships. Despite the apparent (in plan) huge scale of this cosmopolitan campus[5], the individual student or casual visitor can move from classroom to classroom, even across the large quandrangle, and still feel a comfortable sense of "belonging." Whether one's sense of "human" scale is engendered by the colorful mosaics covering the facades of the major buildings, by the sensation of visual order, or the fact that spatial relationships vary from obviously public to intimate is difficult to tell. One only knows that the campus of the University of Mexico, despite its obvious national scale, relates to its most important users, the students, and to their perception of their academic environment.

[5]The scale of the University may be illustrated by noting that in 1964 the School of Architecture (No. 15, Fig. 142) alone enrolled 5,000 students.

# 23

# Perception
## (Behavior and Images, 1950–1965)

The design professional has consistently, throughout history, acted as form giver. Beginning with the earliest known town planner, Hippodamus of Miletus (fifth century, B.C.) designers, particularly in the Western World have concerned themselves with the intricate geometry of spaces for people.

The relatively simple grid patterns of Hippodamus became almost universal throughout the Greek and Roman world, overlaid, in the later centuries of Rome and Byzantium, with scale differences and elaboration of form concomitant with the sense of power and authority of that complex society known as the Roman Empire.

In the Middle Ages, a period of social reorganization, rectilinear geometric forms gave way to a more complex geometry (cf. Carcassonne, Figure 55) based on individual and group needs for survival in a turbulent world. During and after the Renaissance (1400–1600 A.D.), the forms of people-spaces tended again toward rectilinear geometry made more complex as wealth and power demanded flamboyancy (cf. Villa d'Este, Fontainebleau, Vaux-le-Vicomte, Versailles).[1]

With the eighteenth century, the industrial revolution induced a sense of revulsion against previously popular rigid geometry.

As technology created urbanism, a new social conscience emerged in society, exemplified in Olmsted's planning for Central Park, a park for all people.

Although, at the end of the ninteenth century and during the first decades of the twentieth century, society seemed to lose track of socially conscious planning, rapidly expanding technological advances spawned by the military-industrial complex of World Wars I and II created the extremely complex society we know today.

Modern society, involved as it is with superb, yet involuted devices for world communication seems not to have unified world thought, but increasingly tends to fragment it into a multilevel system of pressure groups, each seeking dominance. Perhaps the most influential factor producing this splintering effect is the knowledge explosion. New kinds of devices for collecting, storing, and collating scientific data have made us aware of just how complex our world is.

[1]Figs. 71, 78, 79, 80, 81.

A major outgrowth of the knowledge explosion is the fact that form-givers, though dimly aware in past centuries that they were designing for people, now accept with enthusiasm concepts psychologists and sociologists have begun to document through their research.

Robert Woods Kennedy,[2] wrote:

> In recent years the trend toward mass housing and the planned community has become increasingly marked. Since 1934 when the government first became actively engaged in housing, a long series of projects both public and private, have been planned and built.
>
> A remarkably large fraction of our population is already living in such planned communities and it now appears certain that this number will increase steadily. Yet, we have no idea of how well or poorly the existing projects function, socially speaking. The planning professions, faced for the first time with entire neighborhoods to design, find that they are dealing in a new dimension—that of the family's whole social life. Yet, they have little or no idea how this new dimension might affect physical design.[3]

The sudden influx, at the end of World War II, of returning veterans into institutions of higher learning, created a situation simple enough in form that sociologists could provide a beginning of understanding of the complex relationships among families in planned communities.

The Massachusetts Institute of Technology, in 1945, faced with the overwhelming task of providing educational facilities for married veterans, found it necessary to provide housing for returning servicemen and their families. The first of a large number of housing projects, in a period of acute housing shortage, was built, starting in the fall of 1945, near M.I.T. Westgate and Westgate West (see Fig. 143), designed by architectural students, financed in part by the University and the remainder by the federal government, attracted considerable attention, as meeting an immediate need.

Sociologists recognized the projects as an opportunity to investigate and document social interaction under controlled conditions with relatively well-defined parameters. Here was a relatively large sampling (270 families) of people whose economic status, goals and life styles were uniform enough so that these variables would not significantly complicate a scientific study of social interaction. By a series of surveys, the sociologists documented some significant facts relevant to social interaction of families as it related to the physical form of the community.

[2]Kennedy, Robert Woods, *The House and the Art of its Design*, New York, Reinhold, 1953.

[3]Quoted in Festinger, Leon, Schacter, Stanley, and Back, Kurt, *Social Pressures in Informal Groups; A Study of Human Factors in Housing*, Palo Alto, Calif., Stanford University Press, 1963, p. 202.

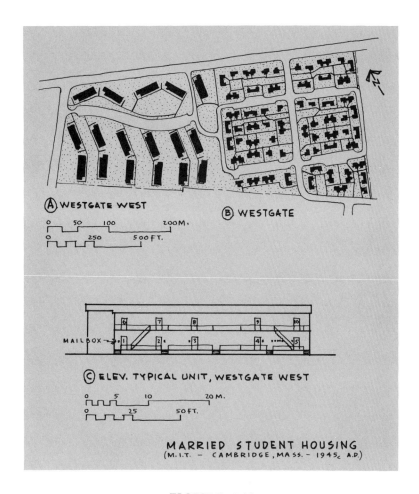

FIGURE 143

We must emphasize that this case study does not truly reflect the social interactions of the usual neighborhood. Westgate and Westgate West communities were, to say the least, extremely homogeneous as to economic status, social class, interests, and aspirations.[4]

However, the study documents the concept that given a relatively homogeneous population, physical relationships of housing units (the spatial characteristics of the environment) enhanced or diminished the possibilities of social relationships, depending on geographic distance. The effect of physical distance on the formation of friendships, in both Westgate and Westgate West was found by the investigators to be an important factor.

For instance, a study of the typical Westgate West unit (see Fig. 143) revealed that, for either floor, those living in adjacent apartments socialized with each other with much greater frequency than with those of more remote units, on a descending scale

[4]Ibid.

depending on whether the units were one, two, three, or four units removed from the case studied. This phenomenon occurred, despite the fact that the entire building was no more than 37 meters (120 feet) in length. Correspondingly, relationships between floors allowed for casual meetings of persons. At the cluster of mail boxes, social relationships took place with higher frequency.

Similar results were obtained from surveys of residents of Westgate (Fig. 144). Physical distance tended to control sociometric choices within a single court, and as well, between courts. Thus, in Figure 144, families "a" and "b" tended to get together for conversation, meals, or bridge more often than families "a" and "c". Less fraternizing took place, the more remote the units were from one another.

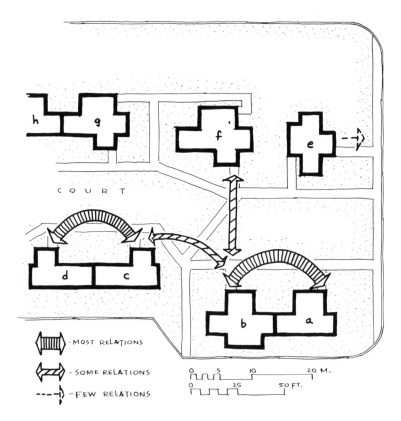

PLAN-TYPICAL COURT
WESTGATE

FIGURE 144

The investigators discovered an additional locational phenomenon as well. Unit "e" (Fig. 144), placed on the perimeter of the court and facing the encircling roadway, seemed, because of its physical location, to have the fewest opportunities in any court for establishing friendships. At first glance, most site planners will say: "Why, of course, that's obvious. The way one locates and orients buildings to one another is something we've known for years."

On the other hand, a survey of building groupings, especially housing complexes, will reveal that many times the sociological implications of structural relationships are neglected in favor of engineering implications, such as economy of utility location, and, with even greater frequency, the relation of buildings to vehicular communication routes and customary delivery services.

It is possible to gain a great deal of insight into social relations among dwellers in planned communities, in which socioeconomic differences among residents have been eliminated as variables. In a "normal" community, however, social relations become much more complex, since the occupants come from widely varied backgrounds, and pursue heterogeneous interests.

Ignoring for the moment the matter of neighborhood image, which we have found in large measure responsible for the informal social connections among residents of Westgate and Westgate West, the mere functional arrangement of housing units has been found by at least one group of planners to be extremely complex.

Chermayeff and Alexander, in *Community and Privacy*[5], attempted to correlate functional relationships affecting optimum dwelling-unit arrangement. They asked a computer to provide these relationships. It spewed out a systematic listing of relations among 33 elements necessary for adequate housing amenity. Thus, it became theoretically possible for site planners, through this kind of complex correlation, to create housing arrangements forming neighborhoods conducive to that neighborliness many find lacking in urban situations. [6]

The urban scene, prevalent as it is today in the United States, has created its own problems. A fairly large segment of New York City's urban population has been found to be at least neurotic, while a smaller portion has been found to have developed psychotic tendencies, almost to the point of requiring hospitalization. At least a part of these mental disturbances we may attribute to a sense of disorientation, in an environment so complex as to defy resolution of visual sense out of apparent chaos.

Kevin Lynch,[7] in *Image of the City*, states that urban dwellers visualize their environment in terms of landmarks, nodes, paths, and edges. That is, the resident of a place understands it in a way different from that of the planner, architect, engineer, and landscape architect. Designers are taught to be aware of precise relationships of scale, pattern, form, proportion and spatial distances, as in the scaled plan (Fig. 145) of the campus of the Ohio State University.

The visual character, however, of the campus in the minds of a group of architectural students is quite different (see Mental Image, Fig. 145). In this case, Lynch's "edges" for the student users of the campus, were High Street and the Olentangy River. The "oval" and Brown Hall became "nodes" to this specialized group of students, the oval being the dominant campus open space, Brown Hall being the building where they spent most time.

---

[5]Chermayeff, Sergius Ivan, Alexander, Christopher: *Community and Privacy; Toward a New Architecture of Humanism*, Garden City, N.Y. Doubleday, 1963.

[6]Chermayeff and Alexander, *op. cit.* pp. 160, 161.

[7]Lynch, Kevin; *Image of The City*, Cambridge, Mass. M.I.T. Press, 1960.

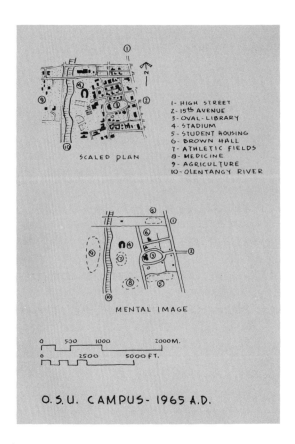

FIGURE 145

"Paths" to this group were only those ways they traversed to and from "home." Other paths, though clearly existent on the scaled plan, tend to become vague, or are nonexistent as mental images. So, too, are building groups rarely frequented by architectural students. In the survey from which the campus maps were prepared, architectural students knew that agriculture was "over there across the River" but its mental image, to them, was extremely vague. It would be interesting, some time, to survey a like group of agriculture students. Certainly their mental image of their environment would be quite different from that of the group used in the experiment.

Realizing the importance of mental image to urbanites in structuring their daily lives, planners are beginning to design with people and their needs in mind.

Lawrence Halprin, San Francisco landscape architect, was called in by the Portland, Oregon, Planning Commission to assist in a massive urban renewal project encompassing an eventual 54 downtown city blocks.

The core of the project was to consist of superblocks, containing apartments, shops, office and public buildings, and parks, all connected by tree-lined pedestrian-path systems. Halprin's open-space plan called for three park-like nodes, two as active, paved plazas filled with the sound of rushing waters, the third, in contrast, a quiet, earth-mounded retreat from urban sights and sounds.

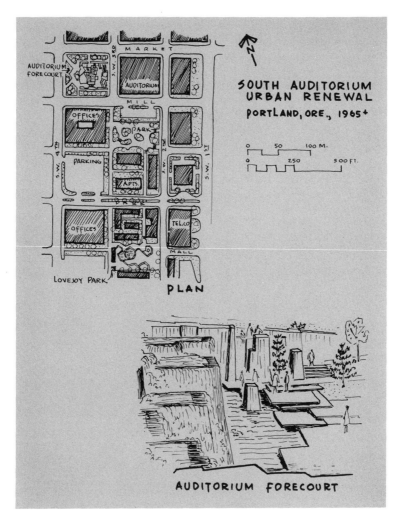

FIGURE 146

The greenways, plazas, fountains and waterfalls (see Auditorium Forecourt) were, in Halprin's words, to capture "the vigor and excitement associated with the City, to meet both the changeless and changing needs and to reveal in some degree the measureless possibilities of the urban landscape."[8]

That Halprin was concerned with the image is inherent in his design concept, particularly that for the Auditorium Forecourt. The plaza reflects, in urbanized form, the mountainous terrain of Oregon, and through the excitement of moving water on a grand scale, proves a major attraction in the city's core.

[8]Halprin, Lawrence, *South Auditorium Urban Renewal Project* Portland, Oregon Planning Commission, 1964.

Halprin's understanding of basic human needs is illustrated by the pools associated with the waterfalls, which nearly always find barefooted urbanites walking and splashing in them. Whether in daylight or under artifical light at night, Portland's plazas provide a central stage for the life of Portland's people.

Urban design today, in contrast to the earlier "City Beautiful" movement, begins to create spaces for the interaction of people.

Yet, the earth still abides, while we, with our highly efficient tools, have learned to exploit her. We are just beginning to learn that "we may modify our environment only so far without initiating chains of irremediable disaster; water, soil, and atmosphere may be tampered with only so much before they become unusable."[9]

[9]Levenson, David *A Sense of the Earth*, Garden City, N.Y. The Natural History Press. 1971, p. 31.

# 24             Earth Day Every Day
(United States, 1965–1970)

"I wish to speak a word for Nature, for absolute freedom and wildness, as contrasted with a freedom and culture merely civil,—to regard man as an inhabitant, or a part and parcel of Nature, rather than a member of society. I wish to make an extreme statement, if so I may make an emphatic one, for there are enough champions of civilization: the minister and the school-committee and every one of you will take care of that."[1]

"Whereas (others) think that the earth made man, man in fact made the earth."[2]

"Tomorrow is a day, and the past is a 'bucket of ashes.' The American Frontier has ceased to recede, so at last we have come to that dead-end marked by the 'No Trespassing' sign at the boundary of the last few thousand acres of natural landscape."[3]

"The unprecedented power man has achieved for modifying or destroying ecosystems at will, coupled with our slender knowledge of the ramifying consequences of such activity, is appalling in view of our continued dependence on the proper functioning of many ecosystems."[4]

"There are many people who look to nature for meaning and order, peace and tranquility, introspection and stimulus. Many more look to nature and activity in the outdoors as the road to restoration and health."[5]

"Modern earth knowledge and the beginnings of geology as a science originated from the establishment of a different set of ground rules, those formulated by James Hutton in the eighteenth century, subsequently known as the Doctrine of Uniformitarianism. According to this doctrine, nature and the earth are not arbitrary or capricious, but follow knowable, predictable and unchanging patterns of cause and effect. Earth processes, it was claimed, are understandable—if we but have the patience and ingenuity to understand them—and from earth forms evolved by earth processes, earth

---

[1]Thoreau, Henry David, from his essay entitled "Walking," first published in *The Atlantic Monthly* in 1862. Quoted here from *Walden*, New York, The Modern Library, 1937, p. 597.

[2]Marsh, George Perkins, *Man and Nature*, Cambridge, Mass., Belknap Press, Harvard University Press, 1965. p. 20. Originally published 1864.

[3]Lewis, Phillip H., *Recreation and Open Space in Illinois*, Division of Landscape Architecture and Community Planning, University of Illinois, Urbana, Illinois, September, 1961. p. xiii.

[4]Daubenmire, Rexford, *Plant Communities*, New York, Harper & Row, 1969. p. x.

[5]McHarg, Ian L., *Design With Nature*, Garden City, New York, p. 5.

229

history may be inferred. Thus, the mountain, the valley, the curiously balanced rock are not gods or their imprint but the result and record of earth movement and erosion, a statement of the present, momentary balance achieved between creation and decay."[6]

The statements you have just read span a century of concern for the quality of environment in the narrow bank of air space, land, water and soil occupied by mankind. This same concern prompted the "Aquarian" generation, in April 1970, to sponsor Earth Day and to coin the motto, "Earth Day Every Day".

These young people, considered by the "establishment" as rebels against society, in reality, expressed the same feelings as Thoreau, and, in much the same way, made "an extreme statement (to) make an emphatic one, for there are enough champions of civilization."[7]

Each of the men previously quoted, further, had an all-consuming curiosity about natural systems, which in their complex ways, make up the only environment we know that is capable of permitting mankind to survive on "Space-ship Earth."

Thus, McHarg could say:

> Many of the problems that society confronts are of such inordinate complexity that it takes the greatest dedication and zeal to assemble the necessary data, analyze and prescribe. Happily there are other problems, where a very small perception can produce astonishing results. If one accepts the simple proposition that nature is the arena of life and that a modicum of knowledge of her processes is indispensable for survival and rather more for survival, health and delight, it is amazing how many apparently difficult problems present ready resolution.
>
> . . . Clearly the problem of man and nature is not one of providing a decorative background for the human play, or even ameliorating the grim city: it is the necessity of sustaining nature as a source of life, milieu, teacher, sanctum, challenge, and, most of all, of rediscovering nature's corollary of the unknown in the self, the course of meaning.
>
> . . . Where else can we turn for an accurate model of the world and ourselves but to science? We can accept that scientific knowledge is incomplete and will forever be so, but it is the best we have and it has that great merit, which religions lack, of being self-correcting.[8]

In illustration of the principles inculcated by McHarg and other contemporary landscape architects and land planners, examine a series of studies prepared by fourth and fifth year students in landscape architecture, conducted at The Ohio State University during the academic year 1968–1969.

[6]Leveson, David, *op. cit.* p. 28.

[7]Thoreau, *op. cit.*, p. 597.

[8]From *Design with Nature* by Ian L. McHarg. Copyright © 1968 by Ian L. McHarg. Reprinted by permission of Doubleday & Company, Inc.; pp. 7, 19.

The University's School of Natural Resources at that time felt the need to establish a Field Study Center of sufficient acreage to permit student and faculty research and practical class exercises within the five disciplines drawn together in the School. These disciplines include: Forestry; Fish and Wildlife Management; Resource Development; Park Administration and Recreation; and Outdoor Education.

The students posed these questions to themselves and to the chairmen of the five divisions of the school:

1. What kind of topography would best suit the teaching-research needs of all five disciplines?
2. How much land would acceptably accommodate the studies each discipline would want to conduct?
3. How far away from the central campus could the center lie, and still meet teaching-research programs conveniently?
4. What level of land-purchase costs could be acceptable to the School's budget?

A series of conferences with personnel of the School of Natural Resources established the following site location and selection criteria:

1. The site selected should have:
   a. As wide a variety of topographic features as possible, including open fields; successional and mature forested areas; steep, rolling, and relatively flat topography; ample pure surface and underground water supplies.
   b. A diversity of geologic and soil features, which in turn would produce diverse vegetation and native animal life.
   c. Reasonably high levels of amenity in terms of aesthetic quality, since the field study center would be a semipublic facility.
2. Site acreage to accommodate the diversity of potential activities should be no less than 500 acres, preferably closer to 1,000 acres. The site should also be so located as to be protected from incompatible adjacent land uses.
3. The site should lie close enough to the main campus in Columbus so that faculty and students could reach it within one hour's driving time. Any further distance would create unacceptable travel times.
4. Land-purchase economics indicated that, for the intended uses, land costs should be kept to a minimum.

On the basis of the established criteria, the site selection process began with qualitative analyses of the entire state of Ohio (see Figs. 147–155).

Study of program requirements indicated that, due to the widely diverse needs of the five disciplines included in the School of Natural Resources, the optimum site should be one with the greatest diversity in topographic and geologic features. Examination of geologic maps of Ohio showed that (see Fig. 147) the greatest diversity occurred along the line established millennia ago at the edge of glacial activity. The basic geology to the west of this line included limestone bedrock. To the east of the line lay sandstone bedrock. Ecological studies revealed that the greatest diversity in superficial features (including admixtures of different plant and animal species) would occur along such an edge, or ecotone.[9]

OHIO · MAJOR ECOTONE

FIGURE 147

Minor edges, or ecotones, also occurred along the zones where subsidiary glacial moraines had been deposited, as well as in areas along the shores of Lake Erie and the Ohio River (see Fig. 148).

Analysis of vegetative maps of the state revealed certain areas to be heavily forested, others to have less dense woodlands, while large portions had been virtually denuded of forest by man's activities. Since Forestry is a discipline vital to the School of Natural Resources, one of the selection criteria included picking a site which contained reasonable forest cover (Fig. 149).

[9]An "ecotone" is an area where differing plant and animal species meet and tend to overlap; thus an ecotone becomes a series of overlapping "edges."

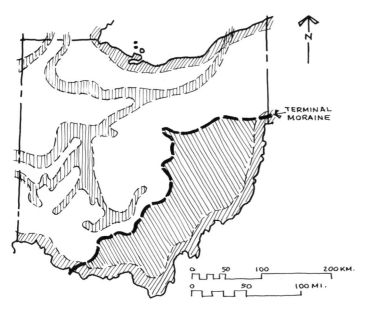

OHIO - MINOR ECOTONES

▨ - GLACIAL MORAINES
▨ - STREAM, LAKE EDGES
▨ - STEEP TOPOGRAPHY

**FIGURE 148**

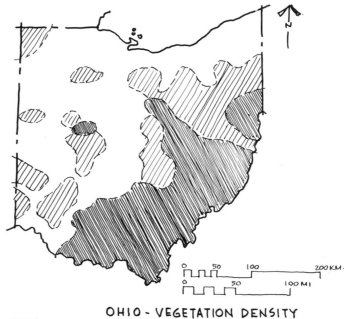

OHIO - VEGETATION DENSITY

□ - SPARSE
▨ - MEDIUM
▨ - DENSE

**FIGURE 149**

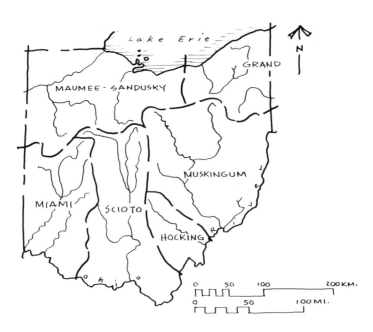

OHIO - RIVER BASINS

FIGURE 150

The matter of unpolluted surface water supply next became important as a selection guide. It seemed logical that surface water would tend to be less polluted in the upper parts of river basins. Discussions with personnel in the State Division of Water Resources proved this conclusion to be reasonable. Therefore (Fig. 150), careful examination of the headwaters of the six river basins greatly assisted site selection.

Fish and wildlife management being an important field of study in the School, underground water supplies for supplementing stream flow (necessarily less in upstream portions of watersheds) had to be considered for the establishment of ponds and to assure year-round water supplies. Figure 151 illustrates where the most adequate supplemental water supplies in the state lie.

Consideration of the needs of the Parks division of the School, and discussions with its director, Dr. Harold Schick, indicated that it probably would be impractical to include public parklands within the scope of the proposed Field Study Center. The State of Ohio has an already existent broad range of parks and forests. It remained, therefore, to establish the Field Study Center in a location near existing parks or forests, rather than to create a new park or forest within the field study center acreage (see Fig. 152).

Several factors involving site selection were next considered. First, the large acreage requirement meant the selected site should be in a relatively rural area, where large land holdings were prevalent. In view of travel time limitations, the site should, though in a rural area, be reasonably close to a major transportation artery (see Fig. 153).

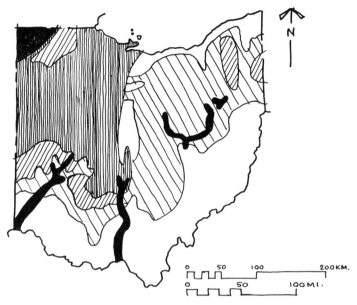

OHIO - UNDERGROUND WATER RESOURCES

- over 500 gallons/min.
- 500 - 100   "   "   "
- 100 - 25   "   "   "
- 25 - 5   "   "   "
- UNDER 5   "   "   "

FIGURE 151

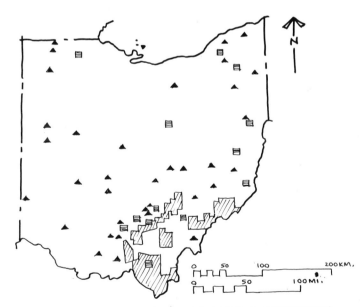

OHIO - PARKS & RECREATION RESOURCES

FIGURE 152

▲ - STATE PARK
☰ - STATE FOREST
▨ - NATIONAL FOREST

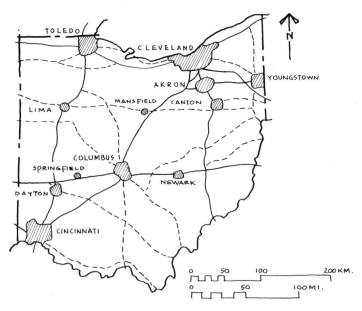

OHIO - TRANSPORTATION NETWORK

—— - INTERSTATE HY.
---- - U.S. HY.
▨ -CITY

**FIGURE 153**

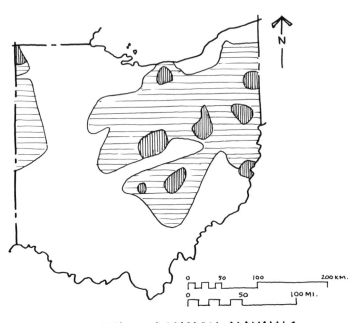

OHIO - COMMON MAMMALS

**FIGURE 154**    ▥ -MAJOR CONCENTRATION
▤ -MINOR CONCENTRATION

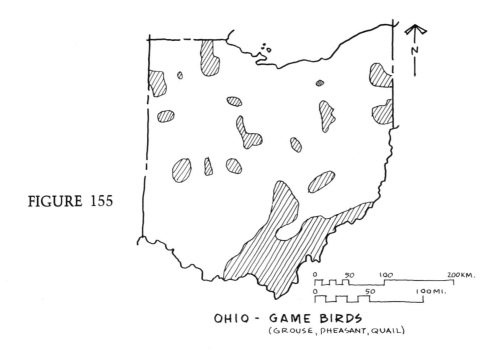

FIGURE 155

**OHIO – GAME BIRDS**
(GROUSE, PHEASANT, QUAIL)

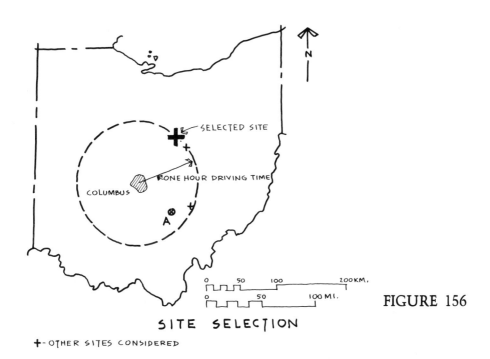

SELECTED SITE

ONE HOUR DRIVING TIME

COLUMBUS

A

FIGURE 156

**SITE SELECTION**

✝ – OTHER SITES CONSIDERED

Wild animal and bird life go hand-in-hand with nature study, fish and wildlife management, development of resources, forestry, and park management. A knowledge of the prevalent habitats of wildlife was therefore a concomitant study (see Figs. 154 and 155).

Collecting base data, from widely dispersed sources, and recording it as a uniform system for analysis, made the resultant site selection possible. Numerous further studies of U.S.G.S. topographic maps (7½ minute quadrangles) and aerial photographs in stereopairs, enabled students to narrow their selection to a much smaller area than the entire state. A circle, drawn on the state map representing one hour's driving time showed that, in the eastern half of the circle, some four to six sites came reasonably close to meeting all the requirements of the program (see Fig. 156).

The site finally selected by the student group was one which conceivably could be easily purchased by assembling two farms, contained within a limiting road network, and thereby creating a controlled site. In addition, it met reasonably well all the selection criteria.

| Reasons for Site Selection | Site Values |
|---|---|
| 1. Within glacial ecotone | Diverse wildlife habitats |
| 2. Dense vegetation | Suited to forestry studies |
| 3. In upper watershed | Pure surface water |
| 4. Excellent ground water supply | Adequate supplemental water supply |
| 5. Near State Forest | Recreation studies |
| 6. Rural area | Land economics |
| 7. Near highway network | Ease of access |
| 8. Away from urban centers | Protected environs |
| 9. Major wildlife concentration | Wildlife studies |
| 10. Within stipulated driving time | Convenience of access |
| 11. Acreage | 279–283 hectares (690–700 acres) |

The site selected from among several, all of which had many of the necessary qualities, showed on analysis to be an admirable choice, because of the location, the wide diversity of land forms within it, and the diversity of open and forested lands (see Fig. 157).

The most significant fact of the student selection of this site, based on the methods of ecological determinism was that it proved the value of the method. It is of interest that the then-Director of the School, Dr. Charles Dambach commented on the selection: "Oh, that site includes Arbutus Glen." Arbutus Glen, a sandstone ravine lined with hemlocks, had long been noted as a prime natural studies site.

Studies of topographic maps and aerial photographs of the selected site, supplemented by personal inspection on the ground by the students concerned, reinforced their feeling that the site would be admirably suited to its intended purposes. Evaluation of topography, vegetation, and natural resources inherent to the site (Fig. 157, 158), proved that Arbutus Glen and its surrounding environs could well supply the various research and study needs of the School of Natural Resources.

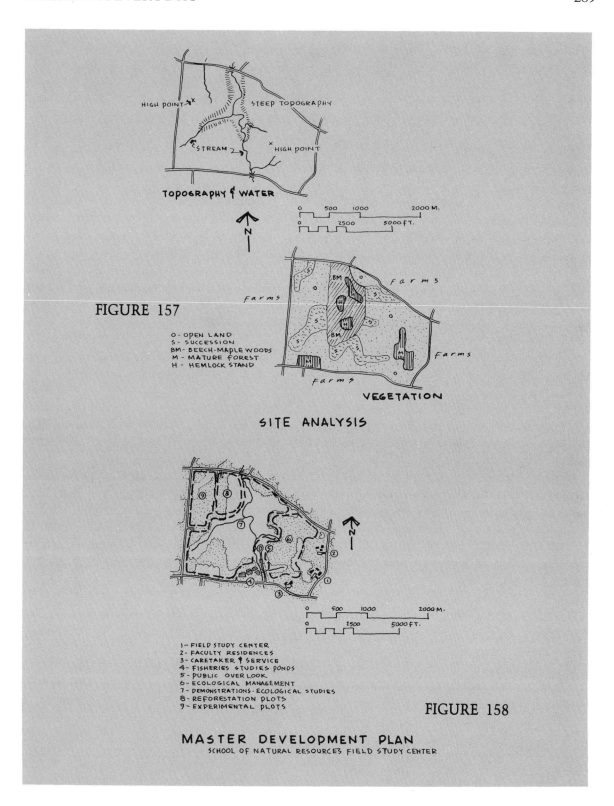

FIGURE 157

TOPOGRAPHY & WATER

O - OPEN LAND
S - SUCCESSION
BM - BEECH-MAPLE WOODS
M - MATURE FOREST
H - HEMLOCK STAND

VEGETATION

SITE ANALYSIS

1 - FIELD STUDY CENTER
2 - FACULTY RESIDENCES
3 - CARETAKER & SERVICE
4 - FISHERIES STUDIES PONDS
5 - PUBLIC OVERLOOK
6 - ECOLOGICAL MANAGEMENT
7 - DEMONSTRATIONS - ECOLOGICAL STUDIES
8 - REFORESTATION PLOTS
9 - EXPERIMENTAL PLOTS

FIGURE 158

MASTER DEVELOPMENT PLAN
SCHOOL OF NATURAL RESOURCES FIELD STUDY CENTER

On this informational and qualitative base, a Master Development Plan (Fig. 158) was prepared to demonstrate the site's land-use capabilities for its intended purposes.

Though the illustrated site did not become the final choice for a Natural Resources Field Study Center, the inherent values of the method of site selection, evaluation, and planning were proven to students and teachers alike.

Of further interest is a site-selection factor which has nothing to do with the scientific site-selection process, but which often produces desired results. This factor is serendipity, or the accidental discovery of a happy resultant, while searching for other conclusions.

A friend of the University, Mr. Barnebey, having learned of the search by the School of Natural Resources for a site for a Field Study Center, deeded some 364 hectares (900 acres) he owned south and west of Lancaster, Ohio, to the University, with the express intent these acres be used as a Natural Resources Field Study Center.

Now known as the Barnebey Center, this magnificent field study center contains within its boundaries almost all the qualities the students had discovered valuable for such a center. In fact, in defense of the study methodology, the Barnebey Center lies approximately at point A, Figure 156. Its natural features include at least one complete watershed, an all-year stream (Clear Creek), and, interestingly enough, sandstone cliffs and hemlock groves. That it is an esthetically pleasing natural site is indicated by the fact that for years Mr. Barnebey had leased it as a summer camp for church groups.

In these days of concern for environmental quality, we can, and do, through application of scientific knowledge, select and arrange land for man's use and delight.

As our awareness increases, we can improve man's lot on earth as we accept and apply the results of improved consciousness of our role here as stewards of our environment rather than as the most powerful predators the world has ever seen.

In this journey through time and place, we have observed man engaged in a desparate struggle for survival in an environment inimical to his comfort and safety.[10] As his numbers increased, as he multiplied mightily, man, according to Biblical injunction "subdued the earth." Finally (and we all hope not too late), we stand on the threshold of a future, in which we make use of expanding scientific and technologic resources to place ourselves in a proper, compatible perspective with our environment, "a part and parcel of Nature."[11]

---

[10]High winds, volcanic action, floods, drought, disease, all have been, and remain, unpredictable restraints to mankind's search for his earthly paradise.

[11]Thoreau, *op. cit.*

# BIBLIOGRAPHY

Asimov, Isaac, *Asimov's Guide to The Bible*, Vol. I, *The Old Testament*, New York, Doubleday, 1968.

Asimov, Isaac, *The Greeks, A Great Adventure*, Boston, Houghton Mifflin, 1965.

Balsdon, J. P. V. D, ed., *Roman Civilization*, Baltimore, Md., Penguin Books, 1965.

Batsford, Harry, and Fry, Charles, *Homes And Gardens Of England*, New York, Scribner, 1933.

Beck, Gus, "The Rise and Fall of Arabia Felix," *Scientific American*, December 1969.

Blumenfeld, Hans, "Scale In Civic Design," *Town Planning Review*, vol. 24, no. 1, (April 1953).

Cellini, Benvenuto, *The Life of Benvenuto Cellini;* trans. John Addington Symonds, New York, Liveright, 1930.

Chermayeff, Sergius I., and Alexander, Christopher, *Community and Privacy: Toward A New Architecture of Humanism*, Garden City, N.Y., Doubleday, 1963.

Childe, V. Gordon, "The Urban Revolution," *Town Planning Review*, Vol. 21 (April 1950).

Choay, Francoise, *The Modern City: Planning In The Nineteenth Century*, New York, George Braziller, 1969.

Church, Thomas, *Gardens Are For People*, New York, Reinhold, 1955.

Clifford, Derek, *A History of Garden Design*, New York, Praeger, 1963.

*Colonial Gardens, The Landscape Architecture of George Washington's Time*, Boston, American Society of Landscape Architects, 1932.

*The Columbia Encyclopedia*, 3rd ed., New York, Columbia University Press, 1963.

Craeger, Hubert K., *A Restoration of Pliny's Laurentine Villa*, Bachelor of Architecture Thesis, The Ohio State University, 1927.

Crisp, Sir Donald, *Medieval Gardens*, Plymouth, England, Mayflower Press, 1924.

Daubenmire, Rexford, *Plant Communities*, New York, Harper & Row, 1969.

Downing, Andrew Jackson, *Cottage Residences, A Series of Designs for Rural Cottages and Cottage Villas, and their Gardens and Grounds Adapted to North America*, New York, Wiley, 1853.

Eckbo, Garrett, *Landscape For Living*, New York, F. W. Dodge Corp., 1950.

Eckbo, Garrett, *The Landscape We See*, New York, McGraw-Hill, 1969.

Eckbo, Garrett, *Urban Landscape Design*, New York, McGraw-Hill, 1964.

Eliot, Charles, *Charles Eliot, Landscape Architect*, 2 vols., Boston, Houghton Mifflin, 1902.

Elwood, Philip H., *American Landscape Architecture*, New York, Architectural Book Publishing Co., 1924.

Fabos, Julius Gy; Milde, Gordon T; and Weinmayr, V. Michael, *Frederick Law Olmsted, Sr., Founder of Landscape Architecture in America*, Amherst, Mass., University of Massachusetts Press, 1968.

Festinger, Leon; Schachter, Stanley; and Back, Kurt, *Social Pressures In Informal Groups: A Study of Human Factors in Housing*, Palo Alto, Calif., Stanford University Press, 1963.

Fox, Helen M., *André Le Nôtre, Garden Architect to Kings*, New York, Crown, 1962.

Frome, Michael, *Whose Woods are These?*, New York, Doubleday, 1962.

*Garden Lore of Ancient Athens*, Princeton, N.J., American School of Classical Studies at Athens, 1963.

Gerould, Gordon Hall, ed., *Beowulf and Sir Gawain and the Green Knight*, New York, Ronald, 1935.

Goode, J. Paul, *World Atlas*, New York, Rand McNally, 1953.

Gothein, Marie Luis, *A History of Garden Art*, 2 vols., New York, Dutton, 1928.

Gray, Richard N., *Iran*, New York, Holt, Rhinehart and Winston, 1953.

Green, David, *Gardener to Queen Anne*, London, Oxford University Press, 1956.

Greenough, Horatio, *Form and Function; Remarks on Art*, ed. by Harold A. Small, Berkeley, University of California Press, 1947.

*Handbook of Mt. Vernon*, Washington, D.C., Mt. Vernon Ladies Association of the Union, 1940.

*Holy Bible; Revised Standard Version*, New York, Nelson, 1952.

Hookman, Hilda, *A Short History of China*, New York, St. Martin's, 1970.

Howard, Ebenezer, *Garden Cities of Tomorrow*, London, Faber & Faber, 1945.

Hubbard, Henry Vincent, and Kimball, Theodora, *An Introduction to the Study of Landscape Design*, Boston, M.I.T. Press, 1959.

Hussey, Christopher, *English Gardens and Landscapes 1700–1750*, New York, Funk & Wagnalls, 1967.

Irving, Washington, *The Alhambra: Tales of A Traveler*, New York, Macmillan, 1925.

Ishimoto, Tatsuo, *The Art of the Japanese Garden*, New York, Crown, 1958.

Lamb, Harold, *Constantinople, Birth of an Empire*, New York, Knopf, 1957.

Lavedan, Pierre, *Histoire de L'Urbanisme*, 2 vols., Paris, Henri Laurens, 1966.

Letarouilly, Paul, *Vatican I, The Basilica of St. Peter*, London, Alec Tiranti, 1953.

Leveson, David, *A Sense of the Earth*, Garden City, N.Y., The Natural History Press, 1971.

Lewis, Phillip H., *Recreation and Open Space In Illinois*, Division of Landscape Architecture and Urban Planning, Urbana, Ill., University of Illinois, 1961.

Lloyd, Seton, *The Art of the Ancient Near East*, New York, Praeger, 1961.

Lynch, Kevin, *Image of the City*, Cambridge, Mass., M.I.T. Press, 1960.

Lynch, Kevin, *Site Planning*, Cambridge, Mass., M.I.T. Press, 1962.

Maiuri, Amedeo, *Pompeii*, Novara, Italy, Instituto Geografico de Agostini, 1951.

Marsh, George Perkins, *Man And Nature*, Cambridge, Mass., Belknap Press, Harvard University Press, 1965 (originally published in 1864).

Mauricheau-Beaupre, Charles, *Versailles*, Monaco, Documents d'Art, 1948.

McEvedy, Colin, *Penguin Atlas of Ancient History*, Baltimore, Md., Penguin, 1968.

McEvedy, Colin, *Penguin Atlas of Medieval History*, Baltimore, Md., Penguin, 1968.

McHarg, Ian, *Design With Nature*, Garden City, N.Y., Natural History Press, 1969.

Mencken, H.L., McDavid, Alfred, *The American Language*, New York, Knopf, 1963.

Moore, Charles, *Daniel H. Burnham, Architect, Planner of Cities*, Vol. II, Boston, Houghton Mifflin, 1921.

Moore, Charles, ed., *Plan of Chicago*, Chicago, The Commercial Club of Chicago, 1909.

Nelson, Beatrice Ward, *State Recreation, Parks, Forests, and Game Preserves*, Washington, D.C., National Conference on State Parks, Inc., 1928.

Olmsted, Frederick Law, Sr., *Forty Years of Landscape Architecture*, Vol. II, edited by F.L. Olmsted, Jr., and Theodora Kimball; New York, Putnam, 1928.

*A Place To Live*, Yearbook of Agriculture, Washington, D.C., U.S. Department of Agriculture, 1963.

Porter, Elliot, *In Wildness Is the Preservation of the World*, New York, Ballantine, 1967.

Rosenau, Helen, *The Ideal City in Its Architectural Evolution*, Boston, Boston Book & Art Shop, 1959.

Sandars, Nancy K., *The Epic of Gilgamesh*, Baltimore, Md., Penguin, 1968.

Shepherd, William R., *Historical Atlas*, Holt, Rinehart and Winston, 1929.

Schmitt, Peter J., *Back To Nature: the Arcadian Myth*, New York, Oxford University Press, 1969.

Simonds, John O., *Landscape Architecture; The Shaping of Man's Environment*, New York, F.W. Dodge Corp., 1961.

Singer, Holmyard, Hall, *A History of Technology*, Vol. II, *The Mediterranean Civilization and the Middle Ages*, Oxford University Press, New York, 1957.

Siren, Osvald, *China And the Gardens of Europe of the Eighteenth Century*, New York, Ronald, 1950.

Smith, Richard Alan, "Crowding In the City: The Japanese Solution," *Landscape*, Vol. 19 no. 1 (July 1971).

Sorensen, C. Th, *The Origin of Garden Art*, Copenhagen, The Danish Architectural Press, 1963.

*South Auditorium Urban Renewal Project*, Portland, Oregon Planning Commission, 1964.

Steele, Fletcher: *Design In The Little Garden*, Boston, The Atlantic Monthly Press, 1924.

Stein, Clarence S., *Toward New Towns For America*, Liverpool, University Press, 1950.

Tange, Kenzo, *Kenzo Tange, 1946–1949, Architecture and Urban Design*, ed. by Udo Kulterman, New York, Praeger, 1970.

Tanzer, Helen H., *The Villas of Pliny the Younger*, Columbia University Press, 1924.

Thoreau, Henry David, *Walden*, The Modern Library, New York, 1937. Originally published as *Walden, or Life in the Woods*, 1854.

Triggs, H. Inigo, *The Art of Garden Design In Italy*, London, Longmans, 1906.

Triggs, H. Inigo, *Town Planning*, London, Methuen, 1909.

Troedsson, Carl Birger, *The Growth of the Western City During the Middle Ages*, Goteborg, Sweden, Elanders Boktryckeri Aktiebolaq, 1959.

Tunnard, Christopher, *Gardens In The Modern Landscape*, London, The Architectural Press, 1938.

Wagar, W. Warren, *The City of Man*, Baltimore, Md., Penguin, 1967.

Wilbur, Donald N., *Persian Gardens and Pavilions*, Rutland, Vt., Tuttle, 1962.

Wright, Richardson, *The Story of Gardening*, New York, Dodd, Mead, 1935.

# APPENDIX A

## Geologic Timetable

Current information indicates the geologic age of the earth as some 5,000,000,000 years. The history is summarized below:

I.   5,000,000,000 years ago: *Precambrian Era*

   1. Earth largely molten.
   2. Cooling: crust, atmosphere, and oceans formed.
   3. *Archeozoic Era* (earliest life forms).
      Primitive multicellular life forms.
   4. *Proterozoic Era:* Algae, other complex but primitive organisms, including annelid worms.
   5. End of Proterozoic Era: Glaciation of parts of South America, Africa, Asia, India, Australia.

II.  600,000,000 years ago: *Paleozoic Era* (Ancient Life)

   1. Mild climate.
   2. Few mountains.
   3. Wide, shallow seas covered today's continents.
   4. Intervals of mountain building.

   A. Periods:

      1. 600,000,000 to 500,000,000 years ago: *Cambrian* (Refers to early discoveries in Wales, formerly Cambria).
         a. Fossil record begins.
         b. Invertebrates and plants in oceans. Trilobites, corals, sponges, crinoids.

      2. 500,000,000 to 425,000,000 years ago: *Ordovician* (from Ordovices, a tribe in Wales)
         a. Invertebrates.
         b. First jawless fishes.
         c. Corals, crinoids, brachiopods.

      3. 425,000,000 to 405,000,000 years ago: *Silurian* (Silures, a people of Britain)
         a. Many jawless fishes.
         b. Highly developed invertebrates (including ancestors of modern mollusks).
         c. First jawed fishes.

      4. 400,000,000 to 345,000,000 years ago: *Devonian* (from Devonshire)
         a. The age of fishes.

      b. Plants move into swamps, followed by scorpions, spiders, early insects, lobe-finned fishes.

      c. First amphibians.

5. 345,000,000 to 310,000,000 years ago: *Mississippian* (first coal-forming period of Paleozoic Era in North America)

      a. Coal in lowland swamps.

      b. Many amphibians.

      c. Spiders, land snails, insects, mollusks.

6. 310,000,000 to 280,000,000 years ago: *Pennsylvanian* (second coal-forming period in North America)

      a. Continuing development amphibians.

      b. Giant club mosses.

      c. First reptiles.

      d. Cockroaches, mollusks, crustaceans.

7. 280,000,000 to 230,000,000 years ago: *Permian* (after Perm, a former province of Russia)

      a. Uplift of mountains produced deserts, cold regions, variable climates.

      b. Conifers in dry regions.

      c. Reptiles diversify, dominate dry areas; amphibians in moist places.

      d. Many earlier plants die off.

III.   230,000,000 years ago: *Mesozoic Era* (middle period)

      a. Age of reptiles.

      b. Reduction of mountains.

      c. Gradual return to uniform tropical condition.

  A. Periods:

1. 230,000,000 to 180,000,000 years ago: *Triassic* (named for threefold division of the period in Germany)

      a. Mountains, deserts.

      b. Reptiles dominate.

      c. Some dinosaurs, pterosaurs, marine reptiles.

2. 180,000,000 to 135,000,000 years ago: *Jurassic* (Jura mountains between France and Switzerland)

      a. Mild climate; many reptiles.

      b. A few primitive mammals; first birds (Archaeopteryx).

      c. Ammonites, dinosaurs, ichthyosaurs, plesiosaurs.

3. 135,000,000 to 63,000,000 years ago: *Cretaceous* (of the nature of chalk)
   a. Hardwood forests; flowering plants.
   b. Continued dominance of highly specialized reptiles: triceratops, brontosaurs, ichthyosaurs, plesiosaurs, mosasaurs.
   c. First marsupials; first placental mammals.
   d. Period ends with mountain building and extinction of giant reptiles.

IV.  63,000,000 years ago: *Cenozoic Era* (Recent Life)

1. Rockies and Coastal ranges appear.
2. Gradual appearance of grassy plains.
3. Age of mammals, modern orders of mammals gradually replace ancient types and extinct reptiles.
4. Series of four ice ages near the end.

A. Periods:

1. 63,000,000 to 58,000,000 years ago: *Paleocene* (Early period)
   a. Archaic mammals: creodonts, amblypods.
   b. First rodents and primates.

2. 58,000,000 to 36,000,000 years ago: *Eocene* (Dawn period)
   a. Lemurs and tarsiers.
   b. Other modern-mammal types.
   c. Early even and odd-toed hoofed mammals.
   d. Advanced carnivores.
   e. Ancestral pigs, camels, whales, eophippus.

3. 36,000,000 to 25,000,000 years ago: *Oligocene* (New period)
   a. Modern orders of mammals replace archaic.
   b. First anthropoids.
   c. Ancestral dogs, cats, horses.
   d. Propliopithecus.

4. 25,000,000 to 13,000,000,000 years ago: *Miocene* (Less-new period)
   a. Appearance of true anthropoid apes.
   b. Mastodons, rhinoceroses, sharks, whales.
   c. Dryopithecus.

5. 13,000,000 to 3,000,000 years ago: *Pliocene* (More-recent period)
   a. Beginnings of extreme of zonal temperatures.
   b. More advanced man-apes: Australopithecus.

6. 3,000,000 to 11,000 years ago: *Pleistocene* (Most-recent period)
   a. Earth covered with ice in many areas.
   b. Four ice ages.
   c. First primitive men (Java, Peking).
   d. Homo sapiens.

7. 11,000 years ago to present: *Recent*
   a. Rapid spread of modern man.
   b. Agriculture and civilization.

# APPENDIX B
# CHRONOLOGIES

## Greece and Persia

| | |
|---|---|
| 3000–B.C. | Crete enters Bronze Age. |
| 2000–B.C. | Greeks enter Greece from North. |
| 1700 B.C. | Knossos (Crete) leveled by earthquake. |
| 1400 B.C. | Myceneans destroy Knossos. |
| 1184 B.C. | Trojan War. |
| 1100 B.C. | Dorians invade Southern Greece. End of Mycenean age. |
| 1000 B.C. | Greeks begin to colonize coast of Asia Minor. |
| 850 B.C. | Iliad of Homer. |
| 814 B.C. | Carthage founded by Phoenicians. |
| 776 B.C. | First Olympic games. |
| 753 B.C. | Legendary date, founding of Rome. |
| 734 B.C. | Syracuse (Sicily) founded by Corinthians. |
| 700 B.C. | Attica (Athens territory) unified. |
| 687 B.C. | Kingdom of Lydia (Asia Minor) founded. Produced first coinage. |
| 660 B.C. | Byzantium founded. Colonization by Greeks of Black Sea coasts. |
| 612 B.C. | Medes and Chaldeans destroy Nineveh. |
| 605 B.C. | Nebuchadnezzar becomes king of Babylon. |
| 550 B.C. | Cyrus the Great of Persia conquers Media; establishes Persian Empire. |
| 546 B.C. | Cyrus conquers Lydia. |
| 540 B.C. | Greek fleet defeated off Sardinia by Carthaginians, and Etruscans; end of major period of Greek colonization. |
| 538 B.C. | Cyrus conquers Chaldea (Originally Sumer). |
| 525 B.C. | Cambyses (successor to Cyrus) conquers Egypt. |
| 521 B.C. | Darius, son of Hystaspes, royal convert and patron of Zoroaster (570c B.C.), becomes King of Persia. |
| 512 B.C. | Darius conquers Thrace (Northeast of Greece). |
| 499 B.C. | Ionian (Asia Minor coastal cities) revolt against Persia. |
| 494 B.C. | Persians put down Ionian revolt. |
| 490 B.C. | Athenians defeat Persians (under Darius) at Marathon. |
| 480 B.C. | Greek fleet defeats Persians under Xerxes at Salamis off Cyprus. |
| 479 B.C. | Greeks defeat Persian army at Plataea insuring independence of Greece. |
| 460 B.C. | Pericles comes to power in Athens. |
| 458 B.C. | Long walls, connecting Athens with port city Piraeus, completed. |
| 457 B.C. | Sparta defeats Athens. |
| 431 B.C. | Beginning of Peloponnesian wars: conflict between Athens on the one hand, Sparta and Corinth on the other. This conflict damaged Greece beyond repair, and marked the end of Greece's Golden Age under Pericles of Athens. |
| 404 B.C. | End of Peloponnesian wars. |

| | |
|---|---|
| 394 B.C. | Athens defeats Sparta, regains sea power. |
| 356 B.C. | Birth of Alexander the Great, Macedonia. |
| 336 B.C. | Alexander becomes king of Macedonia. |
| 335 B.C. | Alexander destroys Thebes. Athens submits to Alexandrian control. |

## Alexander's Conquests

| | |
|---|---|
| 359 B.C. | Philip II (father of Alexander) controls Macedon; marries Olympias, niece of the King of Epirus, a country to the west of Macedon. |
| 358 B.C. | Philip adapts the Theban phalanx, a Greek military formation, of foot soldiers ranked 16 deep. Each rank carried spears, the spears of the rear rank being 7.3 meters (24 feet) long. Known as the "Macedonian Phalanx", Alexander used it to great effect in conquering all the near east. This formation was utilized until the Romans in 168 B.C. demonstrated its weakness by defeating the Macedonians at Pydna, in Macedonia, thus bringing to an end Alexander's empire. |
| 356 B.C. | Birth of Alexander, son of Philip II. |
| 337 B.C. | Philip II in control of all Greece. Greeks vote war against Persia; elect Philip commanding general. |
| 336 B.C. | Philip II assassinated. Rumor has Alexander responsible, but fact indicates the rumor untrue. Alexander becomes King of Macedonia. |
| 334 B.C. | Alexander invades Persia. |
| 333 B.C. | Alexander defeats Persians. Besieges and takes Tyre, stronghold of Phoenicia in the eastern Mediterranean. |
| 331 B.C. | Alexander, having taken Egypt the year before, founds Alexandria. |
| 330 B.C. | Alexander burns Persepolis, having ended the Persian empire in a final battle at Gaugamela (on the Tigris, north of Nineveh) on October 1, 331 B.C. |
| 327 B.C. | Alexander, seeing himself, not as King of Macedonia, but as universal monarch over all men, marries Roxana, a Persian Princess, and begins training 30,000 Persians in Macedonian fashion for service in his army. Alexander invited into India. |
| 326 B.C. | Alexander's forces meet the forces of Porus, a Punjabi monarch, whose army included 200 elephants.<br><br>In the centuries that followed, Macedonian monarchs often used elephants in warfare, somewhat as modern armies use tanks.<br><br>Although after this battle, Alexander expressed the intention to move his army across India to the ocean which geographers of the time thought lay at the end of the world, Alexander's troops failed him. They just wanted to go back. |
| 323 B.C. | June 13 Alexander died at the age of 33 in Babylon. |

## Rise and Decline of Roman Empire

| | |
|---|---|
| 753 B.C. | Legendary date for founding of Rome, as an Etruscan enclave. |
| 509 B.C. | Last Etruscan king (Tarquinius) expelled. Republic of Rome established. |
| 396 B.C. | With the capture of Veii, an Etruscan stronghold, about 19 kilometers (12 miles) North of Rome, Etruscan culture absorbed by the Latins. |
| 390 B.C. | Gauls sack and burn Rome. |
| 378 B.C. | Servius Tullius erects defensive walls. |
| 343–290 B.C. | Samnite Wars. Absorption of Greek cities in Southern Italy. These wars firmly established the Roman military system. |
| 287 B.C. | Lex Hortensia firmly establishes the Republic, marking equality in relations of patricians and plebeians. |
| 264–146 B.C. | Punic Wars. Military and naval struggles against Carthage. Sicily, Sardinia, Greece, Spain, Macedonia added to republic. |
| 206–– B.C. | Establishment of Han Empire in China. Boundaries of China pushed westward across Tarim Basin. "Silk Road" opened. Grapes and clover introduced to China from West. Chinese silks enter Rome by way of Parthia (Persia) and Asia Minor. |
| 193 B.C. | Rome a major cosmopolitan city, the center of Mediterranean commerce. |
| 146–50 B.C. | Expansion northward into Gaul, Germany, Britain. Julius Caesar (first consulship 59 B.C.) acquires reputation as sound military leader. |
| 48–44 B.C. | Julius Caesar first Roman dictator. |
| 27 B.C.–14 A.D. | Principate of Augustus Caesar. |
| 14–200 A.D. | Imperial era. |
| 14–68 A.D. | Julio-Claudian Emperors (Tiberius, Caligula, Claudius, Nero). |
| 43 A.D. | Invasion of Britain. |
| 69–96 A.D. | Flavian emperors, (Vespasian 69–79; Titus 79–81; Domitian 81–96). |
| 97–117 A.D. | Trajan emperor. |
| 117–138 | Hadrian emperor. |
| 161–180 | Marcus Aurelius emperor. |
| 193–235 | Dynasty of the Severi (Septimus Severus; Caracalla, Elagabalus, Alexander Severus). |
| 212 | Grant of citizenship to the whole empire. |
| 250–259 | Persecution of Christians; Valerian. |
| 286–305 | Diocletian emperor in East. (See Fig. 36) Maximian rules West. |
| 312 | Constantine defeats Maxentius in the West, and becomes sole Emperor, ruling from the East. |
| 323–330 | Construction of "new Rome," Constantinople. |

## The Byzantine Period

| | |
|---|---|
| 327 | Constantine (Emperor of Rome 327–337) founds Constantinople, as the new Eastern capital of empire. |
| 395 | Theodosius the Great (Roman Emperor 379–395) divides Roman Empire between his two sons, thus officially creating Eastern and Western Empires (see Map, Fig. 36). |
| 400–500 | Eastern Empire survives pressures from Germanic peoples, thus illustrating the strategic importance of Constantinople's geographic location. Population of the city at this time, 1 million. Exceeded only by Baghdad (see Fig. 49). |
| | Alexandria yields its place as the First City of the Hellenic world to Constantinople. Latin is dying out, while Greek becomes the common language. Monasticism, in the Christian church, both East and West, has its beginning. |
| 500–600 | Justinian (Emperor 527–565), statesman, warrior, administrator, leads the Eastern Empire to new power, recapturing Africa and Italy. During his reign, Justinian recodifies Roman law, thus preserving it. By decree, Justinian establishes Christianity as the State Religion of the Empire. Consulate and senate are eliminated, making the Emperor an absolute monarch in the Oriental tradition. |
| 540–632 | Mohammed the Prophet founds the Mohammedan religion, which has the effect of unifying the Arab world. Rome in this period is at an end, nearly deserted. |
| 632 | Marks the beginning of the Saracen (Moslem) conquest of the Mediterranean world. (see Fig. 51). Constantinople again becomes known as Byzantium. Contact is lost with the west. |
| 800–900 | While the Vikings ravage Northern Europe, Byzantium becomes the seat of Greek monarchy, as a Frank (Charles the Great, or Charlemagne) becomes Emperor of the West, king of semibarbaric knights and peasants. Byzantines, on the other hand, are highly cultured citizens of a great commercial and industrial city. The university at Byzantium is widely known for its scholarship, chiefly in the form of compilation. It was this compilation which preserved knowledge for future generations. |
| 1000–1100 | Venice rules the Adriatic, and challenges Byzantium's position as a center of trade. William the Norman (1066) conquers England, thus setting the stage for later, secular national states in the west. |
| | By 1092, Byzantium calls on the West to furnish mercenaries in its struggle against Islam, thus precipitating the Crusades, and further contacts by the semibarbaric western Europeans with the highly cultured Arab world. |

| 1100–1200 | The Byzantine Empire keeps trade between East and West alive, while the nomadic hordes of Genghis Khan terrify China, and penetrate Europe. |
| 1200–1300 | Impressed with the wealth and grandeur of Byzantium, Crusaders besiege and capture it. For a short time thereafter, the Byzantines reassert commercial control over the eastern Mediterranean, but soon begin to lose that control to the Italian city-states (Venice, Florence, Genoa). |
| 1300–1400 | Byzantine Empire in decline, engages in a death struggle with the Ottoman (Turkish) Empire. |
| 1453 | Byzantium is finally captured by the Turks. Hagia Sophia, originally built by Justinian, and rebuilt after a disastrous earthquake, becomes a mosque. |

## Europe

| 732 | Charles Martel stops Islamic advance on Europe at Poitiers. |
| 800–814 | Charlemagne Holy Roman Emperor. Takes offensive against Moslems in northeast Spain. |
| 800–900 | Monasteries centers of learning. *Certosa di Pavia*. Viking raids on North Europe. A period of decentralization, feudalism. Europe largely agricultural, with a landed gentry. |
| 900–1000 | Height of feudalism. Venice and Genoa centers of trade with the East. Monasteries oases of peace, learning, and stability. |
| 1000–1100 | Vikings dominate North Sea trade in fish, wine, beer, salt, and metals. International trade developing through annual fairs at such centers as Paris, Cologne, London. Rise of nationalism. |
| 1066 | Britain becomes part of Europe. (William the Conqueror.) |
| 1100–1200 | Rise of merchant class (guilds). Expansion in trade, population. Great period of castle building. Crusades bring in new ideas through contact with Moslem culture. |
| 1200–1300 | New towns: Montpazier. The age of cities. Populations upward of 100,000 (Paris, London, Palermo, Florence, Venice, Pisa, Genoa, Bruges). Louis IX of France rebuilds an ancient Roman town as a strategic fortress (Carcassonne). Shift from small self-contained population units to interdependence, brought on by extensive trade. Bourgoisie rivalling agrarian feudal aristocracy. Hanseatic league (Fig. 52) gets its start by monopolizing herring trade. Arabic numerals from India by way of Arabic Africa make computation of accounts easier. |

Italian Renaissance

I.   *1200–1400* A.D., *the stage is set:*

1214–1294   Friar Roger Bacon, of Oxford.
Studied Aristotle as well as the Bible.
Interested in natural science and believed in controlled experiment. "It is the intention of philosophy to work out the nature and properties of things."

1265–1321   Dante (Durante Alighieri).
Italian poet, author: *Divine Comedy*, Florentine cavalryman, councilman, elector; student of classic philosophy.

1304–1374   Petrarch (Francesco Petrarca) poet and humanist.
Grew up in Tuscany; lived at Avignon and Bologna. In 1341 crowned laureate in Rome. Among the first to realize that platonic thought and Greek studies provided a new cultural framework, and therefore helped to spread the Renaissance point of view.

1313–1375   Giovanni Boccaccio, Tuscan-born author. His most famous work *Decameron*, a collection of 100 witty and sometimes licentious tales set against the somber background of the Black Death (Plague). The tales brilliantly reveal man as sensual, tender, cruel, weak, selfseeking, and ludicrous (i.e., Human).

1320        "Invention" of gunpowder, changing technology of war.

1348        Black Death (Plague) decimates city populations.

1350        Rise of city-states—Genoa, Venice, Florence—as trade centers. Establishment of merchant princes.

1377        Return of papacy to Rome from Avignon.

II.  *Fifteenth century: 1400–1499:*

1389–1464   Cosimo de Medici, ruler of Florence.

1397–1473   Michelozzo Michelozzi, artist, architect.

1419–1424   Brunelleschi (1377–1446) designed Loggia, Spedale degli Innocenti, Florence; first Renaissance piazza. (See Fig. 69)

1431        Joan of Arc burned at the stake in Orléans, France, convicted of heresy.

1443        Alphonso V, King of Spain and King of Naples, introduces Islamic use of water in gardens to Italy.

| 1449–1492 | Lorenzo (*Il Magnifico*) de Medici, Merchant prince, Florence. |
| 1450 | Leon Battista Alberti writes "de Architectura." |
| 1450 | Michelozzi designs Medici Villa, Fiesole (see Fig. 70). |
| 1452–1498 | Savonarola (Florence) denounces corruption in church and state. |
| 1452–1519 | Leonardo da Vinci, painter, sculptor, architect, engineer, scientist. |
| 1454 | Johannes Gutenberg invents movable type, Mainz, Germany. |
| 1469–1527 | Machiavelli, Florentine statesman. His *Il principe* (*The prince*, probably modeled on Cesare Borgia) describes the means by which a prince gains and maintains power. The deviousness of the methods depicted has given us the adjective "Machiavellian," a synonym for amoral cunning. |
| 1475–1507 | Cesare Borgia, Soldier, politician, Cardinal at age 17. |
| 1480–1519 | Lucrezia Borgia, Cesare's sister, suspected poisoner for political reasons. |
| 1492 | Cristoforo Colombo, Genoese navigator, under commission from Ferdinand and Isabella of Spain, discovers a new world, while seeking the old. |
| 1497–1499 | Vasco da Gama, Portuguese navigator, sails to India around Africa. |
| 1497 | Giovanni Caboto (John Cabot), Venetian navigator, under commission of Henry VII of England, discovers North American continent (Newfoundland). |

### III.   *Sixteenth century: 1500–1599:*

| 1473–1543 | Copernicus, Polish-Prussian astronomer develops new theory of motion of planets, diametrically opposed to Aristotle (384–322 B.C.). Whereas Aristotle's geocentric thesis, by way of Alexandria, the Ptolemies, and Islamic scholars, became the basis of European astonomy, Copernicus' theories were heliocentric. (See further note under seventeenth century, below.) |
| 1500–1571 | Benvenuto Cellini, artist in metal; autobiographer. |
| 1504 | Hernando Cortes goes to Hispaniola (Spanish possessions in the Caribbean). |
| 1517 | Martin Luther posts his 95 theses on the cathedral door, |

Wittenberg, to invite debate as a means of reformation within the church.

1519–1521   Cortes captures Tenochtitlan (now Mexico City) and kills Montezuma (Aztec emperor 1502–1520) in the New World.

1520        The turkey, chocolate, and cocoa introduced to Europe from Mexico. Luther breaks away from Roman Catholic Church.

1534        Society of Jesus (Jesuits) formed by St. Ignatius of Loyala begins reforms within Roman Catholic Church.

1538        Michelangelo designs Piazza del Campidoglio, Rome.

1547        Michelangelo architect, St. Peter's Cathedral, Rome.

1550        Olivieri and Ligorio design Villa d'Este for Cardinal Ippolito d'Este at Tivoli. (See Figs. 71, 72).

1560        Villa Lante, Bagnaia (See Fig. 73).

1585–1590   Pope Sixtus V redesigns Rome in Renaissance patterns.

## IV.   *Seventeenth century (1600–1700): Baroque:*

1600        Marie de Medici, Queen of Henry IV of France, 1600–1610. Regent for Louis XIII, King of France 1610–1643.

1609        First shipment of tea from China by Dutch East India Company.

1633        Galileo Galilei (1564–1642), astronomer, mathematician, physicist, professor at University of Pisa, publishes *Dialogue on the two chief systems of the world—Ptolemaic vs. Copernican;* a turning point in science and philosophic thought.
            Galileo tried by inquisition for heresy.

1632–1671   Isola Bella, Lago Maggiore (Fig. 74, 75).

1643–1715   Louis XIV King of France: "L'état c'est moi."

1656        Bernini (1589–1680) designs elliptical piazza before St. Peter's, Rome.

## Three Eras of Italian Garden Design

1450–1503   The Philosopher's Garden. Begins with the writings of Alberti; ends with Bramante's plan for the Belvedere in the Vatican gardens. Example: Villa Medici at Fiesole (Fig. 70).

1503–1573    Unity; Harmony; Use of Water. From the Belvedere to the death of Vignola. Examples: Villa d'Este (Fig. 71), Villa Lante (Fig. 73).

1573–1775    Baroque. Long decline; shift of emphasis to France. Example: Isola Bella (Fig. 74).

See Fig. 68 for geographic relationships.

## France

1226–1270    Louis IX. Crusades, Treaty of Paris settles English claims to a portion of France.

1270–1285    Philip III. Increases power of royalty.

1285–1314    Philip IV. Increases power of monarchy. Papacy (1309) headquartered at Avignon.

1314–1316    Louis X. A confused period, marked by feudalism and some loss of royal control.

1316         John I.

1316–1322    Philip V.

1322–1328    Charles IV. Some success in reducing English holdings on French soil.

1328–1350    Philip VI. Beginning of Hundred Years' War against England.

1350–1364    John II.

1364–1380    Charles V. Weakening of feudal nobles' position.

1380–1422    Charles VI. Papal schism; Popes still at Avignon (until 1418).

1422–1461    Charles VII. English driven from France. Joan of Arc burned at Orléans.

1461–1483    Louis XI. Strong central monarchy established; feudal power further reduced.

1483–1498    Charles VIII. Charles briefly holds Naples; returns to France with Renaissance ideas, put to use at his palace at Amboise.

1498–1515    Louis XII. Further contacts with Italian culture.

1515–1547    Francis I. Thirty years' War with Italy.
             Francis builds castle at Fontainebleau, adapting Italian garden art to France.

1547–1559    Henry II. Catherine de Medici Henry's Queen.
             Chenonceaux's gardens made more Italian, as well as expanded gardens at Fontainebleau.

1560–1574    Charles IX. Struggle with Holy Roman Empire for mastery of Europe. (The Holy Roman Empire included Spain.)

1574–1589    Henry III. Continuation of struggle.

1589–1610    Henry IV. Victory over Spain. Religious conflict with Huguenots. Marie de Medici the second wife of Henry IV. Grand Canal built at Fontainebleau.

| | |
|---|---|
| 1610–1643 | Louis XIII. Era of peace, prosperity, except for Thirty Years' War, resulting in the breakup of The Holy Roman Empire. Cardinal Richelieu, as first minister, establishes France as an international power. |
| 1643–1715 | Louis XIV. Fouquet completes Vaux-le-Vicomte. Le Nôtre's garden opened at Versailles. French court becomes the envy of all Europe. |
| 1715–1774 | Louis XV. Age of stirring revolution. Beginnings of industrial revolution, science and modern technology. "The Age of Reason" (Voltaire, Rousseau). |
| 1774–1793 | Louis XVI. Marie Antoinette Louis' Queen. France, impressed with American Revolution, and angered against oppressive (54 percent) taxes, overthrows monarchy. |
| 1793–1804 | Republic. The Reign of Terror, 1793–1794. In 1795, civil war erupts in Paris. In 1799 consular government established. |
| 1804–1815 | Napoleon Emperor. France the master of Europe. Overextension in war with Russia 1813. Germany, Austria, Russia, England ally against France. "Hundred Day's War." Napoleon defeated by Wellington at Waterloo. |
| 1815–1824 | Louis XVIII. Rise of industry. |
| 1824–1830 | Charles X, a reactionary. |
| 1830–1848 | Louis Philippe. A "Middle-class King." Revolt against royalty. In 1845 Louis abdicates in favor of his grandson Louis Philippe, Comte de Paris, who failed in his candidacy for the throne, went to America and fought in the United States Civil War. |
| 1848–1852 | Republic. |
| 1852–1870 | Napoleon III. The Second Empire. France preoccupied with arts and letters, science, and industry. Baron Haussmann rebuilds Paris. |

## England

| | |
|---|---|
| 1461–1470 | Edward IV. War of the Roses, 1455–1485. Internal struggle for the throne between the royal houses of York and Lancaster, resolved by the marriage of Henry VII to the daughter of Edward IV. |
| 1470–1471 | Henry VI. Continuation of the War of the Roses. |
| 1471–1483 | Edward IV. Haddon Hall, Derbyshire (Fig. 85). Derbyshire-Lancastrian alliance with French nobility. |
| 1483 | Edward V. Internal power struggle. |
| 1483–1485 | Richard III. |
| 1485–1509 | Henry VII. Beginning of the House of Tudor. Cardinal Wolsey, Prime Minister, moves England into international relationships. |
| 1509–1547 | Henry VIII. (Tudor). Breach with Rome. Dissolution of Monasteries. Distribution of monastic holdings to Henry's favorites. |
| 1547–1553 | Edward VI (Tudor). Little influence. Conflicts between Roman Catholics and Protestants. Montacute, Somersetshire (Fig. 85). |

| | |
|---|---|
| 1553–1558 | Mary I (Tudor). Known as "Bloody Mary" for her persecution of Protestants. Marries Philip II of Spain, producing brief alliance with Spain. |
| 1558–1603 | Elizabeth I (Tudor). Shrewd politician. Spanish Armada, launched by Philip II of Spain as a great Catholic crusade against the leading Protestant power of Europe, defeated 1588. England becomes European power and enters period of greatest brilliance—William Shakespeare; Sir Walter Raleigh; Sir Francis Bacon. Levens Hall (Fig. 85). |
| 1603–1625 | James I (Stuart). Centralized royal authority. Scotland made part of Empire. Misunderstanding on James' part of Parliament and changing political, social and religious conditions laid groundwork for later English Civil War. Hatfield House (Fig. 86). |
| 1625–1649 | Charles I (Stuart). The great rebellion of the commoners against royalty. |
| 1649–1660 | The Commonwealth (Republic). Military government. |
| 1653–1658 | Oliver Cromwell Lord Protector. "His whole course directed by God." Puritanism-austerity. |
| 1658–1659 | Richard Cromwell, son of Oliver, Lord Protector. |
| 1660–1685 | Charles II (Stuart). Restoration of monarchy. Great plague of 1685. Great London Fire of 1666. Transfer of power to parliament. |
| 1685–1688 | James II (Stuart). Revolution of 1688. |
| 1689–1702 | William III (of Orange) and Mary II (Stuart). Parliamentary constitution question settled. Dutch influence. Advances in human and social relations. Expansion of empire. |
| 1702–1714 | Anne (Stuart). Controlled monarchy. Addison and Pope. Blenheim; Melbourne Hall; Derbyshire (Fig. 87). |
| 1714–1727 | George I (Hanover). Whigs vs. Tories. Beginnings of industrial revolution. Development of scientific disciplines. |
| 1727–1760 | George II (Hanover). Austrian war. "The English Landscape School." Stowe (Figs. 90, 91). |
| 1760–1820 | George III (Hanover). Conservatism. Humane penology. Growth of democracy. Revolution in the American colonies. Stowe (Fig. 93). |

## The New World

| | |
|---|---|
| 1492 | Ferdinand and Isabella (rulers of Spain 1474–1504), having united Spain, send Columbus to West. Columbus lands in the Bahama Islands. |
| 1497 | John Cabot, under patent from Henry VII (King of England 1485–1509) lands at Newfoundland or Cape Breton. |
| 1499 | Amerigo Vespucci sails for Spain. Explores coast of South America to lat. 50° south. |

| | |
|---|---|
| 1513 | Balboa, Spanish conquistador, discovers Pacific Ocean. Ponce de Leon lands near St. Augustine, Florida. |
| 1515 | Havana, Cuba founded. |
| 1519–1522 | Ferdinand Magellan circumnavigates the globe. Cortes conquers Mexico. Founds Vera Cruz, 1519, Mexico City 1521. |
| 1528 | Cabeza de Vaca, Spanish explorer, shipwrecked on Texas coast. He and three other survivors wander through west Texas, New Mexico, Arizona, thence south to Mexico. Tales lead to Coronado's search for the seven cities of Cibola. |
| 1532 | Pizarro conquers Peru; founds Lima. |
| 1541 | De Soto, then governor of Cuba with the right to conquer Florida, explores Florida, Georgia, South Carolina, Tennessee, Alabama; crosses the Mississippi, travels up Arkansas River into Oklahoma. Coronado explores the Southwest as far east as Kansas, as far west as South California (Spanish *Alta California*). |
| 1542 | Cabrillo takes possession of *Alta California* (as opposed to *Baja*, or lower California). |
| 1565 | Spanish found St. Augustine, Florida. |
| 1579 | Sir Francis Drake claims the California region for Elizabeth I (Queen of England 1558–1603). |
| 1603 | Champlain, French explorer under Henry IV (King of France 1589–1610) sails to New France. |
| 1607 | Sir Walter Raleigh, under James I (King of England 1603–1625), establishes Jamestown in Virginia. |
| 1608 | Champlain founds Quebec. |
| 1609 | Spanish found Santa Fe. |
| 1615 | Champlain discovers Lake Champlain, explores Great Lakes to Georgian Bay, Lake Huron. |
| 1620 | Plymouth Colony founded in Massachusetts. Beginning of decline of Spanish Empire |
| 1625 | Dutch establish New Amsterdam, now New York. |
| 1626 | Salem, Mass. established. |
| 1630 | Boston established as main colony of the Massachusetts Bay Company. Center of American Puritanism. |
| 1632 | Middle Plantation founded in Virginia, between James and York Rivers. Name changed to Williamsburg and becomes capital of Virginia colony 1699. |
| 1634 | Nicolet, French explorer, discovers Wisconsin territory and upper-Mississippi. |
| 1642 | Ville Marie de Montreal (later Montreal) founded by French. |
| 1670 | English settle Albermarle Point, 7 miles from present Charleston, South Carolina. Colony moved 1680 to present site (Charles II, King of Britain 1660–1685). |

| 1681 | La Salle (under Louis XIV of France) explores Mississippi River to its mouth. |
|------|---|
| 1682 | William Penn founds Philadelphia, (on the site of a former seventeenth-century Swedish settlement). |
| 1693 | College of William and Mary founded at Williamsburg. |
| 1700 | Charleston becomes most important seaport in the Southern Colonies, exporting indigo, rice, deerskins. The leading center of wealth and culture in the South. French Huguenots add a cosmopolitan touch. |
| 1714 | John Harrison, Yorkshire carpenter wins British government prize for development of a practical marine chronometer capable of determining a ship's longitude within 30 nautical miles at the end of a 6-week voyage. |
| 1722 | Williamsburg (named for William III, King of England 1689–1702) incorporated. |
| 1733 | Savannah, Ga. founded by James Oglethorpe. Colonial seat of government. |
| 1740 | Moravian (Evangelical Christian communion originated 1457 in Bohemia) communities of Bethlehem, Nazareth, Lititz, Pa. founded. |
| 1747 | Mt. Vernon, home of George Washington until his death in 1799. Named for Admiral Edward Vernon, Lawrence (George's half brother) Washington's commander in British Navy. George Washington inherits estate 1754. Additions to house and grounds completed following revolution. |
| 1756–1763 | Seven Years War, a world conflict fought in Europe, North America, and India between France, Austria, Russia, Saxony, Sweden, and Spain on one side, and Prussia, Great Britain, and Hanover on the other. Part of the struggle was due to colonial rivalry between France and England. Result in North America was the loss of most of the French Colonial Empire (Louis XV King of France 1715–1774). |
| 1765 | British Stamp Act, a direct demand by Britain for revenue from the colonies leads directly to colonists' assertions that "Taxation without representation is tyranny." |
| 1770 | Boston Massacre. |
| 1773 | Boston Tea Party. |
| 1774 | Quebec Act places the region between the Ohio and Great Lakes within the boundaries of Canada, thus balking the interest of the colonists in the western lands. |

|               | Continental Congress meets to persuade British government to recognize Colonies' rights. The Congress agrees to boycott British goods. |
|---------------|---|
| 1775–1783     | The American Revolution. French under Louis XVI (King 1774–1793) assist the American colonies to break away from Britain. |
| 1783          | Treaty signed in Paris recognizes the new nation and cedes the Ohio country to the Confederation of States. The Revolution has great influence on liberal thought throughout Europe. |
| 1785          | Virginia passes first Turnpike Act, establishing the concept of self-supporting highways. |
| 1787          | A steamboat built by James Rumsey demonstrated on the Potomac River. |
| 1789          | Federation of 13 original states established. George Washington first President of United States (1789–1797). |
| 1792          | First American operated private turnpike in Pennsylvania (Lancaster Turnpike). |
| 1797–1801     | John Adams, second President. |
| 1791–1800     | Vermont, Kentucky, Tennessee added to the roster of states. |
| 1801–1809     | Thomas Jefferson, third President. |
| 1803          | Louisiana Purchase more than doubles United States territories. |
| 1809–1817     | James Madison, fourth President. |
| 1812–1815     | War with England, caused by aggressive American maritime trade. |
| 1815          | National Road (first federal highway) begun, Cumberland to Wheeling. |
| 1815–1820     | Henry Clay (Lexington, Ky. 1777–1852) Senator and Representative establishes federal aid to internal improvements and tariffs on imports. |
| 1821          | Missouri Compromise pairs Maine, a free state, with Missouri as a slave state. |
| 1825          | Erie Canal completed. Opens trade and communications between New York and Lake Erie. |
| 1825–1833     | National road completed to St. Louis. |
| 1825–1850     | "Hudson River School" flourishes under the leadership of Thomas Cole, American Landscape painter born in England. |
| 1800–1840     | Great boom in turnpikes, as well as canals, permitting further expansion and consolidation of land control. |
| 1826          | First United States railroad, employing horse-drawn wagons to transport granite from Quincy, Mass., to Neponset, R.I. |
| 1829          | First steam locomotives imported from England prove too heavy for existing tracks; from now on engines produced domestically. |
| 1836          | Sleeping cars introduced on long run (i.e., Philadelphia-Harrisburg) rail lines. |

| | |
|---|---|
| 1840 | Railroad mileage exceeds canal mileage. |
| 1850– | Growth of slums in U.S. cities, acute in urban areas, due, in large part to heavy immigration from Europe. |
| 1850 | Atlantic coast connected by rail with the Great Lakes. |
| 1850 | Samuel F.B. Morse develops Morse Code, making rapid telegraphic communication possible. |
| 1850–1861 | Fillmore, Pierce, and Buchanan, Presidents. |
| 1851 | Electric Street Railway in operation near Washington, D.C. |
| 1858 | "Greensward" plan for Central Park, New York; Olmsted & Vaux. |
| 1860–1865 | Civil War. *Olmsted* secretary U.S. Sanitary Commission, does much to establish American Red Cross. |
| 1861–1865 | Abraham Lincoln, President. |
| 1862–1869 | Authorization and building of transcontinental railroad, completed at Promontory Point, Utah, May 10, 1869. |
| 1865– | Great battles among leading financiers for control of commercial empires: Cornelius Vanderbilt, Jay Gould, Daniel Drew, James Fisk, James G. Hill, Henry Villard, Edward H. Harriman. |
| 1865–1869 | Andrew Johnson, President. |
| 1869 | General Plan for Riverside, a railroad subdivision outside Chicago; Olmsted & Vaux. |
| 1869–1877 | Ulysses S. Grant, President. |
| 1876 | Alexander Graham Bell constructs first practical telephone. |
| 1877–1881 | Rutherford B. Hayes, President. |
| 1879 | Edison produces electric lamp. |
| 1880 | First commercial electric lighting. |
| 1881 | James A. Garfield, President. |
| 1881–1885 | Chester A. Arthur, President. |
| 1885–1889 | Grover Cleveland, President. |
| 1886 | Benz, Daimler produce automobile in Germany. |
| 1889–1893 | Benjamin Harrison, President. |
| 1893 | World's Columbian Exposition, Chicago. Plans prepared by Daniel Burnham, F.L. Olmsted. |
| 1893–1897 | Grover Cleveland, President. |
| 1895 | Marconi produces first Hertzian wave (radio) transmitter receiver. |
| 1898 | Spanish-American War. |
| 1899 | Preparation of plans for Metropolitan Boston Park System, Olmsted and Charles Eliot. |
| 1900 | Incandescent gas lighting firmly established (first public use, London, 1807). |

## The "City Beautiful" Era

| | |
|---|---|
| 1893 | World's Columbian Exposition, Chicago. |
| 1893–1897 | Grover Cleveland, President. |

| | |
|---|---|
| 1894 | Pullman strike put down by Federal troops. |
| 1897–1901 | William McKinley, President. |
| 1898 | Spanish-American War causes United States to emerge as a world power. |
| 1900 | Adoption by United States of gold standard. |
| 1901 | National Capital Commission (Daniel Burnham, chairman) attempts to carry out Pierre L'Enfant's plan for Washington. |
| 1903 | Death of Frederick Law Olmsted, Sr. |
| 1903 | Wilbur and Orville Wright successfully fly the first gasoline-powered airplane at Kitty Hawk, N.C. |
| 1901–1909 | Theodore Roosevelt, President. Conservation of natural resources; preservation of millions of acres of land in national parks and forests for the nation. |
| 1902 | Sherman Anti-Trust Act (passed in 1890) influential in "trust-busting." |
| 1904–1914 | Panama Canal connects Atlantic with Pacific through Panama Isthmus. |
| 1906 | Burnham plan of San Francisco. |
| 1908 | Henry Ford produces Model T and establishes assembly-line procedures for automobile manufacture. |
| 1909–1913 | William Howard Taft, President. |
| 1910 | London Town Planning Conference attended by Burnham as Chairman of U.S. Commission of Fine Arts. |
| 1912 | Death of Daniel H. Burnham. |
| 1913 | Sixteenth Amendment to the U.S. Constitution establishes Federal income tax. |
| 1913 | First commercial gasoline-cracking process in operation. |
| 1914 | Clayton Anti-Trust Act excludes labor organizations by declaring that "the labor of a human being is not a commodity or article of commerce." |
| 1913–1921 | Woodrow Wilson, President. |
| 1914–1918 | World War I establishes United States military-industrial empire. |
| 1916 | Punitive expedition into Mexico led by John J. Pershing, later, in World War I generalissimo of American Expeditionary Forces. |
| 1917 | United States enters war in Europe. Emergency measures centralize U.S. economy. |
| 1918 | World War I terminates with armistice, November 11. |
| 1919 | League of Nations established at Paris Peace Conference, with headquarters at Geneva, Switzerland. |
| 1920 | Eighteenth Amendment to U.S. Constitution begins prohibition era and its concomitant, bootlegging (repealed by twentieth Amendment, 1933). |
| 1920 | Nineteenth Amendment gives women right to vote. |

## The Age of Technology

| | |
|---|---|
| 1920 | U.S. population 54.7 percent urban; 46.3 percent rural. Barnstormers, using surplus World War I aircraft, evoke rising interest in aviation. |
| | First commercial radio broadcasting, station KDKA, Pittsburgh. |
| 1921–1923 | Warren G. Harding, President. |
| 1923 | Teapot Dome scandal involves lease of government oil lands to private enterprise without competitive bidding. |
| 1923–1929 | Calvin Coolidge, President. An advocate of laissez-faire business policy. |
| 1925 | First airmail service. |
| 1928 | Electronic scanning device perfected, presaging the age of television. |
| 1929–1933 | Herbert C. Hoover, President. |
| 1929 | Great depression begins with stock market crash in October. |
| 1930 | Television mechanism perfected. |
| | Great drought creates agricultural havoc. |
| 1930 | Commercial air travel begins period of expansion. |
| 1933–1945 | Franklin D. Roosevelt, President |
| 1934 | Pan American Airways inaugurates commercial air travel across Pacific to Manila. |
| 1935 | Social Security Act sets up a system of compulsory old-age insurance. |
| 1939 | First trans-Atlantic mail and passenger air service. First flight utilizing rocket power. Jet aircraft engine developed. Word War II begins. |
| 1940 | Complex computer perfected, laying the groundwork for the development of the electronic computer. |
| 1941 | Japanese attack on Pearl Harbor precipitates United States into World War II. |
| 1944 | Germans perfect V2 rocket, first long-range guided missile. |
| 1945–1953 | Harry S. Truman, President. |
| 1945 | World War II ends with explosion of atomic bombs over Hiroshima and Nagasaki, Japan. |
| | United Nations established at San Francisco. |
| 1946 | Electronic numerical integrator and calculator becomes first computer to use electronic tubes. |
| 1947 | National Security Act places Army, Navy, Air Force under U.S. Department of Defense. |
| | Marshall Plan instituted to assist European recovery following World War II. |
| 1948 | Bell Telephone laboratories announce development of the transistor, as replacement for vacuum tubes in electronic devices. |

| | |
|---|---|
| 1949 | Point Four Program provides technical assistance to under-developed countries. |
| 1950 | Truman sends U.S. troops into Korean conflict. |
| | U.S. population 63.8 percent urban; 36.2 percent rural. |
| | 5.7 million farms averaging 89 hectares (220 acres) per farm. |
| 1952 | United States explodes hydrogen bomb in the Pacific. |
| 1953–1961 | Dwight D. Eisenhower, President. |
| 1957 | Russia orbits first artificial satellite. |
| 1959 | Alaska becomes 49th state; Hawaii 50th. |
| 1960 | U.S. population 69.8 percent urban; 30.2 percent rural. |
| | 4 million farms averaging 121 hectares (300 acres) per farm. |
| 1961–1963 | John F. Kennedy, President. |
| 1963–1969 | Lyndon B. Johnson, President. |
| 1964 | Civil Rights Act becomes law. |
| 1965 | United States begins major military commitment in Vietnam. |

## The Dawning of the Age of Aquarius

| | |
|---|---|
| 1967 | Almost 3 percent of U.S. population owns second (vacation) home. |
| 1968 | U.S. population passes 200-million mark. Projections for year 2000 estimate 266 million to 231 million. |
| 1969– | Richard M. Nixon, President. |
| 1969 | Mobility of U.S. population is indicated by 1969 being a peak year in production of modular housing (prefabricated). 99 percent of U.S. households have TV, 95 percent of U.S. households have telephones, 77 percent of U.S. households have one or more cars, 30 percent of U.S. households have two or more cars. |
| 1970 | Peak year for civil disturbances. |
| | "Earth Day" emphasizes need to preserve and enhance environmental quality. |
| | The United States and two small African nations the only world governments not using or converting to the International (metric) System of measurement. |
| | U.S. population 73.4 percent urban; 26.6 percent rural. 2.9 million farms averaging 157.9 hectares (390 acres) per farm. |
| 1971 | Shifts in international relations include mainland China's entry into United Nations. Economic controls found necessary in U.S. |
| | Use of unmanned orbiting satellites (ERTS) for remote sensing of earth's ecological status. U.S. involvement in Vietnam much reduced. |
| 1973 | U.S. involvement in Vietnam begins to phase out. Inflationary economics continue to plague federal, state, and local environmental quality programs. |

# APPENDIX C

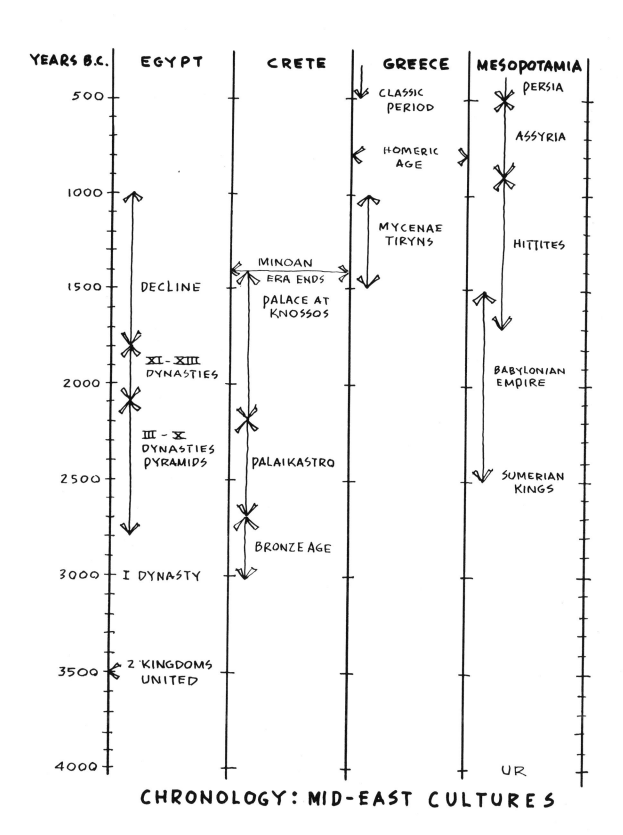

| YEARS B.C. | EGYPT | CRETE | GREECE | MESOPOTAMIA |
|---|---|---|---|---|
| 500 | | | CLASSIC PERIOD | PERSIA |
| | | | HOMERIC AGE | ASSYRIA |
| 1000 | | | MYCENAE TIRYNS | HITTITES |
| 1500 | DECLINE | MINOAN ERA ENDS | | |
| | | PALACE AT KNOSSOS | | |
| | XI-XIII DYNASTIES | | | BABYLONIAN EMPIRE |
| 2000 | | | | |
| | III-X DYNASTIES PYRAMIDS | PALAIKASTRO | | |
| 2500 | | | | SUMERIAN KINGS |
| | | BRONZE AGE | | |
| 3000 | I DYNASTY | | | |
| 3500 | 2 KINGDOMS UNITED | | | |
| 4000 | | | | UR |

# CHRONOLOGY: MID-EAST CULTURES

# INDEX

Page numbers in *italics* indicate illustrations.

This book is set in 11/13 Trump, a linotype face designed in 1954 by George Trump as Trump Mediaval, and later adapted for use in photocomposition and computer typesetting.

The type was set in the United States by Unitron Graphics, Inc., New York City, on their Linotron 505 CRT system.

The book was printed in offset lithography by Rae Publishing Company, Inc., Cedar Grove, New Jersey, and bound at Chas. H. Bohn and Co., Inc., New York City. The paper is Westvaco Deerskin Opaque, and the bookcloth was manufactured by The Columbia Mills Incorporated.

This book was designed by Ellen Blissman.